ALMOST HISTORY

ALMOST

CLOSE CALLS, PLAN B's, AND
TWISTS OF FATE IN AMERICAN HISTORY

HISTORY

By Roger Bruns

A Stonesong Press Book

New York

HYPERION
77 West 66th Street
New York, NY 10023-6298

Copyright © 2000
THE STONESONG PRESS
11 East 47th Street, New York, NY 10017
ISBN 0-7868-6663-2
Book design by Bob Antler, Antler Designworks

Library of Congress Cataloging-in-Publication Data
Bruns, Roger.
    Almost history : close calls, plan Bs, and twists
of fate in American history/by Roger Bruns.
      p. cm.
    "A Stonesong Press book."
    Includes index.
    ISBN 0-7868-6663-2
    1. United States—History—Anecdotes. 2. United States—History—Sources.
    3. Disasters—United States—History—Anecdotes. 4. Crises—United States—
    History—Anecdotes. I Title.

E179 .B92 2000
973—dc21   00-040769

A Stonesong Press book
FIRST EDITION
10 9 8 7 6 5 4 3

Photo Credits: Bettmann/Corbis: 268; William L. Clements Library, University of Michigan: 207; Dwight D. Eisenhower Library, Abilene, Kansas: 3; Reproduced by permission of The Huntington Library, San Marino, California: 147; John Fitzgerald Kennedy Library: 35, 39, 91, 99; Library of Congress: 23, 32, 49, 58, 114, 116, 176, 178, 180, 217, 223, 233, 251, 260, 263; National Archives and Records Administration: 18, 20, 28, 66, 68, 96, 104, 129, 153, 186, 220, 239, 241, 245, 266; National Archives and Records Administration, Mid-Atlantic Region, Philadelphia: 73; National Archives and Records Administration, Records of the Coast and Geodetic Survey: 111; Courtesy of the North Carolina Division of Archives and History: 54; Smithsonian Institution, National Air and Space Museum: 119; Smithsonian Institution, National Museum of American History: 174, 269; Harry S. Truman Library, Independence, Missouri: 190; UPI/Corbis-Bettman: 159.

Foreword by Douglas Brinkley

When I became assistant professor of history at Hofstra University, landing my first tenure-track position a decade ago, I had the great good fortune to become friends with Robert Sobel, who was then the Lawrence C. Stessin Distinguished Professor of Business History at Hofstra and working on his fortieth book: a study of the Wall Street investment firm Dillon Read & Co. Inc. Some who didn't know him well considered Bob just a congenial contrarian, an intellectual whose favorite president was Calvin Coolidge and his favorite financier disgraced ex-junk bond king Michael Milken. He had written the corporate histories of ITT, IBM, RCA, and Anheuser-Busch, among many others—but the book of which Sobel was proudest was his "what if" history, *For Want of a Nail: If Burgoyne Had Won at Saratoga* (1973). That extraordinary volume is based on the premise that if just one battle in the American Revolution had gone the other way, there might never have been a United States as we know it. In truth, a major turning point in the Revolution came when British general John Burgoyne, his forces heavily outnumbered by American troops, surrendered his army to General Horatio Gates at the Battle of Saratoga in 1777. In *For Want of a Nail*, however, Sobel postulates that redcoat reinforcements arrived at Saratoga, Gates's men fled, and Burgoyne won the day.

In consequence, rather than openly allying with the seemingly hapless American rebels, France in fact withdrew its support, as did Spain, and the colonies surrendered. Erstwhile rebels who refused to live in the Confederation of North America subsequently established by the British left their homes and resettled in what would become the United States of Mexico. From then on the two new nations were locked in military, political, and economic conflict.

Every time we had lunch together Sobel prodded me to consider "what if" scenarios beyond the Battle of Saratoga, including alternative outcomes to Abraham Lincoln's assassination, Woodrow Wilson's Zimmerman telegram spurring America's entry into World War I, and Richard Nixon's resignation. These speculations were for fun, meant to stimulate conversation and trigger debate. It was a hobby, really: some people do *The New York Times* crossword puzzle, others read Zane Grey pulp Westerns, still others collect obscure foreign stamps in their leisure time; Bob liked to envision historical "what ifs" undergirded by his encyclopedic facility with America's past. Sometimes he used to forewarn that he was going to compile a book of actual documents that would inspire readers to ponder the randomness of historical events and the role luck plays in world affairs—a volume, he said, that would be devoted to the old maxim that "history is a matter of inches."

Unfortunately, my friend Robert Sobel died in 1999 at the age of 68, leaving behind a shelf bulging with books on business history and a raft of unanswered "what ifs." Well, if he were still alive Sobel would be delighted by the publication of *Almost History: Close Calls, Plan B's and Twists of Fate in America's Past*, edited by Roger Bruns, deputy executive director of the National Historical Publications and Records Commission at the National Archives. Each of the 90 documents included in this riveting anthology could serve as the launchpad for a "what if" narrative like that in *For Want of a Nail*. Bruns's concise explanatory text accompanying the selections in *Almost History* provides the historical context in which each was composed—but what makes this book truly valuable is that every one of the documents cited is an authentic work, written either as policy-making background or for periodical publication. As a result, the various and sometimes startling documents and anecdotes here underline just how tenuous historical achievements are.

The very first selection in *Almost History*, for example, is a note Allied Commander Dwight D. Eisenhower wrote to himself on June 5, 1944, and carried in his pocket just in case the D-Day invasion of Normandy turned disastrous. "Our landings in the Cherbourg-Havre have failed to gain a satisfactory foothold and I have withdrawn the troops," the general wrote. "My decision to attack at this time and place was based upon the best information available. The troops, the Air [Corps.] and the Navy did all that bravery and devotion to duty could do. If any blame or fault attaches to the attempt it is mine alone."

Eisenhower's note raises fascinating questions: what would have happened had the Americans not been successful at Omaha and Utah Beaches, or the Canadians at Juno, or the British at Gold and Sword? Would Hitler's Germany have won World War II, or at least been afforded enough time to develop their own atomic bomb? If so, how would the Nazis have used it, and to what outcome? The commanding general's handwritten one page, now under glass at the Eisenhower Library in Abilene, Kansas, encapsulates the uncertainty in every moment in history, and particularly at its turning points.

Almost History also includes the powerful speech William Safire wrote and President Nixon never had to deliver about the failure of the *Apollo 11* mission, prepared just in case astronauts Neil Armstrong and Edwin "Buzz" Aldrin died on the moon instead of returning safely to Earth as they did. "Fate has ordained that the men who went to the moon to explore peace will stay on the moon to rest in peace," Safire's draft began. "In ancient days, men looked at stars and saw their heroes in the constellations. In modern times, we do much the same, but our heroes are epic men of flesh and blood. Others will follow, and surely find their way home. Man's search will not be denied. But these men were the first, and will remain the foremost in our hearts. For every human being who looks up at the moon in the nights to come will know that there is some corner of another world that is forever mankind." What powerful words, happily never spoken. Yet the mere existence of the speech jolts us to remember just how grandly risky the *Apollo 11* mission was, and how impossibly brave its astronauts were. Today we take their epochal moonwalk of July 20, 1969, for granted, because it occurred without a hitch. Reading the speech the president would have delivered otherwise forces us to recall just how dangerous the enterprise was, and thus just how important.

Perhaps the most unsettling document in *Almost History* is of more recent vintage: an urgent January 11, 1994, cable from Major General Romeo Dallaire, the U.N. Force Commander in Rwanda, warning of imminent genocide in that strife-torn Central African nation. An informant had warned Dallaire of the majority Hutu faction's intent to exterminate their Tutsi rivals, but nobody listened. As the Hutus launched their grisly attempt at systematic ethnic eradication—murdering somewhere between 500,000 and 1 million Tutsis—the U.S. government tried to downplay the genocide as a mere tribal conflict. Recently, however, President Bill Clinton told a group of survivors of the massacre that the United States had reason to be ashamed of its moral failure in Rwanda, and that in hindsight it is clear his administration should have acted to stop the wholesale slaughter. "All over the world there were people like me sitting in offices who did not fully appreciate the depth and the speed with which you were being engulfed by this unimaginable terror," Clinton lamented; had he read and acted upon General Dallaire's urgent missive, thousands of Rwandan lives might have been spared.

Almost History compels us to remember that chance—and the free will of individuals—determines history, which makes it instructive to study not only actual decisions and their results but what poet Robert Frost called "the road not taken." Whether it's a thankfully ignored recommendation that the United States use nuclear weapons in the Vietnam War; John F. Kennedy's prepared address justifying his bombing Cuba during the missile crisis, or a document outlining Abraham Lincoln's plans for post–Civil War Reconstruction, which differed radically from those actually implemented by his successor President Andrew Johnson, the selections in *Almost History* captivate the imagination into pondering the past from a startling "what if" perspective. It's too bad Robert Sobel can't see this book he dreamed of.

Douglas Brinkley
May 21, 2000
New Orleans, Louisiana

Contents

TWISTS OF IRONY

Introduction

What if the South had won the Civil War? What if the Battle of Midway had gone the other way? Most of the fiction, screenplays, films, and other artistic creations rooted in such themes did not originate from actual evidence of an occurrence or near occurrence that could have literally produced a different history. But here, in this collection, is such evidence, documents that give power and integrity to a discussion that begins "Suppose. . . ."

The idea of "what if" has always been around as a topic, not only for novelists but for historians and philosophers. Nearly every aspect of the past can be subjected to such discussion, from the most consequential events to the mundane. *Almost History* is a collection of original source documents that looks at many turning points in American history when events might have taken a different road or taken on a different cast. It presents materials that shed light on ways in which history has been distorted and wrongly perceived. Here are urban legends turned into fact, sorry prognostications, and other aberrations showing that the knowledge of the past is less than a science and more a mélange of inference, speculation, and perception.

Gathered from public and private manuscript repositories, libraries, and archives, from published sources of documentary materials, and from recently declassified State Department, FBI, and other federal records, these historical documents are a direct link to the past, giving us firsthand testimony. This is not secondhand, legend-filled history; this is history's sinew. The materials give us answers and raise new questions.

In revealing significant new information and insights, documents can change the way we look at our past. What sets this collection apart as we consider history's twists and turns and might-have-beens is that it is not based merely on supposition. Here are actual texts, documentary examples of the paths that history could have taken.

If history is not a continuum, if the shape of the past is affected by chance and error, and even the weather is not preordained, then it is fair to imagine a Europe after a Nazi victory, an independent Confederate South, a 20th century in which the names of Stalin and

Mao mean nothing, or even the kind of world that may have existed if the Mediterranean had never filled with water.

Recently, the writing of such historical speculation has expanded into "alternate history," a unique genre. Alternate history—the description of a historical "what if" and its possible consequences—is experiencing a surge of popularity among readers who debate history's different scenarios. Writers of alternate history have developed a jargon that uses such terms as "counterfactuals" and "points of divergence." They chat on the Internet and present new creations at meetings of professional science-fiction writers.

Authors such as Harry Turtledove specialize in writing alternate history. Historians such as James McPherson are entering the field in quickly rising numbers. Scholars such as Niall Ferguson and Mark Conway have recently published anthologies composed of alternate-history writings. While the speculations are interesting, provocative, and enjoyable, they will always be debatable.

Almost History differs in that it presents documents that provide actual scenarios and evidence of "decision points"—any of which could have led to a battle lost instead of won, lives saved instead of sacrificed. It presents records of legends born, myths created, and crimes and lies exposed. For example, you will read about the pivotal Battle of Saratoga during the American Revolution and British general William Howe's shocking decision not to fortify Gen. John Burgoyne's position, as his own fellow officers had assumed he would. If Howe had helped defeat the Continental army at Saratoga, would we now be singing "God Save the Queen" at baseball games? Would there even be such a game as baseball?

Want to speculate on the absence of key world leaders at critical times? What if Winston Churchill had not narrowly escaped death in a traffic accident in New York in 1931? What British statesman, if any, could have rallied his country against Nazi aggression?

The documents in *Almost History* provide the nexus that can drive an alternate story—that point at which change in fact could have begun. The documents speak to the sometimes chilling fragility of history, the seemingly innocuous and serendipitous events that had enormous repercussions but that could have been altered. One of Yogi Berra's insights is appropriate here: "When you come to a fork in the road, take it." This book offers a number of forks.

These documents strip away secrecy and provide a look into history's close calls and touches of irony. In these notes, memos, speeches, agendas, letters, plans, drawings, and press releases, there is a kind of counterhistory, powerful documentary evidence that only slight changes of time, chance, weather, or a second thought could have altered history's fabric. Here is hard evidence from historical roads nearly taken, triggers of fate nearly pulled. We are familiar with what has come down to us as history. Let the evidence show what was *Almost History*. And let the reader imagine the rest.

Acknowledgments

The idea of this book came from the fertile imagination of Paul Fargis, president of The Stonesong Press, a man of many worthy ideas. Paul had seen an article in the *New York Times* by William Safire, in which the former speechwriter for Richard Nixon reminisced about a speech he had composed, one that, thank God, never had to be delivered—a message notifying the world that the Apollo 11 astronauts had been lost on their journey to the moon. Poignant but not maudlin, patriotic and human, the speech was a jarring reminder of how dangerous moon exploration had been and how tenuous had been the success of this particular mission to myriad uncertainties and unknowns. And, as an actual document that could have been used had it been necessary, it was especially powerful.

What about a book of similar speeches, letters, reports, and other historical records that would reveal other instances in which the nation might have experienced different historical outcomes given other exigencies, other dice rolls, other flirtations with danger and fate? The marvelous thing about American history is its richness and diversity. Take a journey of discovery like this back through the country's past and rewards will certainly be there. This book is a compilation of some of what we found.

In that journey I received much help. Mary Giunta and Timothy Connelly, fellow staff members of the National Historical Publications and Records Commission at the National Archives in Washington, D.C., provided many fine suggestions. My wife, Carrie E. Bruns, was particularly helpful in sorting out examples that worked well from those that did not.

Ellen Scordato and Sarah Parvis at Stonesong Press provided their substantial editorial skills. My good friend Laura Kreiss did her usual outstanding photographic research, managing to come up with some material that I had no idea existed.

I especially want to acknowledge the help of David Rudgers, historian and former analyst at the CIA, whose broad range of knowledge of American history I gratefully tapped and most of whose editorial suggestions I respectfully followed.

To these individuals and to the team at Hyperion Books, one of the planet's most professional and classy book publishing organizations, I offer my hearty thanks.

ALMOST

PLANNING FOR THE WORST

HISTORY

If D-Day Had Stood for Disaster—1944

**Personal note of Dwight D. Eisenhower
in case of D-Day disaster**

G roup Capt. James Stagg, chief meteorologist for the Royal Air Force, made what some believe was one of the most important weather predictions in military history: gradual clearing on June 6, 1944, in Normandy, France. Against an entrenched German army, mounds of hedgerows and sunken roads, Gen. Dwight D. Eisenhower, Supreme Commander of the Allied Expeditionary Forces, had prepared a massive assault, "the opening phase," he said, "of the campaign in Western Europe." An invasion force called Operation Overlord consisting of 4,000 ships, 11,000 planes, and nearly three million soldiers, airmen, and sailors assembled in England for the assault. But everything depended on a break in the bad weather that was plaguing the English Channel, a window of opportunity for the assault to take the Germans by surprise.

General Eisenhower trusted in Captain Stagg's prediction and went forward with the plans. The dismal, rainy days that preceded June 6—which did force Eisenhower and the Allies to delay the landing by one day—finally lifted, and more than 150,000 troops stormed the beaches. Their objective: to open a second major European front in the battle against the Germans. Victory was uncertain. The day before the landing, Eisenhower drafted a note in his own hand on a small sheet of paper, a message to be delivered in the event the invasion failed. In the rush of the moment, he wrote July on the bottom, rather than June, and put the note in his wallet.

As the attack began, Allied troops faced not only withering fire on the beaches from artillery and machine guns but a maze of tangled barbed wire and other barriers designed to prevent landing craft from reaching shore. About 4,900 soldiers—American, British, and Canadian—became casualties that momentous day on beaches called Utah, Omaha, Juno, Gold, and Sword. But at its end, the Allied troops were firmly ashore and in control of 80 square miles of French coast. The final destruction of Hitler's Third Reich had begun. The value of the message in General Eisenhower's wallet was not in its utility but in its symbolism: the Allies had turned history in their favor.

But what if the break in the rain and fog had not occurred, and the Allies had attempted the invasion in bad weather, thus placing their troops at even greater risk, or instead had delayed the invasion for many days, thus jeopard-

izing the advantage of surprise they had carefully constructed? The note that Eisenhower carried in his pocket that day was not based on unreasonable fear of failure but on a distinct possibility that Operation Overlord could have brought tragic loss.

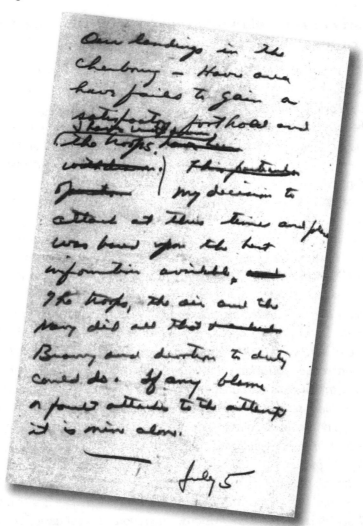

Personal Note of Dwight D. Eisenhower, June 5, 1944

Our landings in the Cherbourg-Havre have failed to gain a satisfactory foothold and I have withdrawn the troops. My decision to attack at this time and place was based upon the best information available. The troops, the air and the Navy did all that Bravery and devotion to duty could do. If any blame or fault attaches to the attempt it is mine alone.

Operation Unthinkable and World War III—1945

Report of British plan to invade Soviet Union with British, American, and German troops

As World War II entered its final phase with Allied armies driving deeper into Germany, the "grand alliance" between the western democracies and the Soviet Union was already unraveling. As discord began to surface, a number of western leaders began to see Josef Stalin as a new postwar menace. Foremost among them was British prime minister Winston Churchill. With his long view of history and reflexive anti-Sovietism, he saw the massive Red Army that forced the Germans out of Eastern Europe as a major threat and manifestation of Stalin's aggressive ambitions, now that it had marched farther west than any Russian army since the days of Napoleon.

Over the years many historians have suspected that Western leaders formulated contingency plans to face the Soviet threat. Now, more than half a century following the war, documents have been uncovered in British public archives showing that a few days after Germany's surrender, Prime Minister Winston Churchill directed his aides to draft plans for an Anglo-American invasion of the Soviet Union. Code-named Operation Unthinkable, the plan included the use of up to 100,000 German troops to back up 500,000 British and American soldiers attacking through northern Germany. Although Churchill regarded the plan as "a purely hypothetical contingency," he considered the Soviet problem serious enough to have his staff prepare detailed estimates of losses and probable outcomes. "The overall or political object is to impose upon Russia the will of the United States and British Empire," declared the report, given to Churchill by Lt. Gen. Sir Hastings Ismay, on May 22, 1945.

Although discounting the idea of "total war" against the Soviet Union, the plan assumed that World War III would begin on July 1, 1945, with a first strike by 47 British and American divisions. The report also suggested the rearming of up to 10 German divisions, a suggestion that proclaimed in stark relief just how great the vicissitudes of war could actually be. Thus, soldiers of the recent great Nazi evil empire, men who had a few weeks earlier killed Allied soldiers, would now fight side by side with them to extinguish the latest evil empire. The report planners recognized the anomaly but pointed out that "ingrained fear of the Bolshevik menace and of reprisals by the Russians should make the German civil population prefer Anglo-American to Russian occupation and therefore incline it to side with the Western allies."

The postwar plan to take on the Soviet Union envisioned a surprise attack by the Allies between Dresden and the Baltic. Stalin, the planners concluded, would probably invade Turkey, Greece, Norway, and the Iranian and Iraqi oil fields and then launch sabotage operations in France and the Netherlands. With Soviet troops outnumbering Allied forces by more than two to one, the planners cautioned against waging a full-scale drive into Russia, an exercise in folly that had been tried by other armies with disastrous consequences.

After considering the assessments provided by the report, Churchill wrote to Lt. Gen. Ismay conveying his concerns that an offensive strike against the Red Army might produce results more deleterious than if the British were merely to plan for an effective defensive posture. War planners informed Churchill that they believed the Soviets would not be ready to invade for several years because of Britain's superiority at sea but could mount a vicious air assault.

Less than two months after this report was prepared, Churchill's government was ousted by the British electorate. Great Britain, exhausted by war and shorn of its empire, had neither the will nor the resources to pursue such an adventure, and the United States, now the world's dominant power, would never have cooperated. Nevertheless, this gem of Churchillian thinking represents a fascinating alternative to the history of international conflict in the postwar world, and fortunately a "road not taken."

Excerpts from Operation Unthinkable Report, 1945

To achieve the decisive defeat of Russia in a total war would require, in particular, the mobilisation of manpower to counteract their present enormous manpower resources. This is a very long-term project and would involve: a) the deployment in Europe of a large proportion of the vast resources of the United States. b) the re-equipment and re-organisation of German manpower and of all the Western European Allies. . . .

Superior handling and air superiority might enable us to win the battle, but there is no inherent strength in our strategic position and we should, in fact, be staking everything upon the tactical outcome of one great engagement. . . .

If we are to embark on war with Russia, we must be prepared to be committed to a total war, which will be both long and costly. Our numerical inferiority on land renders it extremely doubtful whether we could achieve a limited and quick success, even if the political appreciation considered that this would suffice to gain our political objective. . . .

When Bomb Shelters Were In: The ABCs of Surviving an A-Bomb Attack—1954, 1962

A 1954 article on survival and a 1962 Civil Service Commission memorandum on federal employees' response to a nuclear attack

When you joined the federal government in the 1960s, you received a memorandum from the Civil Service Commission explaining steps you, as a government employee, should take in the case of a nuclear attack. The procedure was actually quite simple. After the nuclear explosion, you were to go to the nearest post office where a postal official would, amid the rubble, dutifully give you a registration card to fill out. After the cards from all the surviving members of the federal workforce were organized and tallied, each employee would be notified where to report again for work. Life would be changed by the bomb, certainly, but the government would march forward, orderly, organized, and as unfazed as possible by the conflagration and dislocation heaped on American society.

The nuclear havoc at Hiroshima and Nagasaki had unveiled to the world the possibility of sudden extermination by technology. American government officials, civic leaders, and social planners attempted to cope. Although nuclear devastation in a cold war society was possible (many believed probable), the nation could be prepared. Children in elementary schools and high schools soon learned the techniques, such as ducking under their desks should they see the ominous first sign of nuclear explosion—the blinding flash of light. Families, if they could afford it, invested large sums of money on underground bomb shelters, where, like the Morlocks in H.G. Wells's The Time Machine, they could live for an extended period underground, safe from the deadly radioactive clouds that would envelop the planet. Civic leaders prepared civil defense plans and conducted drills. Television featured test announcements that would appear, viewers were instructed, if nuclear war exploded.

The high-stakes gamesmanship over Cuba in 1962 reinforced fears that the nation was on the brink—that all of the preparation, all of the bunker-making and body-tucking, all of the drills and public service announcements had been on the mark—that nuclear horror was, indeed, almost history.

Albuquerque Journal, 1954

Before Bomb Falls:

A. Keep at a minimum exposed inflammable material around premises. . . .

B. Keep trash cans covered.

C. Rake up and destroy dry leaves and trash around buildings, clear attics and basements of combustible materials.

D. Have flashlights handy.

E. At first alarm, shut off oil burners, gas pilot lights, furnaces, water heaters.

F. At alert make dwelling as near airtight as possible. Close doors, shut windows and draw blinds as a protection against fire sparks, glass splinters and nuclear radioactivity.

G. Put family auto in closed garage or at least close all car windows. . . . Don't stay in auto; its gasoline may ignite.

When Bomb Bursts:

A. Fall flat on stomach. Cover face with arms; close eyes tightly. To view dazzling blast may cause temporary blindness. Five miles away the light glares as brightly as 100 suns. If outdoors, seek a ditch, gutter or side of strong wall or tree. If indoors, seek a basement and be next to wall away from windows and middle of room where falling beams may land. . . . The explosion sends out a destructive shock wave—a shell of air compressed so tightly it glows white-hot. Behind this comes an 800-mile-an-hour wind. . . .

B. Shield body from possible flash burns or radioactive wastes. Cover body with few sheets of newspaper, a board, raincoat or a torn strip of awning.

C. Wait for 'all-clear' signal before leaving shelter. Allow lingering radioactivity time to subside. Travel against the wind instead of with it on leaving shelter, if possible.

After Bombing:

A. Obey authorities, remain calm and resist panic.

B. Don't light matches or cigarettes in building that may be filled with gas from broken lines.

C. Avoid touching waste materials when arising. They may contain radioactive bomb ashes.

D. Eat or drink nothing. It may be radioactively contaminated.

Shun unpackaged foods, be wary of bottled or canned foods or medicines, water, until they are checked by Geiger counters. . . .

E. Wear rubbers or cloths on shoes when in bombed areas, remove shoes when entering home. . . . Scrub clothes in disposable tubs; don't contaminate family washing machine. Bathe, scrub body. Vigorously scrub fingernails. . . . Lacking water, vigorously rub skin with uncontaminated paper or cloth. . . .

—————————————————————————

**U.S. Civil Service Commission Memorandum,
November 13, 1962**

UNITED STATES CIVIL SERVICE COMMISSION
WASHINGTON 25, D.C.

November 13, 1962

CSC EMPLOYEE LETTER a-103
        (Supersedes CSC EL B-115)
TO ALL EMPLOYEES

SUBJECT: Nationwide Post-Attack Registration of Federal
        Employees

Each one of us, as citizens and Federal employees, has a responsibility to contribute to the strength of our Nation. Just as we as individuals must work out plans for ourselves and our families in an emergency, so also must our Government maintain plans to make sure it can continue to operate even in the event of an attack on this Country.

Many Commission employees have specific responsibilities and instructions regarding relocation in the event of a national emergency. Those of you who have such a relocation assignment have been formally notified. At the same time, many of you do not have specific assignments in the Commission's emergency staffing plan. However, all Commission employees, with or without specific emergency assignments, should be fully aware of the nationwide post-attack registration system for Federal employees.

In the event of an emergency brought about by an attack on this Country, the Civil Service Commission will operate a registration system for Federal employees in affected areas. The procedure for this system is as follows:

If you are prevented from going to your regular place of work because of an enemy attack—or if you are prevented from reporting to any emergency location—keep this instruction in mind—*go to the nearest Post Office, ask the Postmaster for a Federal employee registration card, fill it out and return it to him.* He will see that it is forwarded to the office of the Civil Service Commission which will maintain the registration file for your area. After the card is received, decision will be made as to where and when you should report back for work. There is another important reason why you should mail in a registration card as soon as you can do so—this card will also enable us to keep you on the roster of active employees, and enable us to forward your pay.

You should obtain and *complete the registration card as soon after enemy attack as possible* but not until you are relatively sure where you will be staying for a few days.

Expiration Date: *Indefinite*

Pricing Quemoy and Matsu—1958

Top-secret memorandum of Gerard C. Smith to Undersecretary of State Christian C. Herter, on defense of Quemoy and Matsu

On October 13, 1960, Americans gathered around their television sets to watch the junior senator from Massachusetts, John F. Kennedy, and the vice president of the United States, Richard M. Nixon, square off in their third debate. One of the most contentious issues argued by the candidates was the policy of the United States should the Communist government of mainland China undertake an assault on two obscure islands—Quemoy and Matsu—located just off the Chinese coast. Although the two islands were within the territorial waters of the People's Republic of China, they were occupied by the Nationalist forces of Chiang Kai-Shek, in exile on Taiwan since his defeat in 1949. Unquestionably and understandably, few viewers that night were familiar with the islands or the issues surrounding them.

In 1958, the Chinese Communists had bombarded Quemoy and Matsu and blockaded the islands against Chinese Nationalist resupply efforts, claiming that the islands had been used by the Nationalists as a base to conduct raids on mainland China. The Eisenhower administration deployed forces to the region, including a large naval contingent in the Taiwan Straits. Both President Eisenhower and Secretary of State John Foster Dulles publicly affirmed the U.S. commitment to defend Taiwan and to counter naval threats in the region. American naval aircraft also helped the Nationalist air force establish control of the region's airspace. Flying American-made fighters, Nationalist pilots defeated their Communist opponents in a series of air battles. Despite Soviet support of the Chinese Communists' claims to the islands, the military skirmishes virtually ceased after Eisenhower again warned that the United States would not retreat "in the face of armed aggression."

During the debate in 1960, Vice President Nixon was asked whether, as president, he would plunge the United States into a war with the Chinese if they invaded the islands and if he would consider the use of nuclear weapons. Mr. Nixon responded that he would honor treaty obligations and stand by our ally, the Republic of China [Taiwan]. But to speculate on what specific military course he might recommend would be inappropriate, the vice president continued. "Now what do the Chinese Communists want? They don't want just Quemoy and Matsu. They don't want just Formosa; they want the world. And the question is, if you surrender or indicate in advance that you're not going to defend any part of the free world, and you figure that's going to satisfy them, it doesn't satisfy them. It only whets their appetite. And then the question comes: When do you stop them?"

Responding to Nixon's remarks, Kennedy accused the vice president not only of saber-rattling but of misrepresenting the treaty obligations under which the United States had pledged to defend the island of Taiwan and the Pescadores, not the islands of Quemoy and Matsu. "Mr. Nixon suggests that the United States should go to war if these two islands are attacked," said Kennedy. "I suggest that if Formosa is attacked or the Pescadores or if there's any military action in any area which indicates an attack on Formosa and the Pescadores then, of course, the United States is at war to defend its treaty."

What Americans did not know at the time of the Kennedy Nixon debates is that the Eisenhower administration had carefully calculated the cost of defending Quemoy and Matsu. A memorandum disclosed in chilling terms the possible nuclear consequences of public commitments by the United States to defend the islands. Pursuing such a policy, the war planners said, might result in nuclear strikes on Shanghai and Canton, resulting in "millions of non-combatant casualties."

The United States did not reach a point in the Cold War in which a decision was necessary to use nuclear power to defend Quemoy and Matsu. To this day the islands remain under the control of Taiwan. Yet the issue, four decades later, has not died. A Global Intelligence Update dated August 16, 1999, of Stratfor, Inc., a private intelligence firm in Austin, Texas, reported that there have been diplomatic rumblings concerning the Chinese Communists' possible "seizure of two islands, Quemoy and Matsu, that are just off the mainland of China but are controlled by Taiwan. The islands were frequently shelled and threatened during the Cold War. Their seizure would be a high-profile, low-risk operation within the amphibious capabilities of China."

Memorandum of Gerard C. Smith to Undersecretary of State Christian C. Herter, August 13, 1958

Top Secret
August 13, 1958

MEMORANDUM FOR MR. HERTER

Subject: August 14 Discussion of Taiwan Straits

The question of the review of US policy on the Offshore Islands was raised yesterday in the Planning Board. After this meeting, I was shown a copy of the memorandum of your meeting on this subject with the Secretary and others on August 8, at which the Secretary indicated that it may be desirable to make a clearer public statement of our intentions.

It may be useful for you to have the following points in mind during tomorrow's NSC discussion:

1. It is our understanding that current JCS war plans call for the defense of Quemoy and Matsu by nuclear strikes deep into Communist China, including military targets in the Shanghai-Hangehow-Nanking and Canton complexes where population density is extremely high.

2. The attached excerpts from the recent "Limited War" study are pertinent. During this study we were advised by representatives of the Joint Chiefs that military planning contained therein was based on the existing contingent war plan.

3. While nuclear strikes would be with "low yield" weapons, this would include weapons having a yield comparable to 20 KT weapons dropped on Hiroshima and Nagasaki. It is my judgment that before such hostilities were over there would be millions of non-combatant casualties. . . .

[4. missing in original]

5. The President recently directed the preparations of a National Intelligence Estimate on Sino-Soviet and Free World Reactions to US Use of Nuclear Weapons in Limited Wars in the Far East. It concludes that if our present military planning was carried out Peiping [Beijing] and its Soviet ally would probably feel compelled to react with nuclear attacks at least on Taiwan and on the Seventh Fleet. Under our present strategic concept, this would be the signal for general nuclear war between the US and USSR.

6. I doubt that Congressional leaders are aware of the implications of exercising the authority under the resolution of January 29, 1955, by the method planned by the JCS. If a decision is taken to issue a clarifying statement, it may be desirable to consult with key Congressional leaders.

In the light of the above considerations, it seems to me that the US does not have a politically feasible capability to defend Quemoy and Matsu. I question whether, in the event of an attack on Quemoy and Matsu, we should or will run the very grave risk of general nuclear war attendant on our present military planning. If the vital security interests of the US require us to defend these islands, we should, on an urgent basis, develop an alternative military capability based on a local defense of these islands which would give some hope of limiting the hostilities. Until we are within sight of such a local defense capability, I question the wisdom of any public clarification of our commitment in regard to Quemoy and Matsu.

Gerard C. Smith

Predelegating Nuclear Terror—1959

Instructions for expenditure of nuclear weapons in emergency conditions

The existence of the atomic bomb produced assorted national neuroses in the 1950s. On one hand, the country had to protect itself from enemy attack. Thus, we designed sophisticated retaliatory systems and announced to all adversaries that a first strike against the United States would result in annihilation of the aggressor. As we built a balance-of-power nuclear deterrent policy, we developed elaborate mechanisms to warn us of possible attack and procedures for reacting to those warnings.

At the same time, we worried about all of this new technology, about the possibility of accidents, of misunderstandings, of treachery, of all kinds of situations in which a mistake could trigger nuclear disaster. We started to learn terms such as "fail-safe" and "defcon." Novelists and moviemakers responded.

In 1964, Stanley Kubrick's masterpiece Dr. Strangelove: How I Learned to Stop Worrying and Love the Bomb, based on the novel Red Alert by Peter George, opened with a deranged General Jack D. Ripper (Sterling Hayden) declaring a "Code Red," sealing off his air force base, and ordering a nuclear attack on the Soviet Union. When his assistant, RAF Group Captain Mandrake (Peter Sellers), advises moderation, Ripper replies that he intends to launch a preemptive strike to stop a Communist infiltration that is "sapping and impurifying all of our precious bodily fluids." Although the U.S. president (an Adlai Stevenson-like figure also played by Sellers) sends army paratroopers under the intrepid Col. Bat Guano (Keenan Wynn) to retake the base commanded by Ripper, it is too late to recall the bombers Ripper sent out, one of which (commanded by actor Slim Pickens) initiates nuclear holocaust.

In the film, the familiar reference to "missile gaps" is expanded to include "mine shaft gaps" and, forebodingly, the "doomsday gap." The story of humanity's meltdown in a nuclear fireball was parody, but the fears evoked in Dr. Strangelove rose from circumstances not as far-fetched or removed from the parody as we might have believed.

Declassified documents show that top military commanders, beginning in the late 1950s, had presidentially authorized advance authority to use nuclear weapons under certain emergency conditions. In 1959, President Eisenhower signed off on predelegation instructions allowing such use if a Soviet attack on Washington killed national command authorities. The instructions remained in *place throughout the 1960s. Similar authority may be in place to this day.*

In Dr. Strangelove, *General Turgidson (George C. Scott) observed that General Ripper's ability to cause a nuclear disaster is a case of "the human element" having "failed us here," but "it's not fair to condemn the whole program because of one slipup." Fortunately, no General Ripper has ever appeared. But what if he had? What about the possibility of an accident? During the Cuban Missile Crisis, the U.S. Air Force accidentally test-fired an intercontinental ballistic missile (ICBM), and Secretary of Defense Robert McNamara told other government officials that he worried that a designated commander might confuse an accidental nuclear launch with an all-out attack. The issue of command and control of nuclear weapons has remained a dilemma that has outlived the Cold War itself.*

Instructions for Expenditure of Nuclear Weapons in Emergency Conditions, December 1959

The Joint Chiefs of Staff
Washington, D.C.

MEMORANDUM FOR COMMANDER IN CHIEF,
STRATEGIC AIR COMMAND

Subject: Instructions for Expenditure of Nuclear
         Weapons in Emergency Conditions (S)

1. The President has authorized certain Commanders of Unified and Specified Commands to expend nuclear weapons in defense of the United States, its Territories, possessions and forces when the urgency of time and circumstances clearly does not permit a specific decision by the President, or other person empowered to act in his stead. Such commanders will be called Authorizing Commanders.

2. This authorization by the President is an emergency measure necessitated by recognition of the fact that communications may be disrupted by an attack (as defined in the Enclosure). Each Authorizing Commander must insure that such delegation of authority is not assumed through accident or misinformation. Further, it should be regarded as an authorization effective only until it is possible to communicate with the President or other person empowered to act for him.

[excised portion still classified]

3. OPERATIONAL LIMITATIONS. Because of the serious international implications of the use of nuclear weapons by U.S. military forces, it is essential that particularly strict command control and supervision be exercised, and that the use of nuclear weapons be limited to circumstances of grave necessity.

Not an Extraterrestrial—1962

Message carried by John Glenn on *Friendship 7*

On February 20, 1962, astronaut John Glenn sat in a 9½-by-6-foot space capsule called Friendship 7 hurtling across the skies 100 miles above the earth. His fellow Americans listened to reports of the historic flight with a sense of both awe and dread.

President Dwight D. Eisenhower had signed into being the National Aeronautics and Space Administration (NASA) on July 29, 1958. One of the first assignments given to the new agency was to launch a man into space and return him safely to earth. Project Mercury was created to fulfill that mission.

On April 9, 1959, NASA formally introduced to the world the seven test pilots who would carry out Project Mercury: Lt. Comdrs. Malcolm Scott Carpenter, Walter Marty Schirra, and Alan B. Shepard of the navy; Capts. Leroy Gordon Cooper, Virgil I. "Gus" Grissom, and Donald "Deke" Slayton of the Air Force; and Lt. Col. John H. Glenn of the Marine Corps.

Born on July 18, 1921, Glenn was the oldest of the group, a veteran of World War II and the Korean War who had flown 149 combat missions and had been awarded the Distinguished Flying Cross five times. In 1957, he set a transcontinental speed record for the first flight to average supersonic speed (seven hundred miles per hour) from Los Angeles to New York.

Project Mercury was daunting, with many unknowns to overcome: weightlessness, problems with mechanical design, setbacks in constructing a satisfactory booster in the Atlas rocket, and the many variables that a project of this magnitude would necessarily face. To add to the mounting tension, poor weather and mechanical problems with the rocket forced NASA to scrub Glenn's scheduled mission nine times. Glenn also worried about another issue. NASA officials had told him that no matter where he landed he would be picked up within 72 hours. The likely landing sites were Australia, the Atlantic Ocean, and New Guinea. Glenn said he imagined an aborigine hearing the noise in the sky, watching "a big parachute with a little capsule on the end" descend, and then seeing a creature in a silver space suit and helmet step out of the craft.

In addition to his undoubted courage and spirit of adventure, Glenn also had a practical, careful streak. Seventy-two hours seemed like an extraordinary amount of time to sit around in a strange country amid curious onlookers. He decided to take with him a short speech translated into several languages with phonetic pronunciations, announcing that he came in peace.

Glenn did not need to use the speech. He splashed down in the Atlantic Ocean, south of Cape Canaveral. How useful this short speech would have been to an astronaut, surrounded by baffled natives, is anyone's guess.

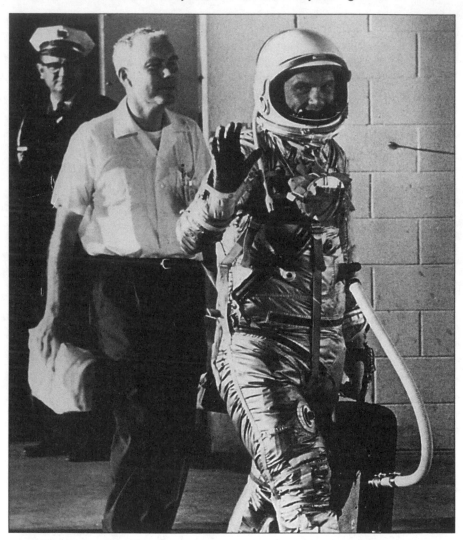

Astronaut John Glenn waves to photographers and others gathered at Cape Kennedy, Florida, prior to his historic Mercury-Atlas 6 Friendship 7 *space-craft flight on February 20, 1962.*

Message carried by John Glenn on *Friendship 7*, February 1962

I am a stranger. I come in peace. Take me to your leader, and there will be a massive reward for you in eternity.

Losing the Astronauts—1969

Draft of speech of President Richard Nixon
on loss of *Apollo 11* astronauts

On July 20, 1969, Neil Armstrong and Edwin "Buzz" Aldrin became the first men to walk on the moon. The feat was of epic dimensions. It could have been one of terrible sadness.

The individuals closest to Apollo 11 were certainly not convinced that the mission was a preordained success. They were confident but not certain that the years of careful calculations and preparations, that the work of 20,000 companies, hundreds of thousands of individuals, and some $2.5 billion, would successfully deliver the spacecraft to the moon surface, that the astronauts would step on the lunar surface, and that they would return safely to earth.

William Safire, a speechwriter for President Nixon, later remembered astronaut Frank Borman approaching him about the prospect of a tragedy. About a week before the launch, Borman suggested to Safire that the administration be prepared for the ceremonial trappings that should occur in case of an Apollo 11 mishap. What words would the president say, both to the widows and to the country? How would the stranded astronauts be treated by Mission Control?

In the days leading up to the launch, Safire and others planned for the tragic contingency that would take place if it became clear that the astronauts' lunar module could not, for whatever reasons, reattach to the command module for the return flight to Earth. If Armstrong and Aldrin had been stranded, the president was to call their wives to express condolences. He was then to deliver a speech to the nation, drafted by Safire. The end of the speech, echoing the British poet Rupert Brooke's words on World War I, was a salute to the men whose bodies ended up on foreign fields but whose spirits made those fields forever part of mankind.

The lost astronauts would "close down communications" with Mission Control in Houston and be left in silence, either to die slowly or, perhaps, to commit suicide with poison they apparently had with them. Finally, a clergyman would, as in a naval burial at sea, commend their souls to "the deepest of the deep."

The speech was not needed by President Nixon. In the president's diary of July 20, 1969, is this entry for 11:45 A.M.: "The President held an interplanetary conversation with Apollo 11 Astronauts, Neil Armstrong and Edwin Aldrin on the Moon." The men returned home as planned.

Safire's speech is a historic relic made even more poignant by the 1986 Challenger tragedy. The words written for Armstrong and Aldrin have the same currency for those who have sacrificed their lives in exploring the unknown, who "stirred the people of the world to feel as one."

Draft of William Safire's Speech for
President Richard Nixon, 1969

Aboard the recovery ship USS Hornet, Apollo 11 astronauts Neil Armstrong, Michael Collins, and Edwin "Buzz" Aldrin are greeted by President Richard M. Nixon on July 24, 1969, following their return from the successful lunar landing.

Fate has ordained that the men who went to the moon to explore in peace will stay on the moon to rest in peace.

These brave men, Neil Armstrong and Edwin Aldrin, know that there is no hope for their recovery. But they also know that there is hope for mankind in their sacrifice.

These two men are laying down their lives in mankind's most noble goal: the search for truth and understanding. They will be mourned by their families and friends; they will be mourned by their nation; they will be mourned by the people of the world; they will be mourned by a Mother Earth that dared send two of her sons into the unknown.

In their exploration, they stirred the people of the world to feel as one; in their sacrifice, they bind more tightly the brotherhood of man.

In ancient days, men looked at stars and saw their heroes in the constellations. In modern times, we do much the same, but our heroes are epic men of flesh and blood.

Others will follow, and surely find their way home. Man's search will not be denied. But these men were the first, and they will remain the foremost in our hearts.

For every human being who looks up at the moon in the nights to come will know that there is some corner of another world that is forever mankind.

ALMOST
FORKS IN THE ROAD
HISTORY

A Road Not Taken to Harper's Ferry —1859

**A newspaper and Frederick Douglass himself
tell why he visited West Virginia**

When a Chambersburg, West Virginia, newspaper reported a visit to the area by the black orator Frederick Douglass in August 1859, it praised his abilities but scoffed at his message of racial equality. But Douglass's visit to West Virginia had another purpose, one about which the newspaper reporter knew nothing. Douglass was there to meet the abolitionist John Brown. They were warriors in a common cause—the driven, messianic guerrilla fighter who had terrorized proslavery forces in Kansas and the young, brilliant ex-slave, orator, and writer, whose autobiography had helped galvanize the abolitionist movement with its harrowing account of life under slavery. The two had met at Douglass's home in Rochester, New York, in 1858 to plot a slave uprising. Brown had recently written Douglass, requesting money and inviting him to another meeting at an abandoned stone quarry near Chambersburg. The plan to set free many slaves, Brown said, was about to be launched.

Douglass made the trip to West Virginia, bringing along "Emperor" Shields Green, a former slave from South Carolina, with whom Brown was acquainted. When Douglass and Green met Brown and another abolitionist, John Kagi, in Chambersburg, Douglass realized that the old man's plan was something far bolder and more dangerous than he had been led to believe. Brown was assembling a tiny army to storm the U.S. arsenal at Harper's Ferry, a show of brazen resistance to strike a blow at slavery's heart, to embolden the slave community to rise up in righteous revolt. He wanted Douglass to join him.

Brown and Kagi tried desperately to convince Douglass; he tried equally as hard to dissuade them from carrying out their plan. No minds were changed. Insisting that the attack was suicidal, that Brown and his men would never escape alive, Douglass left his friends in West Virginia. Douglass was right. His friends lost their lives. Had Brown and the others been able to persuade Douglass to join them, Douglass would surely have been killed or later executed along with them. Had it not been for his decision in West Virginia, the voice and pen of Frederick Douglass would have been extinguished—the long career as journalist, spokesman for racial equality and equal rights for blacks and women, and his service as Charge d'Affaires for Santo Domingo and Minister Resident and Consul-General to Haiti. Because of his critical decision in West Virginia, Douglass did not, along with John Brown, become a martyr in 1859.

The causes for which he fought, Douglass knew, needed not only martyrs but active fighters. He lived to be one.

Chambersburg *Valley Spirit*, August 24, 1859

Fred. Douglass. This gentleman of color paid a visit, on Saturday last, to brighten the prospects of his Republican friends which are now so hopelessly in the *dark*. There is no calling in question the extraordinary ability Mr. Douglass as an Orator. He is an elegant and powerful speaker, and possesses a clear well modulated voice, and a style of elocution effective and impressive. His discourse was well received by a large and attentive audience, and with occasional demonstrations of applause from those who seemed disposed to favor his peculiar doctrine. His aim is to place the Negroes on equality with the white man—to have him eat at the same table, sit in the same pew, and vote at the same ballot box. He would appear to forget altogether the Creator Himself has made a distinction when he established the great and immovable barrier of color between the races. Mr. Douglass certainly does not benefit his cause by opening his vials of wrath on

A contemporary wood engraving depicts the siege of a fire engine house in which abolitionist John Brown and his followers had barricaded themselves during their assault on the federal arsenal at Harper's Ferry, Virginia, on October 17, 1859. Fellow abolitionist Frederick Douglass, who had decided not to join Brown, had left Virginia.

religion, or by representing our leading divines as monsters of inhumanity. They certainly are as capable of knowing what is right and what is wrong as he is, and may be supposed to be as honest in their views. We are constrained to say that portion of his discourse deserves the pointed rebuke of the whole community.

Recollections of Frederick Douglass

His face wore an anxious expression, and he was much worn by thought and exposure. I felt that I was on a dangerous mission, and was as little desirous of discovery as himself, though no reward had been offered for me.

We—Mr. Kagi, Captain Brown, Shields Green, and myself, sat down among the rocks and talked over the enterprise which was about to be undertaken. The taking of Harper's Ferry, of which Captain Brown had merely hinted before, was now declared as his settled purpose, and he wanted to know what I thought of it. I at once opposed the measure with all the arguments at my command. To me, such a measure would be fatal to running off slaves (as was the original plan), and fatal to all engaged in doing so. It would be an attack upon the federal government, and would array the whole country against us. Captain Brown did most of the talking on the other side of the question. He did not at all object to rousing the nation; it seemed to him that something startling was just what the nation needed. He had completely renounced his old plan, and thought that the capture of Harper's Ferry would serve a notice to the slaves that their friends had come, and as a trumpet to rally them to his standard. He described the place as to its means of defense, and how impossible it would be to dislodge him if once in possession. Of course I was no match for him in such matters, but I told him, and these were my words, that all his arguments, and all his descriptions of the place, convinced me that he was going into a perfect steel-trap, and that once in he would never get out alive; that he would be surrounded at once and escape would be impossible. He was not to be shaken by anything I could say, but treated my views respectfully, replying that even if surrounded he would find means for cutting his way out; but that would not be forced upon him; he should have a number of the best citizens of the neighborhood as his prisoners at the start, and that holding them as hostages, he should be able if worse came to worse, to dictate terms of egress from the town. I looked at him with some astonishment, that he could rest upon a reed so weak and broken, and told him that Virginia would blow him and his hostages sky-high, rather than that he should hold Harper's Ferry an hour. Our talk was long and earnest; we spent the most of Saturday and a part of Sunday in this debate—Brown for Harper's Ferry, and I against it; he for striking a blow which should instantly rouse the country, and I for the policy of gradually and unaccountably drawing off the slaves to the mountains, as at first suggested and proposed by him. When I found that he had fully made up his mind and could not be dissuaded, I turned to Shields Green and told him he heard what Captain Brown had said; his old plan was changed, and that I should return home, and if he wished to go with me he could do so. Captain Brown urged us both to go with him, but I could not do so, and could but feel that he was about to rivet the fetters more firmly than ever on the limbs of the enslaved. In parting he put his arms around me in a manner more than friendly, and said: "Come with me, Douglass, I will defend you with my life. I want you for a special purpose. When I strike the bees will begin to swarm, and I shall want you to help hive them." But my discretion or my cowardice made me proof against the dear old man's eloquence—perhaps it was something of both which determined my course. When about to leave I asked Green what he had decided to do, and was surprised by his coolly saying in his broken way, "I b'leave I'll go wid de ole man." Here we separated; they to go to Harper's Ferry, I to Rochester.

Powell's Choice—1869

**Diary entries of John Wesley Powell
during Colorado River journey**

In the summer of 1869, a one-armed Civil War veteran named John Wesley Powell led the historic first expedition on the Colorado River through the Grand Canyon. Facing terrifying rapids and treacherous falls, their food and supplies seriously depleted after several weeks on the river, the men encountered whirlpools in the giant canyon that spun their boats about as if they were toys. On August 27, they faced the most awesome rapids they had ever seen. This was the most critical moment of the expedition.

Powell believed they had nearly reached the end of the canyon. Even if they managed to get through the falls immediately ahead without killing themselves, how much farther did they still have to go? Three of the men decided to leave the party, choosing to climb out of the canyon and to go overland toward an area where they expected Mormon settlements to be, about 75 miles to the north. The three solemnly packed up a few provisions, some guns and ammunition, and wished the others well.

Powell and the others decided to continue down the river. Each of the groups thought that the other was about to take the more hazardous trip. The three who left the expedition never reached their destination. They were soon killed by Native American tribesmen.

Powell rallied the remaining men in his party. Although they were critically low on provisions, unsure of the exact distance still to travel in the canyon, and extremely weary, the intense, driven Powell tried to raise their spirits. Powell's measurements and his own geographic sense told him that they had conquered most of the canyon, that they were perhaps only four days' journey from its end. He gathered the men and tried to convince them that the monstrous whirlpool ahead would be just another of the treacherous traps already conquered by the expedition. For three months, they had survived the river's pounding, had fought mightily to overcome the overwhelming feeling of helplessness against the power of nature. Although physically weakened, they had gained valuable experience in running rapids. They could run this one, he said.

Into the twisting water the boats swirled, oars splintering on the rocks, the men hanging on. George Bradley later wrote how the party "dashed . . . into the boiling tide with all the courage we could muster. We rowed with all our might until the billows became too large to do anything but hold on." The two *boats disappeared for several seconds in the white froth and then reappeared again, with the men still clinging on. They had survived. That night they sat around the campfire swapping stories they would tell and retell to their families for years to come. As it turned out, the treacherous falls they had just managed to navigate were not the last challenge. Six miles farther along, they ran into another falls, and Bradley was almost lost in the rapids. Powell later remembered seeing Bradley swept into "the mad, white foam below." The men, said Powell, had stood frozen, fearing their friend would not reappear. When Bradley suddenly emerged from the swirling water, he waved his hat in the air.*

The river had delivered it last blow. On Sunday, August 29, 1869, the country opened up. Before them now was the parched, brown desert spotted by creosote and greasewood, the desert's hardy plants. The journey was over. They turned to look behind at the majestic walls of the canyon. They had seen its secrets. That night Powell wrote in his diary: "The river rolls by us in silent majesty, the quiet of the camp is sweet; our joy is almost ecstasy."

Powell had succeeded. He did it on a treacherous river, without sophisticated equipment, without maps, without modern gear, without the benefit of modern white-water boating techniques. He succeeded where other seasoned adventurers had not even tried. Years later, a reporter asked Powell to tell him the secret of his success in making it through the canyon. "I was lucky," he said.

This exploration was one of the most honored feats of exploration in American history. Mountains and creeks that no one knew existed now bore the names Powell and his men had given them. Because of the critical decision he made on August 27, these tales of survival were retold in American newspapers across the country, laying the foundation for Major Powell's later explorations. He would return to the Rocky Mountains of the Southwest for more exploration and scientific discovery. From this subsequent research would come the first photographs of the Grand Canyon, the important geological research of the Grand Canyon region, and detailed maps. And from that research would come Powell's vision of conserving the magnificent resources of the West. He would become one of the early environmental leaders, a spokesman for saving the West's natural beauty, a proponent of controlled growth and water use, a pioneer whose career would inspire others.

Diary Entries of John Wesley Powell, August 1869

August 27.—We find that the lateral streams have washed boulders into the river, so as to form a dam, over which the water makes a broken fall of 18 or 20 feet; then there is a rapid, beset with rocks, for 200 or 300 yards, while on the other side, points of the wall project into

When John Wesley Powell rode the Colorado River in 1869, no photographers were along to record the monumental achievement. However, a photographer captured a later embarkation. Powell,with an empty right sleeve, appears in the upper far left.

the river. Below, there is a second wall; how great, we cannot tell. Then there is a rapid, filled with huge rocks, for 100 or 200 yards. At the bottom of it, from the right wall, a great rock projects quite halfway across the river. It has a sloping surface extending up stream, and the water, coming down with all the momentum gained in the falls and rapids above, rolls up this inclined plane many feet, and tumbles over to the left. I decide that it is possible to let down over the first fall, then run near the right cliff to a point just above the second, where we can pull out into a little chute, and, having run over that in safety, if we pull with all our power across the stream, we may avoid the great rock below. On my return to the boat I announce to the men that we are to run it in the morning. Then we cross the river and go into camp for the night on some rocks in the mouth of the little side canyon.

After supper Captain Howland asks to have a talk with me. We walk up the little creek a short distance, and I soon find that his object is to remonstrate against my determination to proceed. He thinks that we had better abandon the river here. Talking with him, I learn that he, his brother, and William Dunn have determined to go no farther in the boats. So we return to camp. Nothing is said to the other men. . . .

We have another short talk about the morrow, and he lies down again; but for me there is no sleep. All night long I pace up and down a little path, on a few yards of sand beach, along by the river. Is it wise to go on? I go to the boats again to look at our rations. I feel satisfied that we can get over the danger immediately before us; what there may be below I know not. From our outlook yesterday on the cliffs, the canyon seemed to make another great bend to the south, and this, from our experience heretofore, means more and higher granite walls. I am not sure that we can climb out of the canyon here, and, if at the top of the wall, I know enough of the country to be certain that it is a desert of rock and sand between this and the nearest Mormon town, which, on the most direct line, must be 75 miles away. True, the late rains have been favorable to us, should we go out, for the probabilities are that we shall find water still standing in holes; and at one time I almost conclude to leave the river. But for years I have been contemplating this trip. To have the exploration unfinished, to say that there is a part of the canyon which I cannot explore, having already nearly accomplished it, is more than I am willing to acknowledge, and I determine to go on.

I wake my brother and tell him of Howland's determination, and he promises to stay with me; then I call up Hawkins, the cook, and he makes a like promise; then Sumner and Bradley and Hall, and they all agree to go on.

August 28.—At last daylight comes and we have breakfast without a word being said about the future. The meal is as solemn as a funeral. After breakfast I ask the three men if they still think it best to leave us. The elder Howland thinks it is, and Dunn agrees with him. The younger Howland tries to persuade them to go on with the party; failing in which, he decides to go with his brother.

Then we cross the river. The small boat is very much disabled and unseaworthy. With the loss of hands, consequent on the departure of the three men, we shall not be able to run all of the boats; so I decide to leave my "Emma Dean."

Two rifles and a shotgun are given to the men who are going out. I ask them to help themselves to the rations and take what they think to be a fair share. This they refuse to do, saying they have no fear but that they can get something to eat; but Billy, the cook, has a pan of biscuits prepared for dinner, and these he leaves on a rock.

Before starting, we take from the boat our barometers, fossils, the minerals, and some ammunition and leave them on the rocks. We are going over this place as light as possible. The three men help us lift our boats over a rock 25 or 30 feet high and let them down again over the first fall, and now we are all ready to start. The last thing before leaving, I write a letter to my wife and give it to Howland. Sumner gives him his watch, directing that it be sent to his sister should he not be heard from again. The records of the expedition have been kept in duplicate. One set of these is given to Howland; and now we are ready. For the last time they entreat us not to go on, and tell us that it is madness to set out in this place; that we can never get safely through it; and, further, that the river turns again to the south into the granite, and a few miles of such rapids and falls will exhaust our entire stock of rations, and then it will be too late to climb out. Some tears are shed; it is rather a solemn parting; each party thinks the other is taking the dangerous course.

The Ascension of "His Fraudulency": John Reid and the Victory of Rutherford B. Hayes—1876

Telegram of John Reid to Republican leaders that turned the presidential election

As the 1876 campaign began, Democrats were favored to win the White House for the first time since before the Civil War. Corruption had plagued the Republican administration of Ulysses S. Grant. With the exception of three states, the South had now returned to home rule following Reconstruction. And the South, as it would for the next century, leaned Democratic.

Both parties nominated state governors: Democrat Samuel J. Tilden, Governor of New York, tough opponent of Tammany Hall and prosecutor of Boss Tweed; and Republican Rutherford B. Hayes, Governor of Ohio, war hero and well-known reformer.

On election night, it looked as if the Democrats, as expected, had won by an electoral vote of 204 to 165. But, at his office at the New York Times, editor John Reid, a staunch Republican, had not given up. After he received a wire from a Democratic operative requesting the vote totals, Reid noticed the extremely close vote from several states and became aware that the totals from Florida, Louisiana, and South Carolina were still very much undecided. This was a century before electronic voting and instant television reporting; it was an age of local precincts counting paper ballots one by one. Reid decided to wire other Republican leaders around the country. The election, he told them, was not over, regardless of what some of the newspapers had begun to claim. If Democrats were unsure of the totals, if several states were still in doubt, then the election was still to be won.

Each telegram was like a giant signal. Party officials nearly leaped from their seats and booked the earliest trains south. They carried with them bribe money and whatever other influence-peddling inducements they had at the ready. Into the three states, both parties invested as much political capital as possible. The result was that Florida, Louisiana, and South Carolina turned in two sets of electoral votes, one from the official election supervisory agency and another from carpetbag Republican governments. Oregon, drowning in political turmoil, also turned in two sets of votes.

As Congress began to sort out the greatest presidential voting mess since the advent of the U.S. Constitution, members found that 20 electoral votes were

An engraving portrays an Electoral Commission meeting by candlelight in the early days of March 1877, as the members try to resolve the muddled imbroglio of a presidential election that brought to the White House Rutherford B. Hayes.

in dispute, just enough to change the outcome of the election. As the legislature began its deliberations, Tilden had 184 certain votes, and Hayes had 165. Hayes had to win all 20 of the disputed votes to win the election.

Although early in its deliberations, Congress awarded a disputed Oregon vote to Hayes, it was unable to reach a settlement on the remaining 19 votes. Members decided to set up an Electoral Commission to decide each of the disputed votes. Comprised of five senators, five representatives, and five members of the Supreme Court, the commission was meant to contain seven members from each of the two parties and one independent. After fevered negotiating and bargaining, the commission finally decided to award all 20 electoral votes to Hayes, thus giving him the election.

But Congress had to approve the decision. Members of both parties threatened to use force, the Republicans to uphold the commission's decision, the Democrats to overthrow it. Angry speeches filled halls and newspaper columns. Could this national election, a little over a decade after the end of the Civil War, turn violent?

The final decision was made on March 2, 1877, just two days before inauguration day. Southern Democrats in Congress were persuaded to vote for the Electoral Commission decision in exchange for a promise of a final end to Reconstruction by the removal of all federal troops from the South. When the southern Democrats voted in favor of the commission decision, that gave a majority in the House to the Republicans, and Hayes was declared elected. President Grant, fearful of violence at the inauguration, arranged for Hayes to take the presidential oath secretly in the Red Room of the White House.

Although more voters in the United States cast their ballots for Tilden, Hayes was the winner in the Electoral College by a count of 185 to 184. Throughout his term, Hayes was referred to as "Old Rutherfraud" and "His Fraudulency." But Hayes proved to be a hardworking and honest caretaker of the office. He removed the last federal troops in the South, ending Reconstruction, and worked hard for civil service reform. If it had not been for John Reid's wire to Republican political leaders, Hayes never would have had the chance.

Telegram of John Reid, *New York Times*, to Republican Leaders in Florida, Louisiana, and South Carolina, November 7, 1876

If you can hold your state, Hayes will win. Can you do it?

A Bombing Order Away from Doomsday: Cuba—1962

Notes of Robert McNamara on meeting with President Kennedy and advisors on plans to bomb Cuba

In the early morning of October 14, 1962, a U.S. U-2 reconnaissance plane, piloted by Maj. Richard Heyser, flying over western Cuba from south to north, found evidence of the construction of bases for Soviet MRBM missiles. The missiles had the capability of reaching targets more than 1,000 miles away, thus threatening major cities and military sites in the United States.

For several days, President John Kennedy and his advisors secretly huddled, poring over the possibilities of how to respond to the threat posed by the missiles. The Joint Chiefs of Staff advised either an air strike to knock out missile sites or an invasion to overthrow Castro and destroy the missiles. But what of the risks? What if Soviet workers were killed in the attacks? Would Soviet premeir Khrushchev respond with a nuclear strike?

Over the next several days in Washington, presidential advisors spun an array of theories and scenarios to Kennedy. Republican lawyer John McCloy suggested an air strike and an invasion. On October 16, Robert Kennedy, dubious about an air strike or invasion, passed a note to the president: "I now know how Tojo felt when he was planning Pearl Harbor." Dean Acheson and Paul Nitze contended that the Pearl Harbor analogy was weak; George Ball and Douglas Dillon found it compelling. When Secretary of Defense Robert McNamara urged a blockade, Acheson and others argued that a blockade would have no effect on the missiles already in Cuba. One of the many papers quickly written for the president on the Cuban situation emphasized "the possibility that the Soviets, under great pressure to respond, would again miscalculate and respond in a way which, through a series of actions and reactions, could escalate into general war."

On October 21, 1962, Robert McNamara took notes of a meeting with President Kennedy and his advisors on the plan to bomb Cuban missile sites. Although the raids would likely be successful, McNamara wrote, "It was not likely that all of the known missiles would be destroyed." The bombing plans, possible ramifications, and alternative approaches all present an eerily disturbing picture of a nation on the brink of war.

The next day, Kennedy announced his plan. The United States would impose a naval blockade to intercept "all offensive military equipment under

Department of Defense aerial reconnaissance photographs of Cuban missile installations in October 1962 provided the Kennedy administration with hard evidence that led the United States and Russia to the nuclear brink.

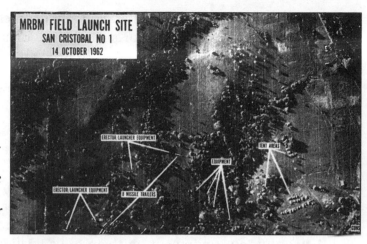

MRBM FIELD LAUNCH SITE
SAN CRISTOBAL NO 1
14 OCTOBER 1962

ERECTOR LAUNCHER EQUIPMENT

TENT AREAS

EQUIPMENT

ERECTOR LAUNCHER EQUIPMENT

8 MISSILE TRAILERS

shipment to Cuba." The United States also demanded the "dismantling and withdrawal of all offensive weapons in Cuba."

On October 24, a force of 19 U.S. warships, supported by aircraft carriers and B-52 bombers, formed a line in the Atlantic, 500 miles from Cuba. There were also troop ships ready for a possible invasion. At one point during the crisis, President Kennedy, speaking by phone with former President Eisenhower, said that the United States might have to invade Cuba and that he worried about the implications for the divided city of Berlin as well as the possibility of the Cubans and Soviets firing missiles in retaliation.

As Soviet ships moved ever closer to Cuba, the nation watched the spectacle as a kind of Super Bowl game of chicken. Indeed, when the Soviet ships reversed course, Secretary of State Dean Rusk remarked, "We're eyeball to eyeball, and I think the other fellow just blinked."

With the brazen brinkmanship played out on television screens in those few days in late October, Americans sensed that events were moving nations out of control. They were right.

Notes of Robert McNamara on Meeting with President Kennedy and Advisors, October 21, 1962

1. The meeting was held in the Oval Room of the White House and lasted from 11:30 a.m. to approximately 12:30 p.m. In attendance were the Attorney General, General Taylor, General Sweeney and the Secretary of Defense.

2. The Secretary of Defense stated that following the start of an air attack, the initial units of the landing force could invade Cuba within 7 days. The movement of troops in preparation for such an inva-

sion will start at the time of the President's speech. No mobilization of Reserve forces is required for such an invasion until the start of the air strike. General LeMay had stated that the transport aircraft, from Reserve and Guard units, which would be required for participation in such an invasion, can be fully operational within 24 to 48 hours after the call to active duty.

3. The Secretary of Defense reported that, based on information which became available during the night, it now appears that there is equipment in Cuba for approximately 40 MRBM or IRBM launchers. (Mr. McCone, who joined the group 15 or 20 minutes after the start of the discussion, confirmed this report.) The location of the sites for 36 of these launchers is known. 32 of the 36 known sites appear to have sufficient equipment on them to be included in any air strike directed against Cuba's missile capability.

4. We believe that 40 launchers would normally be equipped with 80 missiles. John McCone reported yesterday that a Soviet ship believed to be the vessel in which the Soviets have been sending missiles to Cuba has made a sufficient number of trips to that island within recent weeks to offload approximately 48 missiles. Therefore, we assume there are approximately that number on the Island today, although we have only located approximately 30 of them.

5. General Sweeney outlined the following plan of air attack, the object of which would be the destruction of the known Cuban missile capability.

a. The 5 surface-to-air missile installations in the vicinity of the known missile sites would each be attacked by approximately 8 aircraft; the 3 MIG airfields defending the missile sites would be covered by 12 U.S. aircraft per field. In total, the defense suppression operations, including the necessary replacement aircraft, would require approximately 100 sorties.

b. Each of the launchers at the 8 or 9 known sites (a total of approximately 32 to 36 launchers) would be attacked by 6 aircraft. For the purpose, a total of approximately 250 sorties would be flown.

c. The U.S. aircraft covering the 3 MIG airfields would attack the MIG's if they became airborne. General Sweeney strongly recommended attacks on each of the airfields to destroy the MIG aircraft.

6. General Sweeney stated that he was certain the air strike would be "successful"; however, even under optimum conditions, it was not likely that all of the known missiles would be destroyed. (As noted in 4 above, the known missiles are probably no more than 60% of the

total missiles on the island.) General Taylor stated, "The best we can offer you is to destroy 90% of the known missiles." General Taylor, General Sweeney, and the Secretary of Defense all strongly emphasized that in their opinion the initial air strike must be followed by strikes on subsequent days and that those in turn would lead inevitably to an invasion.

7. CIA representatives, who joined the discussion at this point, stated that it is probable the missiles which are operational (it is estimated there are now between 8 and 12 operational missiles on the Island) can hold indefinitely a capability for firing with from 2-1/2 to 4 hours notice. Included in the notice period is a countdown requiring 20 to 40 minutes. In relation to the countdown period, the first wave of our attacking aircraft would give 10 minutes of warning; the second wave, 40 minutes of warning; and the third wave a proportionately greater warning.

8. As noted above, General Sweeney strongly recommended that any air strike include attacks on the MIG aircraft and, in addition, the IL28s. To accomplish the destruction of these aircraft, the total number of sorties of such an air strike should be increased to 500. The President agreed that if an air strike is ordered, it should probably include in its objective the destruction of the MIG aircraft and the IL28s.

9. The President directed that we be prepared to carry out the air strike Monday morning or any time thereafter during the remainder of the week. The President recognized that the Secretary of Defense was opposed to the air strike Monday morning, and that General Sweeney favored it. He asked the Attorney General and Mr. McCone for their opinions:

a. The Attorney General stated he was opposed to such a strike because:

(1) "It would be Pearl Harbor type of attack."

(2) It would lead to unpredictable military responses by the Soviet Union which could be so serious as to lead to general nuclear war. He stated we should start with the initiation of the blockade and thereafter "play for the breaks."

b. Mr. McCone agreed with the Attorney General, but emphasized he believed we should be prepared for an air strike and thereafter an invasion.

Robert S. McNamara 10/21/62

A Federal-State Showdown in Mississippi—1962

Conversation of President Kennedy with Solicitor General Archibald Cox on the possibility of arresting Governor Ross Barnett of Mississippi and army general Edwin Walker for encouraging insurrection against James Meredith entering the University of Mississippi

In the summer of 1961, Attorney General Robert Kennedy sent federal marshals to Montgomery, Alabama, to protect "Freedom Riders" traveling across the state. Until then, the federal government had done little to support the civil rights movement. A year later, in Mississippi, it would act again.

James Meredith, a black Air Force veteran, attempted to attend the all-white University of Mississippi. When he was denied admission to the university, the NAACP filed a suit that was eventually argued before the U.S. Supreme Court. In September 1962, the Court ordered the university to desegregate.

Defying the federal order, Mississippi Governor Ross Barnett, emboldened by such right-wing supporters as Army Gen. Edwin Walker, vowed that he would never allow Meredith to enter the University of Mississippi. Walker, a Korean War hero who had led U.S. troops into Little Rock, Alabama, on a desegregation mission in 1957 on President Eisenhower's orders, was now firmly on the side of the segregationists, encouraging crowds in Oxford, Mississippi, and calling integration "a plot of the anti-Christ."

The Kennedy administration faced an increasingly intractable confrontation between civil rights proponents, states' rights defenders of the status quo, and the conflicting interests of federal and state governments. On October 1, 1962, a day after thousands of protesters surrounding the university clashed with civil rights demonstrators, a flurry of conversations took place between Justice Department officials, the White House, and Governor Barnett. Kennedy told the governor that Mississippi State Police would have to be stationed to ensure Meredith's safety.

Barnett reluctantly cooperated. At one point during the hectic period, President Kennedy called Solicitor General Archibald Cox about the possibility of arresting both General Walker and Governor Barnett, an action that would have seriously exacerbated federal-state tensions. If the president had arrested a sitting governor, the court system would have clashed and constitutional issues of federal and state authority would have reverberated more resoundingly than at any time since the Civil War.

By the time the crisis ended, major rioting had resulted in two deaths. The federal government had dispatched 16,000 army troops to Oxford, a town of 10,000 people. A total of 23,000 troops occupied the general area. Meredith went to school at the University of Mississippi. When he graduated in 1963, he wore a Ross Barnett campaign button that said NEVER, NEVER. Meredith wore the button upside down.

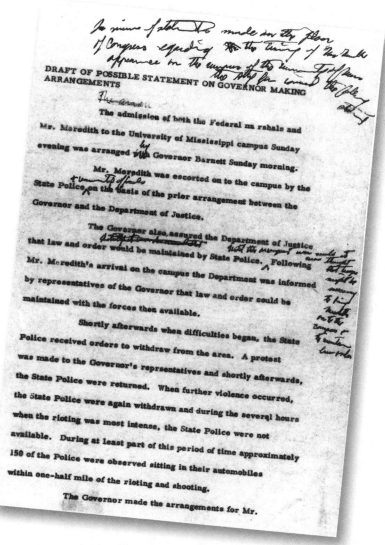

Negotiations between the Kennedy administration and Governor Ross Barnett over James Meredith's enrollment at the University of Mississippi prompted numerous hurried telephone calls and contingency plans. This draft statement of October 1, 1962, blamed the governor for failing to enforce law and order.

Transcript of Taped Conversation of President Kennedy with Solicitor General Archibald Cox, October 1, 1962

JFK: Hello

Cox: Good morning, Mr. President

JFK: Good morning . . . I'm just on my way up there. Now, the only question I had was whether there are any additional proclamations or powers, et cetera, that we might need in the Mississippi matter if it gets worse . . . for arresting people, and under what charge and what legal penalties they face and so on. For example, we want to arrest General Walker, and I don't know whether we just arrest him under disturbing the peace or whether we arrest him for more than that. I wonder if . . . How long are you going to be at the court this morning?

Cox: Not beyond half past ten.

JFK: Yeah, well then I wonder if we can get more precise information on where we are legally on arresting people, including the governor if necessary and others.

Cox: Right.

JFK: And what the penalties are because we might want to announce that on the radio and television that anyone involved in any demonstration or anything would be subject to the, this penalty, and, if not, maybe the general could announce it.

Cox: Right. Good-bye.

JFK: All right. Okay. Thank you.

Cox: Thank you.

To Indict a President?—1974

Memorandum of Watergate prosecution team on whether to indict President Richard Nixon

The Watergate scandal not only brought down President Nixon, it raised constitutional issues for which there had been scant or no precedent. The Office of the Special Prosecutor, created in 1973, twice faced the question of whether to seek an indictment of the president. In March 1974, when the grand jury handed down indictments of seven White House aides for perjury and obstruction of justice, Nixon was named an "unindicted coconspirator." Special Prosecutor Leon Jaworski advised the grand jury at that time that evidence regarding the president should be considered by the House Judiciary Committee, rather than by the courts, for possible impeachment proceedings.

The Judiciary Committee complied and drew up five articles of impeachment, three of which they approved in the summer of 1974. On August 9, 1974, Nixon resigned. Thus, for the second time, the Watergate Special Prosecutor's Office faced the question of whether to seek an indictment. Article I, section 3, clause 7 of the Constitution provides that a person removed from office by impeachment and conviction "shall nevertheless be liable and subject to Indictment, Trial, Judgment and Punishment, according to Law."

When President Gerald Ford issued a pardon to Nixon on September 8, 1974, the question about indictment became moot. But the Special Prosecutor's office, wrestling with these weighty matters, had composed a memorandum outlining the arguments for and against indictment. The document shows how narrowly Richard Nixon had avoided this real possibility.

Many of the arguments for and against formal legal proceedings against the president of the United States or a former president would have a resoundingly familiar ring a quarter of a century later.

**Memorandum of Watergate Prosecution Team,
August 9, 1974**

WATERGATE SPECIAL PROSECUTION FORCE
DEPARTMENT OF JUSTICE

MEMORANDUM

TO : Leon Jaworski
     Special Prosecutor
DATE: August 9, 1974

FROM : Carl B Feldbaum
       Peter M. Kreindler

SUBJECT: Factors to be Considered in Deciding Whether to Prosecute
         Richard M. Nixon for Obstruction of Justice:

In our view there is clear evidence that Richard M. Nixon participated in a conspiracy to obstruct justice by concealing the identity of
those responsible for the Watergate break-in and other criminal
offenses. There is a presumption (which in the past we have operated
upon) that Richard M. Nixon, like every citizen, is subject to the rule
of law. Accordingly, one begins with the premise that if there is sufficient evidence, Mr. Nixon should be indicted and prosecuted. The
question then becomes whether the presumption for proceeding is
outweighed by the factors mandating against indictment and prosecution.

The factors which mandate against indictment and prosecution
are:

1. His resignation has been sufficient punishment.
2. He has been subject to an impeachment inquiry with resulting
articles of impeachment which the House Judiciary Committee
unanimously endorsed as to Article I (the Watergate cover-up).
3. Prosecution might aggravate political divisions in the country.
4. As a political matter, the times call for conciliation rather than
recrimination.
5. There would be considerable difficulty in achieving a fair trial
because of massive pre-trial publicity.

The factors which mandate in favor of indictment and prosecution are:

1. The principle of equal justice under law requires that every person, no matter what his past position or office, answer to the criminal justice system for his past offenses. This is a particularly weighty
factor if Mr. Nixon's aides and associates, who acted upon his orders

and what they conceived to be his interests, are to be prosecuted for the same offenses.

2. The country will be further divided by Mr. Nixon unless there is a final disposition of charges of criminality outstanding against him so as to forestall the belief that he was driven from his office by erosion of his political base. This final disposition may be necessary to preserve the integrity of the criminal justice system and the legislative process, which together marshaled the substantial evidence of Mr. Nixon's guilt.

3. Article I, Section 3, clause 7 of the Constitution provides that a person removed from office by impeachment and conviction "shall nevertheless be liable and subject to Indictment, Trial, Judgment, and Punishment, according to Law." The Framers contemplated that a person removed from office because of abuse of his public trust still would have to answer to the criminal justice system for criminal offenses.

4. It cannot be sufficient retribution for criminal offenses merely to surrender the public office and trust which has been demonstrably abused. A person should not be permitted to trade in the abused office in return for immunity.

5. The modern nature of the Presidency necessitates massive public exposure of the President's actions through the media. A bar to prosecution on the grounds of such publicity effectively would immunize all future Presidents for their actions, however criminal. Moreover, the courts may be the appropriate forum to resolve questions of pre-trial publicity in the context of an adversary proceeding.

ALMOST
FORTUITOUS OCCURRENCES
HISTORY

Manifest Destiny or Lucky Circumstance: Jefferson and Louisiana—1802

Letter of Thomas Jefferson to American minister to Paris, on circumstances leading to the Louisiana Purchase

O n April 30, 1803, the United States purchased from France, at a cost of $15 million, more than 800,000 square miles of land extending from the Mississippi River to the Rocky Mountains. In this single transaction, the United States doubled its size, added an enormous area of land that would be open to settlement, and acquired the free navigation of the Mississippi River. Later, when looking back at the early years of the U.S. government, historians and politicians would popularize the term "manifest destiny," and the Louisiana Purchase would stand as evidence that the country was, indeed, preordained to extend from coast to coast. Was this deal with the French government a product of deft diplomacy, farsighted intuition, divine will, or simple circumstance? Perhaps more than any other diplomatic achievement, the Louisiana Purchase had far-reaching implications for the infant United States. But it was almost an accident of history.

In 1762, France had ceded Louisiana to Spain, but by the secret 1800 Treaty of San Ildefonso, the French had regained the area. Napoleon Bonaparte envisioned a great French empire in the New World, anchored geographically by the Mississippi Valley as a trading center to supply the island of Hispaniola (comprising present-day Haiti and the Dominican Republic), which was to be the empire's heart.

But the French had lost control of Hispaniola to an uprising of Haitian slaves under Toussaint L'Ouverture. In 1802, Napoleon dispatched forces under his brother-in-law, Charles Leclerc, to suppress the rebellion. L'Overture's hold on the island proved more intractable than expected, and the military intervention cost the French army thousands of soldiers, many of them to yellow fever. Reluctantly, Napoleon concluded that the sacrifices made by the French in Hispaniola and the continuing war machinery required to conquer and hold the area would eventually prove more costly to the French government than the possible advantages of establishing a new trading base.

Once he had decided that the Hispaniola venture would be too costly, Napoleon had little use for Louisiana. Facing renewed war with Great Britain, he needed funds to support his military in Europe and, in April 1803, he offered to sell Louisiana to the United States.

President Thomas Jefferson, who had great respect for French institutions *and capabilities, was, nevertheless, quite concerned about French intentions in America, as he indicated in a letter to American Minister to France Robert R. Livingston on April 18, 1802. He had already sent Livingston and James Monroe to Paris to negotiate the purchase of a tract of land on the lower Mississippi or, at least, a guarantee of free navigation on the river. Jubilant, if not dumbfounded, by the French offer of the whole territory, they immediately negotiated the treaty.*

Although the U.S. Constitution did not specifically empower the federal government to acquire new territory by treaty, an enthusiastic Jefferson concluded that the practical benefits to the nation far outweighed the possible violation of the Constitution. The Senate concurred with this decision and voted ratification of the treaty on October 20, 1803. As no other single event, the Louisiana Purchase opened the door for U.S. continential expansion, relatively free of foreign entanglements and guaranted its emergence as a great power a century later.

Excerpt of Letter of Thomas Jefferson to American Minister to Paris, April 18, 1802

The cession of Louisiana and the Floridas by Spain to France works most sorely on the U.S. On this subject the Secretary of State has written to you fully. Yet I cannot forbear recurring to it personally, so deep is the impression it makes in my mind. It completely reverses all the political relations of the U.S. and will form a new epoch in our political course. Of all nations of any consideration France is the one which hitherto has offered the fewest points on which we could have any conflict of right, and the most points of a communion of interests. From these causes we have ever looked to her as our *natural friend*, as one with which we never could have an occasion of difference. Her growth therefore we viewed as our own, her misfortunes ours. There is on the globe one single spot, the possessor of which is our natural and habitual enemy. It is New Orleans, through which the produce of three-eighths of our territory must pass to market, and from its fertility it will ere long yield more than half of our whole produce and contain more than half our inhabitants. France placing herself in that door assumes to us the attitude of defiance. Spain might have retained it quietly for years. Her pacific dispositions, her feeble state, would induce her to increase our facilities there, so that her possession of the place would be hardly felt by us, and it would not perhaps be very long before some circumstance might arise which might make the cession of it to us the price of something of more worth to her. Not so can it ever be in the hands of France. The impetuosity of her temper, the energy and restlessness of her character, placed in a point of eternal friction with us, and our character, which though quiet, and loving peace and the pursuit of wealth, is high-minded, despising wealth in competition with insult or injury, enterprising and energetic as any nation on earth, these circumstances render it impossible that France and the U.S. can continue long friends when they meet in so irritable a position. . . .

Every eye in the U.S. is now fixed on this affair of Louisiana. Perhaps nothing since the revolutionary war has produced more uneasy sensations through the body of the nation. Notwithstanding temporary bickerings have taken place with France, she has still a strong hold on the affections of our citizens generally.

The Five-Spot Would Have Looked Different: The Story of Lincoln's Beard—1860

Correspondence of Grace Bedell and Abraham Lincoln

As he campaigned as the Republican nominee for president in the fall of 1860, Abraham Lincoln received a letter written by 11-year-old Grace Bedell of Westfield, New York. Grace suggested that Mr. Lincoln would be more attractive with a beard. "I have got 4 brothers," she wrote, "and part of them will vote for you any way and if you will let your whiskers grow I will try and get the rest of them to vote for you. You would look a great deal better for your face is so thin. All the ladies like whiskers. . . ."

Beardless all his life, Lincoln seemed amused by the girl's suggestion. He politely responded to her letter but gave no indication that he would consider taking her advice. As he prepared for his trip to the White House in 1861, nevertheless, the girl's impressions must have resonated strongly with the president-elect. When Lincoln stopped in Chautauqua County, New York, on his way to Washington to take the oath of office, he was told that the young girl was in the crowd. When she appeared, Lincoln stepped down from the car, shook her hand, kissed her, and remarked, "You see, Grace, I let my whiskers grow for you." He was fully bearded.

Lincoln's beard soon became the subject of much discussion among political friends and enemies alike. Although most observers thought the president had a more distinguished appearance with a beard, that it complemented his angular face, political enemies found the beard yet another subject for lampooning. On December 27, 1860, an editorialist wrote, "They say Old Abe is raising

Photographer Mathew Brady took this portrait of Abraham Lincoln at New York's Tenth Street Gallery on February 27, 1860, after Lincoln's speech at the Cooper Union. In October, Lincoln took the advice of an 11-year-old girl named Grace Bedell and grew a beard.

---

a pair of whiskers. Some individual of the cockney persuasion remarked that he was 'a puttin' on (h)airs.'"

If it had not been for the letter of an 11-year-old girl, the face of Lincoln, perhaps the most recognizable in all American history, would likely have remained beardless.

Letter of Grace Bedell to Abraham Lincoln, October 15, 1860

N Y
Westfield Chatauque Co
Oct 15, 1860

Hon A B Lincoln
Dear Sir

My father has just home from the fair and brought home your picture and Mr. Hamlin's. I am a little girl only eleven years old, but want you should be President of the United States very much so I hope you wont think me very bold to write to such a great man as you are. Have you any little girls about as large as I am if so give them my love and tell her to write to me if you cannot answer this letter. I have got 4 brother's and part of them will vote for you any way and if you will let your whiskers grow I will try and get the rest of them to vote for you you would look a great deal better for your face is so thin. All the ladies like whiskers and they would tease their husband's to vote for you and then you would be President. My father is going to vote for you and if I was a man I would vote for you to but I will try to get every one to vote for you that I can I think that rail fence around your picture makes it look very pretty I have got a little baby sister she is nine weeks old and is just as cunning as can be. When you direct your letter dir[ect] to Grace Bedell Westfield Chatauque County New York

I must not write any more   answer this letter right off   Good bye

Grace Bedell

Letter of Abraham Lincoln to Grace Bedell, October 19, 1860

Private
Springfield, Ills.
Oct 19, 1860
Miss Grace Bedell
My dear little Miss.

Your very agreeable letter of the 15th. is received.

I regret the necessity of saying I have no daughters. I have three sons—one seventeen, one nine, and one seven, years of age. They, with their mother, constitute my whole family

As to the whiskers, having never worn any, do you not think people would call it a piece of silly affection if I were to begin it now?

Your very sincere well-wisher

A. Lincoln.

How a Cigar Wrapper Smoked the Confederates—1862

Robert E. Lee's Special Orders 191

I n mid-September 1862, on a hillside near Frederick, Maryland, members of the 27th Indiana awaited orders as Confederate units under Gen. Robert E. Lee approached and a major battle seemed imminent. One of the troops suddenly spotted a package on the ground. When he picked it up, he found three cigars wrapped in a piece of paper with extensive writing on it. When he looked at the paper closely, it was clear that it was some kind of battle plan or orders. He took it to a colonel in the regiment, who turned it over to a general. As the men studied the document, they became convinced it was authentic. For an army about to engage the enemy, this was a miraculous find: it was the battle plan of General Lee for the upcoming clash.

The orders had been issued to Gen. D. H. Hill. One of Hill's staff officers had apparently wrapped cigars in the orders and then carelessly stuffed them in a pocket. They ended up on the ground. General Hill had received another copy of the orders from his immediate superior, Gen. Thomas "Stonewall" Jackson, and didn't realize until later that the first set was lost.

By that afternoon, Union general George C. McClellan knew exactly the planned moves of Lee. McClellan sent a telegram on September 13, 1862, to President Lincoln saying "I have all the plans of the rebels. . . ."

These were critical days in the Civil War. On July 22, Lincoln had told his cabinet that he intended to use his war powers as commander in chief to seize enemy property as a rationale for issuing an emancipation proclamation. Although the cabinet agreed with Lincoln's decision, Secretary of State William Seward advised him to make the announcement from a position of strength, after a major victory on the battlefield. Lincoln looked to the impending battle in Maryland as the opportunity he needed.

For Lee, the upcoming battle was also of vital importance. Lee hoped that a decisive victory would convince both the French and British governments that the Confederates had succeeded in establishing a new government and that the foreign nations would officially recognize the Confederacy and offer assistance. Lee's push into Maryland was only the first intended strike against the North in its own territory. A victory near Frederick would allow Lee to aim his army at major northern cities.

Even though McClellan had Lee's plans, he was, as usual, cautious, and his dilatory actions allowed Lee time to pull most of his troops together before

September 17, when the large armies finally clashed. The Union army named the battle after the creek that ran by the battlefield—Antietam. The battle was the single bloodiest day of the entire Civil War. It was not a decisive victory for McClellan, but it turned the Confederate army around, destroying Lee's plan to strike boldly at northern cities. And the victory did allow Lincoln to issue the Emancipation Proclamation.

Lee later told a friend: "I went into Maryland to give battle, and could I have kept Gen. McClellan in ignorance of my position and plans a day or two longer, I would have fought and crushed him."

If it had not been for the discovered battle plan, the Battle of Antietam could very well have been a turning point in the war. If the South had later achieved a negotiated settlement to end the war and had gained independence, it may have looked back at Antietam as McClellan's and Lincoln's Waterloo. But for that damned package of cigars. . . .

Excerpts from Robert E. Lee's Special Orders 191, 1862

HEADQUARTERS, ARMY OF NORTHERN VIRGINIA
September 9th, 1862
Special Orders, No. 191

III. The Army will resume its march tomorrow, taking the Hagerstown road. General Jackson's command will form the advance, and after passing Middletown, with such portions as he may select, take the route toward Sharpsburg, cross the Potomac at the most convenient point, and by Friday night take possession of the Baltimore and Ohio Railroad, capture such of the enemy as may be at Martinsburg, and intercept such as may attempt to escape from Harper's Ferry.

IV. General Longstreet's command will pursue the same road as far as Boonsboro', where it will halt with the reserve, supply, and baggage trains of the army.

V. General McLaws with his own division and that of General R.H. Anderson, will follow General Longstreet; on reaching Middletown he will take the route to Harper's Ferry, and by Friday morning possess himself of the Maryland Heights and endeavor to capture the enemy at Harper's Ferry and vicinity.

VI. General Walker, with his division after accomplishing the object in which he is now engaged, will cross the Potomac at Check's ford, ascend its right bank to Lovettsville, take possession of Loudoun

When a copy of General Robert E. Lee's "Order No. 191," dated September 9, 1862, a battle plan for Southern forces at Antietam, was found by a Union soldier, Lee's troops were hopelessly compromised. The lost orders were probably intended for General D. H. Hill, who had already received the copy at left, written by Stonewall Jackson. Hill, therefore, had no way of knowing that a duplicate set had been lost.

Heights, if practicable, by Friday morning, Keyes's ford on his left, and the road between the end of the mountain and the Potomac on his right. He will, as far as practicable, cooperate with General McLaws and General Jackson in intercepting the retreat of the enemy.

VII. General D.H. Hill's division will form the rear guard of the army, pursuing the road taken by the main body. The reserve artillery, ordnance, and supply trains, etc., will precede General Hill.

VIII. General Stuart will detach a squadron of cavalry to accompany the commands of Generals Longstreet, Jackson, and McLaws, and, with the main body of the cavalry, will cover the route of the army and bring up all stragglers that may have been left behind.

IX. The commands of Generals Jackson, McLaws, and Walker, after accomplishing the objects for which they have been detached, will join the main body of the army at Boonsboro' or Hagerstown.

X. Each regiment of the march will habitually carry its axes in the regimental ordinance-wagons, for use of the men at their encampments, to procure wood, etc.

By command of General R. E. Lee.
R. H. Chilton, Assistant Adjutant-General.
Major-General D. H. Hill, Command Division.

Saved by a Speech—1912

Speech of Theodore Roosevelt delivered after the assassination attempt

Americans had known for some time that former president Theodore Roosevelt took obsessive pride in his physical exploits. Short of stature, big on muscle, he relished vigorous pursuits, from taking on a series of professional boxers to hunting wild game in foreign lands to leading his troops up San Juan Hill. His had been the presidency of the Big Stick, from trust-busting to strident nationalism. And now, in 1912, estranged from the Republican Party, he was back on the campaign hustings running again for president. His party: "The Bull Moose."

Because of his poor eyesight (one of his eyes had been damaged in one of his encounters with a boxer), Teddy often prepared his speeches on small sheets of paper with large words and spaces between the lines to help him see the material during delivery. Thus, the manuscripts of his speeches were often quite thick.

On October 14, 1912, as he arrived at the train station in Milwaukee, Wisconsin, shortly after five o'clock, he made his way through the large crowd to a waiting automobile that whisked him away to a private dinner party at the Hotel Gilpatrick. After dinner, Teddy waved to his admirers, put on his topcoat with the speech stuffed in one of the pockets, and left the hotel to head for the Milwaukee auditorium for a campaign rally. As he prepared to step into the car, a man rushed forward and jammed a gun into the ex-president's chest and fired. As two of Roosevelt's friends seized the shooter, he was heard yelling "Any man looking for a third term ought to be shot." Roosevelt seemed more stunned than injured, but blood began staining his shirt. When Roosevelt took off his coat, it was clear what had happened. The .32-caliber bullet had passed through the thick speech and lodged in his chest. If the speech had not been in Roosevelt's coat pocket, the bullet would have ripped straight into his heart.

The gritty candidate demanded to be taken to the auditorium. There, in his blood-splattered clothes, he climbed on the podium, announced he had been shot, showed off the bloody speech, unfolded it, and, haltingly, began to speak. After assorted asides about his manhood and his toughness and his dedication not to his own safety but to the safety of the nation, Roosevelt finally declared, "It takes more than that to kill a Bull Moose." The former president then spoke for 50 minutes before finally being helped off the platform.

Since the assassination of Abraham Lincoln in 1865, the nation had suffered through two more slayings of presidents—James Garfield and William McKinley. But for the inadvertent but perfect placement of a thick speech, Theodore Roosevelt would have joined their number.

Speech of Theodore Roosevelt, October 14, 1912

I do not care a rap about being shot, not a rap. Friends, I shall have to ask you to be as quiet as possible. I do not know whether you fully understand that I have just been shot, but it takes more than that to kill a Bull Moose.

But fortunately I had my manuscript, so you see I was going to make a long speech. And, friends, the hole in it is where the bullet went through and it probably saved the bullet from going into my heart.

The bullet is in me now, so that I cannot make a very long speech. But I will try my best.

And now, friends, I want to take advantage of this incident to say as solemn a word of warning as I know how to my fellow-Americans.

First of all I want to say this about myself. I have altogether too many important things to think of to pay any heed or feel any concern over my own death.

Now I would not speak to you insincerely within five minutes of being shot. I am telling you the literal truth when I say that my concern is for many other things. It is not in the least for my own life.

I want you to understand that I am ahead of the game anyway. No man has had a happier life than I have had, a happier life in every way. I have been able to do certain things that I greatly wished to do, and I am interested in doing other things.

I can tell you with absolute truthfulness that I am very much uninterested in whether I am shot or not. It was just as when I was Colonel of my regiment. I always felt that a private was to be excused for feeling at times some pangs of anxiety about his personal safety, but I cannot understand a man fit to be Colonel who can pay any heed to his personal safety when he is occupied as he ought to be occupied with the absorbing desire to do his duty.

I am in this case with my whole heart and soul; I believe in the Progressive movement—a movement to try to take the burdens off the man and especially the woman in this country who is most oppressed.

In the summer of 1910, ex-president Theodore Roosevelt, after returning from a long tour of Africa and Europe, decided to reenter politics and challenge his successor, William Howard Taft, who, Roosevelt believed, had betrayed progressive reforms. This photograph was taken on June 27, 1910. Ahead was the Bull Moose campaign and a brush with an assassin.

I am absorbed in the success of that movement. I feel uncommonly proud in belonging to that movement.

Friends, I ask you now this evening to accept what I am saying as absolute truth when I tell you I am not thinking of my own success. I am not thinking of my life, or of anything connected with me, personally.

I am saying this by way of introduction because I want to say something very serious to our people, and especially to the newspapers. I don't know who the man was who shot me tonight. He was seized by one of my stenographers, Mr. Martin, and I suppose he is in the hands of the police now. He shot to kill me. He shot the bullet. I am just going to show you [Col. Roosevelt then unbuttoned his coat and vest showed his white shirt badly stained with blood].

Now, friends, I am going to be as quiet as possible even if I am not able to give the challenge to the Bull Moose quite as loudly. Now, I do not know who he was or what party he represented. He was a coward. He stood in the darkness in the crowd around the automobile, and when they cheered me and I got up to bow, he stepped forward and shot me in the breast.

It is a very natural thing that weak and vicious minds should be inflamed to acts of violence by the kind of foul mendacity and abuse that have been heaped upon me for the last three months by the papers in the interests not only of Mr. Debs, but of Mr. Wilson and Mr. Taft.

Friends, I will disown and repudiate any man of my party who attacks with such vile, foul slander and abuse any opponents of another party.

Now I wish to say seriously to the speakers and the newspapers representing the Republican and Democratic and Socialist Parties that they cannot, month in and month out, year in and year out, make the kind of slanderous, bitter, and malevolent assaults that they have made and not expect that brutal and violent characters—especially when the brutality is accompanied by a not too strong mind—they cannot expect that such natures will be unaffected by it.

I am not speaking for myself at all, I give you my word. I do not care a rap about being shot, not a rap. I have had a good many experiences in my time and this is only one of them. What I do care for is my country. I wish I were able to impress on our people the duty to feel strongly, but to speak truthfully of their opponents. I say now that I have never said on the stump one word against any opponent that I could not substantiate, and nothing I ought not to have said; nothing that, looking back, I would not say again.

Now, friends, it ought not to be too much to ask that our opponents—I am not sick at all. I am all right.

I cannot tell you of what infinitesimal importance I regard this incident, as compared with the great issues at stake in this campaign, and I ask it not for my sake, not the least in the world, but for the sake of our common country, that they make up their minds to speak only the truth, and not to use the kind of slander and mendacity which, if taken seriously, must incite weak and violent natures to crimes of violence.

Don't you make any mistake. Don't you pity me. I am all right. I am all right, and you cannot escape listening to the speech either.

Now, friends, what we who are in this movement are endeavoring to do is to forestall any such movement by making this a movement for justice now, a movement in which we ask all just men of generous hearts to join with the men who feel in their souls that lift upward which bids them refuse to be satisfied themselves while their fellow-countrymen and countrywomen suffer from a veritable misery. Now, friends, what we Progressives are trying to do is to enroll rich or poor, whatever their social or industrial position, to stand together for the most elementary rights of good citizenship, those elementary rights which are the foundation of good citizenship in this great Republic of ours.

My friends are a little more nervous than I am. I have had an A1 time in life, and I am having it now.

I never in my life had any movement in which I was able to serve with such whole-hearted devotion as in this, in which I was able to feel, as I do in this, that common weal. I have fought for the good of our common country.

And now friends, I shall have to cut short much of the speech that I meant to give you, but I want to touch on just two or three of the points.

In the first place, speaking to you here in Milwaukee, I wish to say that the Progressive Party is making its appeal to all our fellow citizens without any regard to their creed or to their birthplace.

We do not regard as essential the way in which a man worships his God or as being affected by where he was born. We regard it as a matter of spirit and purpose.

In New York, while I was Police Commissioner, the two men from whom I got the most assistance were Jacob Riis, who was born in Denmark, and Oliver von Briesen, who was born in Germany, both of them as fine examples of the best and highest American citizenship you could find in any part of this country.

I have just been introduced by one of your own men, Henry Cochems. His grandfather, his father, and that father's brothers served in the United States Army, and they entered it four years after they had come to this country from Germany. Two of them left their lives, spent their lives on the field of battle—I am all right—I am a little sore. Anybody has a right to be sore with a bullet in him.

You would find that if I was in battle I would be leading my men just the same. Just the same way I am going to make this speech.

At one time I promoted five men for gallantry on the field of battle. Afterward it happened to be found in making some inquiries about them that I found two of them were Protestants, two Catholics, and one a Jew. One Protestant came from Germany and one was born in Ireland. I did not promote them because of their religion. It just happened that way. If all of them had been Jews I would have promoted them, or if all had been Protestants I would have promoted them, or if they had been Catholics.

In that regiment I had a man born in Italy who distinguished himself by gallantry; there was a young fellow, a son of Polish parents, and another who came across when he was a child from Bohemia, who likewise distinguished themselves, and, friends, I assure you that I was incapable of considering any question whatever but the worth of each individual as a fighting man. If he was a good fighting man, then I saw that Uncle Sam got the benefit from it. That is all.

I make the same appeal in our citizenship. I ask in our civic life that we in the same way pay heed only to the man's quality of citizenship—to repudiate as the worst enemy that we can have whoever tries to get us to discriminate for or against any man because of his creed or his birthplace.

Now, friends, in the same way I want our people to stand by one another without regard to differences or class or occupation. I have always stood by the labor unions. I am going to make one observation tonight. I have prepared my speech because Mr. Wilson had seen fit to attack me, by showing up his record in comparison with mine. But I am not going to do that tonight. I am going to simply speak of what I myself have done and what I think ought to be done in this country of ours.

It is essential that there should be organization of labor. This is all one organization. Capital organizes and therefore labor must organize. My appeal for organized labor is two-fold. To the outsider and the capitalist I make my appeal to treat the laborers fairly and recognize the fact that he must organize that there must be such organization, that the laboring man must organize for his own protection, and that it be the duty of the rest of us to help him and not hinder in organizing. That is one half of the appeal that I make.

Now the other half is to the labor man himself. My appeal to him is to remember that as he wants just so he must do justice. I want every labor man, every labor leader, every organized union man to take the lead in denouncing crime or violence. I want them to take the lead in denouncing disorder and inciting riot, that in this country we shall proceed under the protection of the law and with all respect to the laws and I want the labor men to feel in their turn that exactly as justice must be done them, so they must do justice. That they must bear their duty as citizens, their duty to this great country of ours, and that they must not rest content unless they do that duty to the fullest degree.

"Don't Forget to Be a Good Boy": A Tennessee Legislator Listens to His Mother and Saves the Vote for Women—1920

Letter to a Tennessee legislator from his mother persuading him to vote for the 19th Amendment

In 1919, American women still did not have the vote. Since the first Women's Rights Conventions before the Civil War, leaders such as Susan B. Anthony and Elizabeth Cady Stanton had lobbied, organized, conducted hunger strikes, picketed, wrote, spoke, endured ridicule, and gone to jail seeking a basic right denied to half of the population. But in 1853, Harper's Magazine had declared, "Nothing could be more anti-Biblical than letting women vote." And in 1905, former president Grover Cleveland had written, "Sensible and responsible women do not want to vote. The relative positions to be assumed by man and woman in the working out of our civilization were assigned long ago by a higher intelligence than ours." The reformers persevered.

In 1919, the U.S. House of Representatives finally voted to send a women's suffrage constitutional amendment to the states for ratification. If 36 of the 48 states voted in the affirmative, the 19th Amendment would become law.

By the summer of 1920, 35 states had ratified, 8 had rejected it, and no other state except Tennessee was even close to holding ratifying votes. If Tennessee failed to ratify, antisuffrage forces could likely stall action on the amendment for many years.

During the sweltering summer of 1920, Tennessee became the scene of one of the most fiercely contested political contests in American history. Many called it the "War of the Roses," with antisuffrage forces wearing the American Beauty red rose depicting their femininity and their efforts "to save Southern womanhood" and the prosuffrage forces countering with the yellow rose, long symbolic of the suffrage movement.

After the Tennessee Senate voted 25 to 4 in favor of the amendment on August 13, prosuffrage leader Carrie Chapman Catt wrote: "We are one-half of one state away from victory." The final showdown would be in the Tennessee House of Representatives, and the outcome looked close.

The vote was held on August 18, 1920. Throughout the week preceding the vote, both the prosuffrage and antisuffrage forces had carefully canvassed the legislators, and both sides believed that the amendment would be defeated by a single vote. On the morning of the vote, Harry Burn, a Republican who was the youngest member of the General Assembly, who had been counted as a certain opponent of suffrage and who had been wearing a red rose, received a letter from his mother. The short note from Febb Ensminger Burn concluded, "Don't forget to be a good boy and help Mrs. Catt put the 'rat' in ratification. Signed, Your Mother."

When his name was called, Harry Burn said, "aye." The hall erupted in screaming, weeping, and singing. Prosuffrage members of the House tore off their yellow boutonnieres and threw them in the air.

The next day, Harry Burn rose on the floor of the House to explain his vote: "I want to take this opportunity to state that I changed my vote in favor of ratification because: 1) I believe in full suffrage as a right, 2) I believe we had a moral and legal right to ratify, 3) I know that a mother's advice is always safest for her boy to follow, and my mother wanted me to vote for ratification."

Letter of Febb Ensminger Burn to Harry Burn, August 17, 1920

Dear Son:

Hurrah, and vote for suffrage! Don't keep them in doubt. I noticed some of the speeches against. They were bitter. I have been watching to see how you stood, but have not noticed   anything yet. Don't forget to be a good boy and help Mrs. Catt put the "rat" in ratification. Signed, Your Mother.

Einstein's Modest Suggestion—1939

Letter of Albert Einstein to President Franklin Roosevelt, recommending U.S. funding of nuclear research

Leo Szilard, like many other foreign-born physicists in the United States, had fled European fascism. Along with M. Joliot in France, Szilard had done extensive research on chain reaction in uranium and was one of the discoverers of neutron emission of uranium. Aware that Germany was conducting similar secret nuclear research at the Kaiser Wilhelm Institute, Szilard was certain that they were developing an atomic bomb. Fearing what would happen if Germany developed a nuclear weapon, he urged his close friend Albert Einstein to convince the American government to support nuclear research.

On August 2, 1939, a month before Germany invaded Poland, Einstein wrote a letter to President Roosevelt, recommending that the United States fund nuclear research, stating that it could result in "extremely powerful bombs" made of uranium. Einstein said that his recommendation was based on the research both of Szilard and Enrico Fermi, who was the first scientist actually to produce nuclear fission in the laboratory, a research triumph that won him the 1938 Nobel Prize for Physics.

Based on Einstein's letter, President Roosevelt authorized a government study on the possibilities of launching the research program recommended by the scientists. Ironically, Roosevelt decided to proceed with the work on December 6, 1941. The next day, Japanese war planes bombed Pearl Harbor.

Under the leadership of Gen. Leslie Groves and a brilliant nuclear physicist from the University of California, J. Robert Oppenheimer, the Manhattan Project, a collaboration of American science and industry carried out under the direction of the U.S. Army, was begun at Los Alamos, New Mexico, a remote location near Santa Fe. Oppenheimer gathered scientists from the most prestigious universities in the United States, including the University of Chicago, Columbia University, and his own University of California. He also recruited several British and Canadian scientists. The U.S. Army Corps of Engineers built power stations, factories, foundries, blast furnaces, steel works, hospitals, laboratories and housing at Los Alamos. The project involved more than 200,000 people and cost the United States $2 million. It was conducted in complete secrecy not only from the enemy but from the American public. From this research came the weapon that exploded with such ferocity over Hiroshima and Nagasaki, Japan.

Leo Szilard, the scientist who suggested to Einstein that he approach President Roosevelt about developing a bomb, later became one of the most ardent spokespeople against the military use of nuclear weapons. Einstein himself, fearful that the work would lead to nuclear conflagration, later took full responsibility for the consequences of his approach to the president, calling it "the greatest mistake" of his life. For the U.S. military, the suggestion of Szilard and Einstein had been one of the greatest fortuitous occurrences in history, even if for both of them it later became an aching source of guilt.

Letter of Albert Einstein to President Franklin Roosevelt, August 2, 1939

Albert Einstein
Old Grove Rd.
Nassau Point
Peconic, Long Island
August 2nd, 1939

F. D. Roosevelt
President of the United States
White House
Washington, D.C.

Sir:

Some recent work by E. Fermi and L. Szilard, which has been communicated to me in manuscript, leads me to expect that the element uranium may be turned into a new and important source of energy in the immediate future. Certain aspects of the situation which has arisen seem to call for watchfulness and, if necessary, quick action on the part of the Administration. I believe therefore that it is my duty to bring to your attention the following facts and recommendations:

In the course of the last four months it has been made probable—through the work of Joliot in France as well as Fermi and Szilard in America—that it may become possible to set up a nuclear chain reaction in a large mass of uranium, by which vast amounts of power and large quantities of new radium-like elements would be generated. Now it appears almost certain that this could be achieved in the immediate future.

This new phenomenon would also lead to the construction of

In August 1939, Albert Einstein warned President Franklin Roosevelt about German efforts to create an atomic bomb and encouraged an American research team to undertake the work. In June 1942, Einstein's fellow scientist J. Robert Oppenheimer was named to head the Manhattan Project.

bombs, and it is conceivable—though much less certain—that extremely powerful bombs of a new type may thus be constructed. A single bomb of this type, carried by boat or exploded in a port, might very well destroy the whole port together with some of the surrounding territory. However, such bombs might very well prove to be too heavy for transportation by air.

The United States has only very poor ores of uranium in moderate quantities. There is some good ore in Canada and the former Czechoslovakia, while the most important source of uranium is Belgian Congo.

In view of this situation you may think it desirable to have some permanent contact maintained between the Administration and the group of physicists working on chain reactions in America. One possible way of achieving this might be for you to entrust with this task a person who has your confidence and who could perhaps serve in an unofficial capacity. His task might comprise the following:

a) to approach Government Departments, keep them informed of further development, and put forward recommendations for Government action, giving particular attention to the problem of securing a supply of uranium ore for the United States;

b) to speed up experimental work, which is at present being carried on within the limits of the budgets of University laboratories, by providing funds, if such funds be required, through his contacts with private persons who are willing to make contributions for this cause, and perhaps also by obtaining the cooperation of industrial laboratories which have the necessary equipment.

I understand that Germany has actually stopped the sale of uranium from the Czechoslovakia mines which she has taken over. That she should have taken such early action might perhaps be understood on the ground that the son of the German Under-Secretary of State, von Weizsäcker, is attached to the Kaiser-Wilhelm-Institut in Berlin, where some of the American work on uranium is now being repeated.

Yours very truly,

A. Einstein

Code Maker's Dream,
Enemy's Nightmare—1942

Letter of Philip Johnston to Commander, U.S. Marine Corps, on using Navajo language as code

On September 12, 1942, Philip Johnston wrote to the commander of the U.S. Marine Corps, asking to serve in the corps in some capacity in communications. The son of missionaries to the Navajo and one of the few non-Navajo who spoke their language fluently, Johnston, who had been reared on the Navajo reservation and had once worked as an interpreter at the White House during Theodore Roosevelt's administration, was a World War I veteran. He knew of the military's search for a code that would withstand all attempts to decipher it. He also knew that Native American languages, notably Choctaw, had been used in World War I to encode messages.

Johnston's offer led to the development of a group of men known later as

In Bougainville, Solomon Islands, Corp. Henry Bake, Jr., and PFC George H. Kirk, Navajo Indians serving with a Marine signal unit, operate a portable radio set in a clearing they have hacked in the dense jungle close to the front lines in December 1943.

----

the Navajo Code Talkers. Guadalcanal, Tarawa, Iwo Jima—the Navajo Code Talkers took part in every assault the U.S. Marines conducted in the Pacific from 1942 to 1945. At Iwo Jima, for example, six Navajo Code Talkers worked around the clock during the first two days of battle, sending and receiving more than 800 errorless messages.

Navajo Code Talkers served in marine Raider battalions and marine parachute units, transmitting messages by telephone and radio in their native language—a code that the Japanese, who were very proficient at decoding, were never able to break. Navajo is an unwritten language of extreme complexity; its syntax, tonal qualities, and dialect make it unintelligible to anyone without extensive exposure and training. It has no alphabet or symbols and is spoken only on the Navajo lands of the American Southwest. The best of the Japanese code breakers could not solve the Navajo language.

Philip Johnston had suddenly and unexpectedly given the marines a breakthrough, a secret weapon of extraordinary use that, ironically, had been developed thousands of years before the existence of the United States.

Letter of Philip Johnston to Commander of U.S. Marine Corps, September 12, 1942

2335 Norwalk Avenue
Los Angeles, Calif.
Sept. 12, 1942

The Commander
United States Marine Corps
Washington, DC

Dear Sir:

I desire enlistment in the Marine Corps Reserve, Class 5-B Specialist, to serve in the capacity of training and direction of Navajo Indian personnel for communication, and to perform duty with them both inside and outside the limits of the continental United States; with non-commissioned rank commensurate with duties assigned.

Your authority for my induction into the service is requested. The basis for this request is as follows:

Twenty-two years of residence among the Navajo Indians, starting when I was four years of age, enabled me to become fluent in the language of this tribe. At the age of nine, I acted as interpreter for President Theodore Roosevelt at the White House; and subsequently, on many occasions, as court interpreter in Arizona. Since establishing my residence here, I have continued my use of the language through frequent visits to the reservation, and lecture work. . . .

Last February, it occurred to me that the Navajo language might be ideally suited to use by the Marine Corps for code in oral communication. I presented this idea to Lieutenant Colonel (then Major) J.E. Jones, Force Communication Officer at Camp Elliott, who agreed the plan was worth considering. I offered to make a search in Los Angeles for enough Navajos to permit a practical demonstration, and Colonel Jones accepted my offer. Two days after my return to the city, I received a letter from him stating that General Vogel was interested and requested further information. . . .

On February 27th, I arrived at Camp Elliott with four Navajos; a fifth had been located in the Naval service at San Diego and brought to Camp Elliott. The following morning at 8:15, Colonel Jones gave me six typical messages used in military operations, and asked me to report at Divisional Headquarters at nine o'clock for the demonstration. These messages contained many terms for which no equivalents exist in the Navajo language, and we had only a short time to devise such terms.

The demonstration was held as scheduled. . . .

Informing on the Veep: The Kickback Revelations that Brought Down Agnew—1973

Deposition of informer to FBI on kickback payments to Vice President Spiro Agnew

During the heat of the Watergate investigation, President Richard Nixon, in a nationally televised address, said of himself that the people of the United States had a right to know whether their president was a crook. He assured the country that he was not a crook. Contextually, the term itself seemed oddly placed in the speech. The word had always carried a connotation of graft, corruption, and slippery deals to line one's pockets. In the Watergate imbroglio, Nixon was not squirming in a web of personal enrichment sins; his transgressions were in nature political and constitutional.

In the matter of Nixon's vice president, Spiro T. Agnew, the story was quite different.

During a political career that rocketed from the office of county executive of Baltimore County, Maryland, to the state governorship and, surprisingly, on to the vice presidency, Agnew had received tens of thousands of dollars in kickbacks from firms awarded state contracts in Maryland. The bags of money did not stop when Agnew became vice president. "I just paid off the Vice President of the United States," one contractor told a friend shortly after he gave Agnew $10,000 in a basement office of the White House.

Agnew's graft was rooted in the shady world of government contracting in Maryland in the 1960s, when state farmland was being divided up for road and construction projects, a time when politicians commonly took a percentage of many state contracts awarded. The case against Agnew stemmed from a corruption investigation initiated in 1973 by U.S. Attorney George Beall, a Republican, whose office struck gold with the testimony of four Agnew associates implicated in the kickback scam: Jerome Wolff, an Agnew staffer and head of the Maryland Highway Administration; I. H. Hemmerman, a Baltimore developer; and engineering firm leaders Lester Matz and Alan Greene. It was Matz who led Beall to Agnew, admitting in a polygraphed interview that he'd given kickback payments to Agnew in his offices both in Baltimore and later in Washington.

According to FBI reports, the vice president also occasionally returned a favor. After Agnew pocketed a $1,500 cash payment intended as a campaign *contribution, he rewarded one of his cronies with an invitation to fly to Florida on the vice president's jet to watch an Apollo moon launch.*

At first, according to the investigation, Agnew received a third of the 5 percent kickbacks on road construction and consulting contracts, with the other two-thirds going to two other unnamed parties. As Agnew's power grew, he was able to take half of the kickback fee, or 2.5 percent of the amount of the contract.

One informer said that Agnew must have received at least $75,000 in one particular transaction because he himself had taken $35,000–$40,000. "There were eight to 10 engineering firms contributing or kicking back in this manner," the informant recalled.

Beall and three attorneys quietly built the case against Agnew until the Wall Street Journal *broke the story in August 1973. Just two months later, on October 10, 1973, Agnew quit. The disgraced vice president pleaded no contest to a single charge that he had failed to report to the Internal Revenue Service $29,500 of income received in 1967. He was fined $10,000 and placed on three years' probation, avoiding a jail term. He was the first vice president to depart with a criminal record.*

Otherwise, President Agnew might have taken the oath of office upon the resignation of President Nixon less than a year later.

Deposition of FBI Informer on Kickback Payments to Vice President Spiro Agnew, 1973

Sometime in 1970, or early 1971, Matz received a telephone call from Jones who advised him that there was an upcoming federal job that the Vice-President would control. This job would generate something on the order of $100,000 in fees, and Jones advised Matz that a payment would be necessary. This job was the (deleted) and Matz wanted it to go to (deleted). The job was awarded to (deleted). He then approached his partner in (deleted) for the purpose of advising him that the job was awarded through Mr. Agnew and that a payment was expected. (Deleted) at first balked, but when Matz later told him that he (Matz) had committed them to make a 5% payment to Mr. Agnew, (deleted) finally agreed to contribute $1,000. Matz arranged an appointment with Mr. Agnew and Jones in the Vice-President's offices in Washington. He then arranged to meet with (deleted) in Washington just before his appointment with the Vice President. Matz met with (deleted) across the street from the EOB and there received from (deleted) $1,000 in cash. Matz added $1,500 in cash

From DS-250
(Ed. 4-26-63)

UNITED STATES GOVERNMENT   DEPARTMENT OF JUSTICE

Memorandum

TO   :   Baltimore County File   DATE: July 20, 1973

FROM :   Russell T. Baker, Jr.
          Assistant U. S. Attorney

SUBJECT: ███████

At 2:00 p.m. on Thursday, July 19, 1973, I met with ████████ in my office. He advised me that his client was willing to explore the possibilities that we had ~~xkix~~ outlined in our discussion earlier this week. He has only had a preliminary opportunity to debrief his client and would appreciate a further opportunity to debrief him on these matters. I delivered to him our negotiation letter, a copy of which he signed in my presence. He indicated to me that his client would sign the original of the letter as soon as possible and that he would return the signed document to me. We agreed to proceed with some preliminary disclosures at this time even though his client had not yet signed the letter.

████████ was associated with ████████. ███ apparently had a major drinking problem and is no longer with the firm. Indeed, ████ does not even know where he is now. He is in contace with ████ and it is possible that ████ may end up representing ████ in this matter. Neither ████ nor ████ had any direct contact with Hammerman but were contemporaneously advised of the situation and apparently participated in the accumulation of cash by the firm. Apparently the firm kept a supply of cash available for such payments as a regular matter and the payments made to Hammerman came out of this supply. ████ disclosed these matters to me even after he had read and signed the letter.

████████ receive a substantial amount of state work, apparently in excess of $200,000 a year in fees. ████ had made a political contribution to Agnew's 1966 election campaign, perhaps through Hammerman. He therefore expected to get some state business and knew that contributions were necessary. Sometime after Agnew took office, ████ received a telephone call from Hammerman who asked ████ to meet with Hammerman in Hammerman's office. This apparently took place around the end of 1967. ████ subsequently met with Hammerman in Hammerman's office. Hammerman advised ████ that his firm was in line for state work and mentioned in particular the upcoming work that was to be done to ████. Hammerman asked ████ if he wanted a piece of the action. When ████ indicated that he was interested, Hammerman advised him that a "commission" of $5,000 would be necessary in order to assure that he got the work. ████ understood this to be a direct solicitation of an illegal payment and not a political contribution. There was no discussion of tickets or any discussion of political contribution. Hammerman told him that the money was to be paid in cash and that there was to be no record of the payment. ████ knew that Hammerman was close to Agnew. He paid the $5,000 and after going through the necessary procedural work, received the contract. Cohen believes that the total fees on the project may have been as great as $150,000. This may be the only occasion upon which ████ paid money to Hammerman. ████ would like a further opportunity to debrief his client on this point.

1491

In the 1973 investigation of Vice President Spiro T. Agnew, Department of Justice attorneys built a steely case of fraud and graft around the testimony of a series of informers who had engaged in corrupt dealings with Agnew since his days in Maryland's state government. This July 20, 1973, Department of Justice memorandum corroborated other evidence that brought the vice president's career to an ignominious close.

and placed the entire sum in an envelope which he took with him to his meeting with Jones and the Vice-President. (Deleted) has been interviewed and confirms Matz's recollection of these events. We have the check by which he generated the $1,000.

Matz met with Jones and the Vice President and placed the envelope on the Vice President's desk saying that this was the money for the job. . . .

John C. Childs is expected to testify in substance as follows: Childs never made any payments to Mr. Agnew, Jones or Wolff. Nevertheless, he was aware from Matz of these payments and of the means by which the cash was generated, and recalls contemporaneous discussions with Matz about the payments. His own experience in Baltimore County had convinced him that the company would never receive any substantial public work unless they made the payments. Under the Agnew administration in Baltimore County, he discussed with Matz the payments to Jones and was involved in the generation of cash by the company. He recalls that during the 1966 election, he and Matz believed that if Mr. Agnew was elected Governor their company would be able to break into the substantial amounts of work awarded by the State Roads Commission. In July of 1968, he assisted Matz in making the calculations that led to the $20,000 payment to Mr. Agnew and knew from his conversations with Matz at the time that the money had come from (deleted) and that Matz paid the money to Mr. Agnew shortly before the Nixon banquet in Annapolis. He did not know in advance of Matz's $10,000 payment to Vice-President Agnew in early 1969, but he recalls that Matz informed him of this payment immediately thereafter. He also recalls that Matz told him at the time of the $2,500 payment made in connection with the (deleted).

ALMOST
CLOSE CALLS
HISTORY

General Washington Under Fire—1783

Response of George Washington to the so-called Newburgh Conspiracy

On March 15, 1783, Gen. George Washington stood to address a group of his officers at the Continental army's camp in Newburgh, New York. Military activities in the American Revolution had all but ended two years earlier with Lord Cornwallis's defeat at Yorktown, but Washington now faced another moment of crisis—a challenge to his own authority.

As Benjamin Franklin, John Jay, and John Adams continued to negotiate a final peace treaty with the British in Paris, many in the army had become restless and disillusioned. The officers complained about back pay owed to them, the failure of the army to settle food and clothing accounts, and Congress's lack of action in settling pension provisions. Amid these grievances, a number of men, including Maj. Gen. Horatio Gates, second in command at Newburgh, were reportedly laying plans aimed at the removal of Washington as commander and the takeover of the Congress and the country by a military coup.

Already aware of the discontent of his officers, Washington had received a letter from Alexander Hamilton of New York alluding to the crisis of congressional finances and the pressures mounting for an overthrow of the government. He warned Washington that he would need to "keep a complaining and suffering army within the bounds of moderation" or the unrest could turn to open rebellion.

In addition, on March 10, Washington was given a written call for a meeting of general and field officers along with an anonymous letter that had been circulated among the officers suggesting that if their demands were not met, they would "retire to some unsettled country" and leave Congress without an army.

On March 11, Washington issued general orders denouncing the "irregular invitation" and the "disorderly proceedings." At the same time, he called for a meeting on March 15 of representatives of all the regiments to decide how "to attain the just and important object in view." Washington reported the developments in a letter to Congress. The next day, a second unsigned letter circulated among the camp expressing the view that Washington's orders made him party to the complaints.

With his career, reputation, and authority on the line, Washington told his men on March 15 not to take any action that would "lessen the dignity and *sully the glory you have hitherto maintained." As he took a letter from his pocket describing the financial problems confronting Congress, Washington had trouble reading the lines in the letter. Pausing to put on his glasses, he said, "Gentlemen, you must pardon me. I have grown gray in your service and now find myself growing blind."*

The gesture seemed to affect the men greatly as they remembered the past days of fighting for the American cause and the leadership of Washington. They listened closely to his words. When he left the meeting, the officers expressed their confidence in Congress and repudiated the "infamous propositions" in the anonymous letter. The possible coup was dead.

When Washington asserted his authority in March 1783, he warded off what could have been a constitutional crisis, a serious disruption in the Paris peace talks, and the future development of the republican form of government adopted four years later.

Letter of George Washington to His Troops, March 15, 1783

Head Quarters, Newburgh, March 15, 1783

Gentlemen,

By an anonymous summons, an attempt has been made to convene you together; how inconsistent with the rules of propriety! how unmilitary! and how subversive of all order and discipline, let the good sense of the Army decide.

In the moment of this summons, another anonymous production was sent into circulation, addressed more to the feelings and passions, than to the reason and judgment of the Army. The author of the piece, is entitled to much credit for the goodness of his Pen and I could wish he had as much credit for the rectitude of his Heart, for, as Men see thro' different Optics, and are induced by the reflecting faculties of the Mind, to use different means, to attain the same end, the Author of the Address, should have had more charity, than to mark for Suspicion, the Man who should recommend moderation and longer forbearance, or, in others words, who should not think as he thinks, and act as he advises. But he had another plan in view, in which candor and liberality of Sentiment, regard to justice, and love of Country, have no part; and he was right, to insinuate the darkest suspicion, to effect the blackest designs.

That the Address is drawn with great Art, and is designed to answer the most insidious purposes. That it is calculated to impress the Mind, with an idea of premeditated injustice in the Sovereign power of the United States, and rouse all those resentments which must unavoidably flow from such a belief. That the secret mover of this Scheme (whoever he may be) intended to take advantage of the passions, while they were warmed by the recollection of past distresses, without giving time for cool, deliberative thinking, and that composure of Mind which is so necessary to give dignity and stability to measures is rendered too obvious. . . .

Thus much, Gentlemen, I have thought it incumbent on me to observe to you, to shew upon what principles I opposed the irregular and hasty meeting which was proposed to have been held on Tuesday last: and not because I wanted a disposition to give you every opportunity, consistent with your own honor, and the dignity of the Army, to make known your grievances. If my conduct heretofore, has not evinced to you that I have been a faithful friend to the Army, my declaration of it at this time wd. be equally unavailing and improper. But as I was among the first who embarked in the cause of our common Country. As I have never left your side one moment, but when called from you on public duty. As I have been the constant companion and witness of your Distresses, and not among the last to feel, and acknowledge your Merits. As I have ever considered my own Military reputation as inseparably connected with that of the Army. As my Heart has ever expanded with joy, when I have heard its praises, and my indignation has arisen, when the mouth of detraction has been opened against, it can *scarcely be supposed*, at this late stage of the War, that I am indifferent to its interests. But, how are they to be promoted? The way is plain, says the anonymous addresser. If War continues, remove into the unsettled Country; there establish yourselves, and leave an ungrateful country to defend itself. But who are they to defend?   Our wives, our Children, our Farms, and other property which we leave behind us. Or in this state of hostile separation, are we to take the two first (the latter cannot be removed),   to perish in a Wilderness, with hunger cold and nakedness? If peace takes place, never sheath your Sword Says he until you have obtained full and ample justice; this dreadful alternative, of either deserting our Country in the extremest hour of her distress, or turning our Arms against it, (which is the apparent object, unless Congress can be compelled into instant compliance) has something so shocking in it, that humanity revolts at the idea. My God! What can this writer have in view, by recommending such measures? Can he be a friend to the Army? Can he be a friend to this Country? Rather is he not an insidious Foe? Some Emissary, perhaps, from New York, plotting the ruin of both, by sowing the seeds of discord and separation between the Civil and Military powers of the Continent? And what Compliment does he pay to our Understandings, when he recommends measures in either alternative, impracticable in their Nature?...

For myself (and I take no merit in giving the assurance, being induced to it from principles of gratitude, veracity and Justice)—a grateful sense of the confidence you have ever placed in me, a recollection of the chearful assistance, and prompt obedience I have experienced from you, under every vicissitude of Fortune, and the sincere I feel for an Army I have so long had the honor to Command, will oblige me to declare, in this public and solemn manner, that, in the attainment of compleat justice for all your toils and dangers, and in the gratification of every wish, so far as may be done consistently with the great duty I owe my Country, and those powers we are bound to respect, you may freely command my Services to the utmost of my abilities.

While I give you these assurances, and pledge myself in the most unequivocal manner, to exert whatever ability I am possessed of, in your favor, let me entreat you, Gentlemen, on your part, not to take any measures, which, viewed in the calm light of reason, will lessen the dignity, and sully the glory you have hitherto maintained; let me request you to rely on the plighted faith of your Country, and place a full confidence in the purity of the intentions of Congress; that, previous to your dissolution as an Army they will cause all your Accts. to be fairly liquidated, as directed in their resolutions, which were published to you two days ago, and that they will adopt the most effectual measures in their power, to render ample justice to you, for your faithful and meritorious Services. And let me conjure you, in the name of our common Country as you value your own sacred honor, as you respect the rights of humanity, and as you regard the Military and National character of America, to express your utmost horror and detestation of the Man who wishes, under any specious presences, to overturn the liberties of our Country, and who wickedly attempts to open the flood Gates of Civil discord, and deluge our rising Empire in Blood. By thus determining, and thus acting, you will pursue the plain and direct road to the attainment of your wishes. You will defeat the insidious designs of our Enemies, who are compelled to resort from open force to secret Artifice. You will give one more distinguished proof of unexampled patriotism and patient virtue, rising superior to the pressure of the most complicated sufferings; And you will, by the dignity of your Conduct, afford occasion for Posterity to say, when speaking of the glorious example you have exhibited to Mankind, "had this day been wanting, the World has never seen the last stage of perfection to which human nature is capable of attaining. . . ."

The "Firebell in the Night" Nearly Rang Early: The Tallmadge Amendment and the Missouri Compromise—1819

Congressional deliberations over the admission of Missouri to the Union

On December 18, 1818, a memorial of the legislature of the Territory of Missouri was laid before the U.S. House of Representatives proposing the admission of Missouri as a state upon "an equal footing with the original States." By the time Congress had resolved the issue of Missouri's statehood, ex-president Thomas Jefferson lamented that "this momentous question, like a firebell in the night, awakened and filled me with terror." The firebell to which he referred was slavery.

Under French and Spanish rule, slavery had been legal in Missouri, and settlers hoped to legalize slavery in the new state, a region that had been part of the Louisiana Purchase. The trend, at least in the North, had been in the opposite direction. By 1818, slavery had been abolished in every state north of Delaware and had been banned in the Northwest Territory. With this new petition to admit Missouri as a slave state, the issue of slavery, always nationally sensitive and potentially explosive, would flare up again.

Representative James Tallmadge of New York, a strong antislavery spokesman, ignited the debate, in February 1819, by proposing an amendment to the legislation. Tallmadge's amendment would prohibit the entry of slaves into the territory "except for the punishment of crimes." He went further: ". . . all children born within the said State, after the admission thereof into the Union, shall be free at the age of twenty-five years."

The arguments over the amendment were fierce ("quite interesting" was the way the House recorder cautiously characterized them in the Annals of Congress). In the end, the Tallmadge Amendment was adopted by the House of Representatives in a straight sectional vote, 79 to 67. The savage, bitter struggle over slavery was now at the center of American political discourse.

When the legislation reached the Senate, where Southern representation was strong, Tallmadge's amendment was narrowly defeated, with enraged Southern senators railing against the attempt by Northern representatives to meddle in the internal life of the South and to strip away the constitutional rights of the states.

For eighteen months, the intense debate stormed on, outside the halls of

Congress as well as within—in newspapers, public speeches, and from pulpits. After much acrimony, the question of Missouri statehood was finally resolved, largely through the maneuverings and legislative dexterity of Henry Clay of Kentucky. The Missouri Compromise provided for the admission of Missouri without any restriction as to slavery but prohibited the institution throughout the United States north of latitude 36 degrees and 30 minutes. The compromise was a palliative, not a solution, and the vituperative debate would march on until the blasts of guns at Fort Sumter four decades later.

What if the Senate had not defeated the Tallmadge Amendment? What if the South had lacked the votes to stop Northern legislators from blocking Missouri statehood with slavery intact? Would the action, considered imperious and unjust by the South, have brought the slavery controversy, secession, and perhaps war to a head much earlier? A war without Abraham Lincoln and Robert E. Lee, U. S. Grant and Stonewall Jackson?

Excerpt from Congressional Deliberations over the Tallmadge Amendment, February 1819

And provided, That the further introduction of slavery or involuntary servitude be prohibited, except for the punishment of crimes, whereof the party shall have been fully convicted; and that all children born within the said State, after the admission thereof into the Union, shall be free at the age of twenty-five years.

Mr. LIVERMORE spoke as follows: Mr. Chairman, I am in favor of the proposed amendment. The object of it is to prevent the extension of slavery over the territory ceded to the United States by France. It accords with the dictates of reason, and the best feelings of the human heart; and is not calculated to interrupt any legitimate right arising either from the Constitution or any other compact. I propose to show what slavery is, and to mention a few of the many evils which follow in its train; and I hope to evince that we are not bound to tolerate the existence of so disgraceful a state of things beyond its present extent, and that it would be impolitic and very unjust to let it spread over the whole face of our Western territory. Slavery in the United States is the condition of man subjected to the will of a master, who can make any disposition of him short of taking away his life. In those States where it is tolerated, laws are enacted making it penal to instruct slaves in the art of reading, and they are not permitted to attend public worship, or to hear the Gospel preached. Thus the light of science and of religion is utterly excluded from the mind that the body may be more easily bowed down to servitude. The bodies of slaves may, with impunity, be prostituted to any purpose, and deformed in any manner by their owners. The sympathies of nature in slaves are disregarded; mothers and children are sold and separated; the children wring their little hands and expire in agonies of grief while the bereft mothers commit suicide in despair. How long will the desire of wealth render us blind to the sin of holding both the bodies and souls of our fellow men in chains! But, sir, I am admonished of the Constitution and told that we cannot emancipate slaves. I know we may not infringe that instrument, and therefore do not propose to emancipate slaves. The proposition before us goes only to prevent our citizens from making slaves of such as have a right to freedom. In the present slaveholding States let slavery continue, for our boasted Constitution connives at it; but do not, for the sake of cotton and tobacco, let it be told to future ages that, while pretending to love liberty, we have purchased an extensive country to disgrace it with the foulest reproach of nations. Our Constitution requires no such thing of us. The ends for which that supreme law was made are succinctly stated in its preface. They are, first, to form a more perfect union, and insure domestic tranquility. Will slavery effect this? Can we, sir, by mingling bond with free, black spirits with white, like Shakespeare's witches in Macbeth, form a more perfect union, and insure domestic tranquility? Secondly, to establish justice. Is justice to be established by subjecting half mankind to the will of the other half? Justice, sir, is blind to colors, and weighs in equal scales the rights of all men, whether white or black. Thirdly, to provide for the common defence, and secure the blessings of liberty. Does slavery add anything to the common defence? Sir, the strength of a Republic is in the arm of freedom. But, above all things, do the blessings of liberty consist in slavery? If there is any sincerity in our profession that slavery is an ill tolerated only from necessity, let us not, while we feel that ill, shun the cure which consists only in an honest avowal that liberty and equal rights are the end and aim of all our institutions, and that to tolerate slavery beyond the narrowest limits prescribed for it by the Constitution, is a perversion of them all.

Slavery, sir, I repeat, is not established by our Constitution; but as part of the States are indulged in the commission of a sin from which they could not at once be restrained, and which they would not consent to abandon. But, sir, if we could, by any process of reasoning, be brought to believe it justifiable to hold others to involuntary servitude, policy forbids that we should increase it. Even the present slaveholding States have an interest, I think, in limiting the extent of involuntary servitude; for, should slaves become much more numerous and conscious of their strength, draw the sword against their masters, it will be to the free States that the masters must resort for an efficient power to suppress servile insurrection. But we have made a treaty with France, which, we are told can only be preserved by the charms of slavery. . . .

An opportunity is now presented, if not to diminish, at least to prevent, the growth of a sin which sits heavy on the soul of every one of us. By embracing this opportunity, we may retrieve the national character, and, in some degree, our own. But if we suffer it to pass unimproved, let us at least be consistent and declare that our Constitution was made to impose slavery, and not to establish liberty. Let us no longer tell idle tales about the gradual abolition of slavery; away with colonization societies, if their design is only to rid us of free blacks and turbulent slaves; have done also with bible societies, whose views are extended to Africa and the East Indies, while they overlook the deplorable condition of their sable brethren within our own borders; make no more laws to prohibit the importation of slaves, for the world must see that the object of such laws is alone to prevent the glutting of a prodigious market for the flesh and blood of man, which we are about to establish in the West, and to enhance the price of sturdy wretches, reared like black cattle and horses for sale on our own plantations.

The question being put on the motion of Mr. TALLMADGE to amend the bill, the vote was—for the amendment 79, against it 67.

So the amendment was agreed to.

Declining an Invitation to Ford's Theatre—1865

Memoirs of U. S. Grant on the invitation from the Lincolns to attend Ford's Theatre on the night of April 14, 1865

The swirling events in the spring of 1865 are forever chiseled in American history: the eloquent second inaugural address of President Abraham Lincoln in March, in which he called for a generous peace, "With malice toward none, with charity for all"; the surrender of Robert E. Lee's Army of Northern Virginia at Appomattox on April 9; and then, six weeks after the inauguration and five days after the Confederate surrender in Virginia, the night when the name of Ford's Theatre, a play called Our American Cousin, and an actor named Booth became infamous.

President Lincoln and Ulysses S. Grant, the general whose determination and forcefulness had finally driven the North to victory, had never been personally close, even though each had great respect for the other. Lincoln's wife, Mary, had little regard for Grant and his wife, Julia. Nevertheless, as Grant arrived in Washington from his meeting with Lee at Appomattox, the Lincolns invited the Grants to sit with them in the presidential box at Ford's Theatre on the night of April 14, 1865. The Grants declined.

In his later memoirs, Grant explained that he and Julia had been anxious to see their children and had left Washington on the train that afternoon for Burlington, New Jersey. When a telegram arrived informing Grant of the events at Ford's Theatre, he sadly handed the paper to Julia, who began to sob. "It was the blackest day of my life," Grant wrote. When he stood at the head of Lincoln's coffin in the rotunda of the Capitol, the New York Tribune reported, "General Grant gave way to a torrent of grief and the tears streamed down his cheeks in a steady stream. He made no motion to wipe them away and was grief stricken, to his very core."

If the Grants had stayed the night in Washington on April 14, they certainly would have accepted the Lincolns' invitation to see the play. Would the presence of the Grants in the presidential box have in any way deterred Booth? Or would Booth have had two principal targets? If both Lincoln and Grant had been killed that night by Booth, who would have succeeded Andrew Johnson in the presidency? Or would the Grants have had others with them who would have provided greater security? If U. S. Grant had been in the presidential box for the play, the years of Reconstruction might have taken on a much different character.

Excerpts from the Memoirs of U. S. Grant

After I left General Lee at Appomattox Station, I went with my staff and a few others directly to Burkesville Station on my way to Washington. The road from Burkesville back having been newly repaired and the ground being soft, the train got off the track frequently, and, as a result, it was after midnight of the second day when I reached City Point. As soon as possible I took a dispatch-boat thence to Washington City.

While in Washington I was very busy for a time in preparing the necessary orders for the new state of affairs; communicating with my different commanders of separate departments, bodies of troops, etc. But by the 14th I was pretty well through with this work, so as to be able to visit my children, who were then in Burlington, New Jersey, attending school. Mrs. Grant was with me in Washington at the time, and we were invited by President and Mrs. Lincoln to accompany them to the theatre on the evening of that day. I replied to the President's verbal invitation to the effect, that if we were in the city we would take great pleasure in accompanying them; but that I was very anxious to get away and visit my children, and if I could get through my work during the day I should do so. I did get through and started by the evening train on the 14th, sending Mr. Lincoln word, of course, that I would not be at the theatre. . . .

It would be impossible for me to describe the feeling that overcame me at the news [of Lincoln's death]. . . . I knew his goodness of heart, his generosity, his yielding disposition, his desire to have everybody happy, and above all his desire to see all the people of the United States enter again upon the full privileges of citizenship with equality among all.

How a Taxicab Accident Nearly Changed World History—1931

Winston Churchill's miraculous escape from death

O n a cold Sunday night in mid-December 1931, a taxicab traveling north on New York's Fifth Avenue struck a man as he was crossing the street. Although he remained conscious, the man suffered a serious gash to his forehead, cracked ribs, assorted bruises, and a crushed right foot, which had been run over as he was struck. He was rushed to Lenox Hill Hospital where he stayed for several days, during which time he contracted a case of pleurisy. When he left the hospital in a wheelchair and was taken to his suite in the Waldorf Astoria Hotel, a press of photographers and newspaper reporters gathered. At the hotel, messages from around the world had been stacked in a large pile, and the hospital lobby and the man's suite were filled with flowers. Winston Churchill had survived.

Churchill had entered Parliament in 1901 at age 26. After 30 years, he had made an extraordinary mark in British politics. He had been Home Secretary and later First Lord of the Admiralty at the outbreak of World War I in 1914. During the war, he had elevated the navy's strategic role in the Flanders campaign in 1914 and had initiated the Allies' effort to outflank the Germans on the Western Front by launching a seaborne expeditionary force against the Turkish Straits, an action that led to one of the worst military defeats in British history.

Despite later cabinet service, he lost his seat in Parliament in the 1922 elections but rebounded to become Chancellor of the Exchequer in Prime Minister Stanley Baldwin's government from 1924 to 1929. But after a falling-out with Baldwin, once again Churchill's political career was in eclipse. As he visited New York in 1931, he was busily engaged in literary pursuits, a career in which he would also make a substantial contribution.

Following that wintry-night accident in 1931, there could have been obituaries lamenting the passing of a world political figure, talking about how tragic his end had been and how a great career had been cut short by fate. Because of a kinder destiny, the obituary writers did not have to write such copy that night. In coming years, the newspapers would, instead, relate yet another political comeback, Churchill's leadership in times of truly great challenge, and his words: "I have nothing to offer but blood, toil, tears, and sweat. . . ."

London Daily Mail, December 24, 1931

MR. CHUCHILL ON HIS ESCAPE
Special Story for the Daily Mail:
His Thoughts and Sensations

From our own Correspondent
New York, Tuesday.

Mr. Winston Churchill, though still very weak from the shock of the accident last week, when he was knocked down by a taxicab in Fifth-avenue, is in excellent spirits.

He tells me that he hopes to strong enough to write the first of a series of American articles for *The Daily Mail* early next week.

I found him sitting up in bed in one of the towers of the new Waldorf Astoria Hotel. With his wife and his daughter he is occupying a suite 39 floors above street level, but their view of the city to-day is obscured by fog almost as thick as that experienced in London.

"I realize," he said to me, "that I have had a miraculous escape from death, the curious thing is that I never once lost consciousness. . . . I shall rest here during the Christmas holidays, and then, if well enough, pay a brief visit to Nassau in the Bahamas, returning to New York in time to deliver my first lecture on: 'The pathway of the English-speaking Peoples' on January 14. . . ."

Mr. Churchill's forehead and nose are still elaborately bandaged, and he is destined to carry a large scar for the rest of his life as a memento of his appallingly narrow escape from death.

The accident was due, he tells me, to his momentary forgetfulness of the rule of the road in the United States, which is exactly the opposite of that in England.

In crossing the road, he explains, he turned his eyes involuntarily to the left instead of to the right, with the result that the taxicab hit him on the right side, catapulting him with terrific force on to his forehead.

A table in the reception room in his suite is piled high with letters and cables from his friends in England and this country. Packages with rare vintages of pre-Prohibition wine are also arriving from American sympathizers anxious to speed his recovery.

Though able to walk a few steps, Mr. Churchill, by the advice of his physician, Dr. Otto C. Pickhardt, is spending the next eight or ten days in bed. "His condition, on the whole," says Dr. Pickhardt, "is very satisfactory, and it can now be safely said that he will suffer no serious after-effects of his injuries. But he must have rest, as he has been badly shaken up."

Mr. Churchill to-day played several games of backgammon in bed, and accepted with a smile the verdict of his doctor that he might read and dictate letters or lectures, and receive his friends "within limits."

Others Didn't Make It—JFK Did—1943

Action report on the loss of the USS *PT-109*

O n August 2, 1943, a U.S. Navy torpedo boat was lost at sea, rammed and sunk by a Japanese destroyer. There was loss of life. The boat, PT-109, was piloted by Lt. John F. Kennedy.

Born in Brookline, Massachusetts, on May 29, 1917, to Rose and Joseph P. Kennedy, he attended the Choate School in Wallingford, Connecticut, and the London School of Economics and graduated cum laude from Harvard University in 1940. He had begun to attend graduate school at Stanford University when the war broke out.

After joining the U.S. Navy, Kennedy served for a time in the Office of Naval Intelligence. After attending Naval Reserve Officers Training School at Northwestern University, he entered the Motor Torpedo Boat Squadron Training Center in Melville, Rhode Island, achieving the rank of lieutenant, junior grade. Upon completing his training, he served in Panama and the Solomon Islands.

He became commander of PT-109 on April 23, 1943, and was ordered to the Russell Islands, where he, along with the other commanders, conducted nightly operations to interdict heavy Japanese barge traffic resupplying the Japanese garrisons on New Georgia. On the night of August 1, 1943, PT-109—commanded by Kennedy with an executive officer, Ensign Leonard Jay Thom, and 10 enlisted men—was one of 15 boats sent on patrol.

The Japanese destroyer Amagiri struck PT-109, cutting it in half. Two men were killed in the collision. The 11 survivors clung to pieces of the boat, managing to swim to a small island three miles away. All 11 made it to the island after having spent a total of 15 hours in the water, including one man whom Lieutenant Kennedy had towed the entire distance. With no food or water on the island, the men, after resting, swam to another, with Kennedy again towing the injured man. Kennedy managed to communicate with some natives on the island who provided food and water and were able to make contact with other Americans. On August 8, Kennedy and the other survivors were rescued.

Kennedy was later awarded the Navy and Marine Corps Medal and the Purple Heart for injuries sustained in the accident. In early 1944, he was released from active duty and he retired from the U.S. Naval Reserve on physical disability in March 1945.

Nearly two decades later, President Kennedy met once again with his rescuers and was toasted by members of the Japanese destroyer crew. It could have been otherwise.

The promising career of a young PT boat commander was almost lost in the seas near the Russell Islands in the summer of 1943. A Navy photographer shot this picture of Lt. John F. Kennedy aboard USS PT-109.

Excerpts from Action Report on the Loss of the USS *PT-109*, August 1–2, 1943

Motor Torpedo Boats, Rendova

From: The Commander
To: The Commander-in-Chief, U.S. Fleet.
Via: Official Channels

Subject: PT Operations night 1-2 August, 1943

    1. FORCE: All available boats (15) on patrol
    2. ENEMY CONTACTS: Five enemy destroyers, attacked in Blackett Strait, five or possibly six torpedo hits scored.

3. WEATHER: Overcast, visibility poor.
4. PATROLS:
AREA B - (BLACKETT STRAITS
DIVISION B - OFF VANGA VANGA

Lt. H.J. Brantingham	PT 159	OAK 27
Lt. (jg) W.F. Liebenow	PT 157	OAK 21
Lt. (jg) J.R. Lowrey	PT 162	OAK 36
Lt. (jg) Jack Kennedy	PT 109	OAK 14

Division B. ...PTs 162 and 109 of Division B with PT 169 of Division A were in Blackett Strait off Vanga Vanga, as was PT 157, which however, was not in contact with them. Around 0215 the three were due East of Gizo Island headed South, in right echelon formation with PT 109 leading, PT 162 second and PT 169 last. PT 162 saw on a collision course, a warship headed Northward about 700 yards away. The PT 162 turned to fire its torpedoes, but they did not fire. The PT 162 finally turned to the Southwest upon getting within 100 yards of the warship to avoid collision. Personnel aboard the PT 162 saw 2 raked stacks, and at least 2 turrets aft, and possibly a third turret. At the time of the turning, PT 109 was seen to collide with the warship, followed by an explosion and a large flame which died down a little, but continued to burn for 10 or 15 minutes. The warship when it was about 3000 yards away headed toward them at high speed. The PT 169 stopped just before the warship hit PT 109, turned toward it and fired two torpedoes when abeam at 150 yards range. The destroyer straddled the PT 169 with shell fire, just after it a collision with PT 109, and then circled left toward Gizo Island at increased speed and disappeared. . . .

RESCUE MISSION: August 6, word was received from the Coastwatcher and by Native Messenger that eleven survivors of PT 109, sunk in a collision with an enemy destroyer on the morning of August 2, were alive and on a small Islet near Cross Island on the West side of Ferguson Passage. Arrangements were made through the Offices of the Coastwatcher Organization for the rescue. . . .

Wernher von Braun: The Soviet Union's Loss—1945

Interview with a member of the team that escorted Wernher von Braun out of Germany

I n the crush and chaos of the final days of Hitler, when Allied forces were overrunning Germany, U.S. government officials were determined that German rocket science and the scientists who developed it would not fall into Soviet hands. The top prize was Wernher von Braun, the man who was responsible for the V-2 rocket that had terrorized Britain late in the war. During those last days of the Third Reich, von Braun's own goal was the same as that of his former enemies.

When Hitler came to power in 1933, there had been a mass exodus of intellectual talent to France and the United States. Wernher von Braun had stayed in Germany, joining the National Socialist Aviation Corps and other Nazi organizations.

At a scientific complex at a small fishing village named Peenemünde on the Baltic sea, von Braun and other scientists conducted sophisticated rocket research. By the early 1940s, they had already produced early designs for a two-stage intercontinental ballistic missile (ICBM) as well the first models of the A-4 rocket, which would eventually become the V-2. By 1944, the A-4 was being mass-produced at the Mettelwork concentration camp with slave labor, and the Germans used them in combat. Joseph Goebbels's propaganda department renamed the A-4 the Vengeance Weapon-2 or simply, the V-2.

With the Soviet army driving toward Berlin, 500 top rocket scientists were moved west under heavy German guard. Von Braun managed to find an abandoned mine in the Harz Mountains to hide data about the rockets. Convinced that his future scientific work depended on his own capture by the Americans, von Braun successfully made his way to a village in Bavaria near the Austrian border. He sent his younger brother, Magnus, a personal assistant, to find the Allies on a bicycle borrowed from a local innkeeper. Magnus located Americans in a nearby valley, and the scientists quickly surrendered.

Under the Yalta agreement, the Soviets would receive the entire region surrounding the scientific complex, and they were rapidly advancing. U.S. troops had to act quickly. With only a few days to spare, they managed to ship out V-2 parts, records, and scientists.

For the next 21 years, von Braun would work with the U.S. Army in peacetime space missions and in the development of the ICBM. The work of von

Braun and other German scientists became essential in American rocket research. The man who had developed the weapons that had terrorized the Allies now turned his work into the invention of the Saturn V.

At the center of the Cold War's scientific research in the 1950s was a race with the Soviet Union in the development of sophisticated weaponry and in the steps toward the control of space technology. If von Braun and the records of his research had not been picked up by U.S. troops in the rush of the Allies to Berlin, the Soviets would have inherited a wealth of talent and information that could have made a dramatic difference in the progress of Cold War strategic and diplomatic activity. In those few days, as the enemy shifted from the defeated Nazi war machine to the Soviet threat, the United States captured a significant weapon.

Excerpt from Interview with Dr. Richard W. Porter

It was getting dark and we had been going all day. . . . The station was full of displaced people who had been released from the camps in the neighborhood. . . . We went to see the station master, but he said that he didn't have a locomotive, but he would give us the first one that came in. . . . After some time, one came in, but it had a busted injector and was just limping along. . . . There was a hill outside Muhlhausen. . . . Finally, a locomotive came in, but it was the smallest I have ever seen, and it could only pull about half of our cars up that hill. . . .

Von Braun wanted to bring over a complete operating group, as I would have, too, in his place. That included draftsmen, tool makers. . . . Being a project manager myself, I knew exactly what he was talking about. He was right, and we ended up with a group of about 500, or maybe even 600.... I went off to Paris to talk to Toftoy, by Jeep. . . . He told me: "Oh, no, that's way too many people." He knew that his higher-ups would never accept such a number. There were weeks of debates and arguments with the people back in Washington, and also with the British who wanted V-2s and a launch crew for test launchings. . . . Certainly plans to ship a number of the Peenemunde people to the United States did not materialize overnight. . . .

A Heartbeat Away—1955

Memorandum on President Eisenhower's heart attack

In the fall of 1955, much of the world's press focused on a small suite of rooms on the eighth floor of Fitzsimons Army Medical Center in Denver, Colorado. While on vacation, President Dwight D. Eisenhower had suffered a heart attack.

He had recently returned from Geneva, Switzerland, where, in an effort to ease world tensions, the heads of the Big Four powers—the United States, Great Britain, France, and the Soviet Union—had met in July. Geneva had been the first top-level conference among the leaders since the Potsdam meeting of 1945.

Following the stressful meetings in which the four governments had aired Cold War positions, the president had gone to Denver to relax and play golf at Cherry Hills Golf Club. On September 23, he complained of indigestion and returned to the home of his mother-in-law, Elivera Doud, where he had dinner that evening with his physician. In the early morning hours, he again complained of pain, and the doctor was summoned. Although the physician suspected a heart attack, he gave the president morphine and delayed sending him to the hospital. Later that morning, Eisenhower was taken to the hospital.

Rushed to room 8002, the president was placed in an oxygen tent and given a combination of drugs. For several weeks, the eighth floor of the Denver hospital became a presidential compound. President Eisenhower survived, despite the fact that physicians had varying opinions about treatment and despite the relatively low state-of-the-art treatment of the 1950s.

The death of Eisenhower in 1955 would have made Richard Nixon president of the United States. It would have been Nixon, and not Eisenhower, facing Adlai Stevenson in the 1956 election, a contest that would have been far closer and much more partisan than Eisenhower vs. Stevenson. A Nixon victory would have established him as a young, towering political figure and, assuming a relatively successful first term, he would have been a far more difficult challenge for the Democrats in 1960.

An Aide's Diary Entry on President Eisenhower's Heart Attack, September 1955

The President spent the four days, September 19th to the morning

---

President Dwight D. Eisenhower, recovering from a serious heart attack, greets the press and well-wishers at Denver's Fitzsimons Army Hospital in late September 1955.

of the 23rd at Fraser. On the morning of the 23rd he got up at 5:00, cooked breakfast for the guests there (George Allen, Bib Biggers—who was an unexpected added starter by Bob Schulz—and of course Aksel Nielsen.) He told me that morning he did not give them wheatcakes, only eggs and bacon. At 6:45 they left Fraser and drove to Denver. President stopped for a few minutes at the Doud house and came to the office at Lowry Air Force Base. *I have never seen him look or act better*—which is a flat statement made not in retrospect but made a few minutes after he left the office. He was delightful, patient with the pile of work, handed a letter from Dr. Milton and said "see what a wonderful brother I have." He sat and talked for a little while after he got through the work before he went to the golf course. On the way out I screamed after him (George Allen was waiting downstairs in the car). "Tell Mr. Allen I shan't forgive him for not coming up to see me." He did so the minute he got in the car—in other words his mind was not preoccupied with anything in particular.

He talked with the Secretary of State, and arrangements were made for the Secretary to call him off the golf course. This was done at about 3:00. For the record apparently he was called off the course, the call was not ready to go through, he went back, was called off again—and was upset.

The next morning General Snyder called me at about 6:45 to say the President would not be in early—he might be in ten o'clock or so. If Murray had to say anything, General Snyder said to call it a "digestive upset." I thought it was one of the periodic upsets he has had and was not in the slightest worried. Around 11 or so Bob Clark called (INS) and said that because of Murray's reluctance to say it was not serious, the wires were blowing it up until some major illness. Could

I call General Snyder and if it was not serious, ask him to tell Murray so. This was accomplished in approximately 45 minutes. General Snyder, for reasons of his own—the President was still asleep—said his digestive upset was not serious and this was carried on the wires. This I accepted face value—of course it was not serious, it would not be serious.

Meantime, at the House, General Snyder was called about 2:00 because the President had a severe pain. As soon as he arrived he gave him morphine and shortly the President went to sleep, sleeping until some time after eleven. General Snyder says he suspected it was a coronary attack but believed it better to let the President sleep and his system to get over the initial shock, rather than to wake him and get him to a hospital immediately. When he did wake, the General ~~called~~ examined him, renewed his suspicions that this was serious thing and I believed called General Griffin and the experts at Walter Reed. I do know that they took an electrocardiogram at the Doud house before taking him to the hospital. When the decision was made that the President was to go to the hospital. General Snyder told him he thought he would be more comfortable there, they wanted to take tests but did not, I believe, tell him what it was. The General urged the President be allowed to walk, with support, down the stairs and to the car, again because of the morale factor and because it would have been extremely difficult to carry a stretcher down the Doud stairs. The president, supported heavily, did manage to walk, and chatted with General Snyder in the car on the way to the hospital. Once there he was put in a wheel chair and taken to the suite. Dick Flohr sensed the seriousness of the attack and told me later in the day.

At 1:45 Murray Snyder, Betty Allen, Ann Parsons and I had gone over to the Famous Chef for lunch. Murray got the first call, told us the diagnosis was "a mild anterior coronary thrombosis" and took one of the cars to beat it back to the field. I got the second call, with which we all paid for our uneaten lunch and left. General Snyder said the President wanted me to call the Attorney General for an opinion as to how he could delegate authority.

Meantime (this of course I found out later) apparently the first time the President knew that he had had a heart attack was when they put him in the oxygen tent at the hospital. General Snyder said his eyes filled with tears. . . .

If the Heat Shield Had Blown—1962

Communication from John Glenn's *Friendship 7*

On February 20, 1962, John Glenn, in a historic moment in the history of flight, rode the space capsule Friendship 7 at a speed of 17,500 miles per hour in an orbit 160 miles above Earth. With all systems running smoothly during his initial circle of the Earth, Mission Control advised him that he "had a go" for at least seven turns. Although space planners had worried about the effects of weightlessness on the astronaut, Glenn worked and ate without any apparent difficulty. Remarkably, his pulse rate and other stress indicators emulated those of an individual who might have been out on a leisurely Sunday stroll in the park. As he looked down at the Earth, Glenn mentioned how fragile it appeared.

After Glenn began his second orbit, the flight team, headed by Chris Kraft, then received a shocking indication: a telemetry signal indicating that the capsule's heat shield, designed to prevent the capsule from burning up during reentry, might be loose. If these indications turned out to be accurate, John Glenn would perish in a blast of 3,000-degree heat.

In an attempt to hold the heat shield in place, Glenn was ordered to retain a retro-rocket pack that normally would be jettisoned. Its titanium straps might hold the shield. Although keeping the pack on the spacecraft made Glenn's job of controlling it more difficult, this seemed to be his only chance. Maintaining a calm demeanor, the scientists and engineers on the ground advised Glenn of their decision to end his flight and ordered him to plan for reentry after his third orbit.

Unwilling to burden Glenn with concern over the possible heat-shield malfunction, Mission Control offered no explanation for their decision. Glenn was suspicious, but all parts of Friendship 7 seemed to be working properly, so he focused on following instructions from the ground. "When I started back in through the atmosphere, when the straps that held the retropack on burned off," Glenn later remembered, "one of them popped up in front of the window. . . . I thought the retropack or the heat shield was breaking up. It was a real fireball. But the heat shield worked fine."

When the capsule splashed down safely in the Atlantic Ocean, few realized the harrowing ordeal that had just occurred. If the large, fiery chunks of debris Glenn saw whistling past the window had been the heat shield, the following transcript of the communication between Mission Control and Friendship 7

On February 23, 1962, three days after Col. John Glenn's earth orbit in Friendship 7, President John F. Kennedy joins Glenn in a hangar at Cape Canaveral, Florida, to inspect the spacecraft. Neither Kennedy nor the general public realized at the time how harrowing had been the final minutes of the heralded flight.

would have been one of the most heartbreaking in American history. The transcript would have contained the last words of a space pioneer.

Transcript of Communication from John Glenn's *Friendship 7*, 1962

04 36 56	0.4 CC	Roger.
04 37 00	9.6 P	There is quite a bit of cloud cover down in this area. I can, ah, right on track, I can only see certain areas. I can see quite a bit on up to the north, however.
04 37 18	2.4 P	This is Friendship 7, going to manual control.
04 37 21	1.3 CC	Ah, Roger, Friendship 7.
04 37 23	2.7 P	This is banging in and out here; I'll just control it manually.
04 37 25	0.4 CC	Roger.
04 37 48	3.1 CC	Friendship 7, Guaymas Cap Com, reading you loud and clear.
04 37 51	2.1 P	Roger, Guaymas, read you loud and clear also.

TEXAS

04 38 06	4.0 CT	Friendship 7, Friendship 7, this is Texas Com Tech. Do you read? Over.

04 38 10	1.3P	Roger, Texas, go ahead.
04 38 13	3.9CT	Ah, Roger. Reading you 5 square. Standby for Texas Cap Com.
04 38 16	0.4P	Roger.
04 38 25	23.8CC	This is Texas Cap Com, Friendship 7. We are recommending that you leave the retropackage on through the entire reentry. This means that you will have to override the 05g switch which is expected to occur at 04 43 _3. This also means that you will have to manually retract the scope. Do you read?
04 38 49	4.0 P	This is Friendship 7. What is the reason for this? Do you have any reason? Over.
04 38 53	3.6CC	Not at this time; this is the judgement of Cape Flight.
04 38 58	2.6P	Ah, Roger. Say again your instructions please. Over.
04 39 01	22.1CC	We are recommending that the retropackage not, I say again, not be jettisoned. This means that you will have to override the 05g switch which is expected to occur at 04 43 53. This is approximately 4-½ minutes from now. This also means that you will have to retract the scope manually. Do you understand?
04 39 25	9.7P	Ah, Roger, understand. I will have to make a manual 05g entry when it occurs, and bring the scope in, ah, manually. Is that affirm?
04 39 35	2.5CC	That is affirmative, Friendship 7.
04 39 39	0.6P	Ah, Roger.
04 39 42	3.6P	This is Friendship 7, going to reentry attitude, then, in that case.
04 40 00	3.8CC	Friendship 7, Cape flight will give you the reasons for this action when you are in view.
04 40 06	2.6P	Ah, Roger. Ah, Roger. Friendship 7.
04 40 09	2.5CC	Everything down here on the ground looks okay.
04 40 12	1.5P	Ah, Roger. This is Friendship 7.
04 40 14	1.4CC	Confirm your attitudes.
04 40 16	0.4P	Roger.

04 40 23	1.7CC	Ah, Friendship 7, this is Cape. Over.
04 40 25	1.5P	Go ahead, Cape. Friend 7.
04 40 27	4.9CC	Ah, recommend you go to reentry attitude and retract the scope manually at this time.
04 40 32	1.9P	Ah, Roger, retracting scope manually.
04 40 36	14.6CC	While you're doing that, we are not sure whether or not your landing bag has deployed. We feel it is possible to reenter with the retropackage on. Ah, we see no difficulty at this time in that type of reentry. Over.
04 40 51	1.6P	Ah, Roger, understand.
04 41 10	1.4CC	Seven, this is Cape. Over.
04 41 12	1.5P	Go ahead, Cape. Friendship 7.
04 41 15	5.4CC	Estimating 05g at 04 44.
04 41 21	0.6P	Ah, Roger.
04 41 23	3.0CC	You override 05g at that time.
04 41 31	2.7P	Ah, Roger. Friendship 7.
04 41 33	13.2P	This is Friendship 7. I'm on straight manual control at present time. This was, ah, still kicking in and out of orientation mode, mainly in yaw, ah, following retrofire, so I am on straight manual now. I'll back it up—
04 41 45	0.8CC	—on reentry.
04 41 47	0.9P	Say again.
04 41 50	0.6CC	Standby.
04 41 53	6.2P	This is Friendship 7. Ah, going to fly-by-wire. I'm down to about 15 percent on manual.
	8.9CC	Ah, Roger. You're going to use fly-by-wire for reentry and we recommend that you do the best you can to keep a zero angle during reentry. Over.
04 42 09	1.2P	Ah, Roger. Friendship 7.
04 42 13	3.4P	This is Friendship 7. I'm on fly-by-wire, back it up with manual. Over.
04 42 18	1.1CC	Roger, understand.
04 42 29	9.2CC	Ah, Seven, this is Cape. The weather in the recovery area is excellent, 3-foot waves, only one-tenth cloud coverage, 10 miles visibility.
04 42 39	1.2P	Ah, Roger. Friendship 7.

04 42 47	1.4CC	Ah, Seven, this is Cape. Over.
04 42 49	2.5P	Go ahead, Cape, you're ground, you are going out.
04 42 52	1.8CC	We recommend that you—
04 43 16	2.9P	This is Friendship 7. I think the pack just let go.
04 43 39	2.4P	This is Friendship 7. A real fireball outside.
04 44 20	1.9P	Hello, Cape. Friendship 7. Over.
04 45 18	1.9P	Hello, Cape. Friendship 7. Over.
04 45 43	2.3P	Hello, Cape. Friendship 7. Do you receive? Over.
04 46 20	2.0P	Hello, Cape. Friendship 7. Do you receive? Over.
04 47 18	1.2CC	—How do you read? Over.
04 47 20	1.5P	Loud and clear; how me?
04 47 22	1.6CC	Roger, reading you loud and clear. How are you doing?
04 47 25	1.0P	Oh, pretty good.
04 47 30	3.8CC	Roger. Your impact point is within one mile of the up-range destroyer.
04 47 34	0.5P	Ah, Roger.
04 47 35	0.2CC	—Over.
04 47 36	0.3P	Roger.
04 47 44	3.4CC	This is Cape, estimating 4 50. Over.
04 47 48	1.5P	Roger, 04 50.
04 47 53	1.6P	Okay, we're through the peak g now.
04 47 55	4.0CC	Ah, Seven, this is Cape. What's your general condition? Are you feeling pretty well?
04 47 59	2.8P	My condition is good, but that was a real fireball, boy.
04 48 05	3.2P	I had great chunks of that retropack breaking off all the way through.
04 48 08	2.1CC	Very good; it did break off, is that correct?
04 48 11	3.4P	Roger. Altimeter off the peg indicating 80 thousand.
04 48 15	1.7CC	Roger, reading you loud and clear.
04 48 17	0.3P	Roger.

What the Public Didn't Know About Three Mile Island—1979

Evidence that the accident at Three Mile Island was far more dangerous than ever admitted to the public

On March 28, 1979, we almost had meltdown. The Three Mile Island Unit 2 nuclear power plant near Middletown, Pennsylvania, scene of the most serious commercial nuclear power plant accident in U.S. history, has become synonymous, along with Chernobyl, with nuclear disaster. On one hand, there were no immediate deaths or even injuries to plant workers or members of the nearby Pennsylvania community. But, among people in the most direct path of the leaked radiation, lung cancer and leukemia rates seriously increased in coming years. And, as reports later concluded, the plant had come within 30 minutes of a major catastrophe. The public never knew the extent of the crisis.

The causes of the accident continue to be debated. Based on a series of investigations, it seems a combination of personnel error, design deficiencies, and equipment failures triggered the near meltdown. It began about 4:00 A.M., when one section of the plant experienced several failures—feed-water pumps and then the turbine stopped running, and some valves malfunctioned. Because adequate cooling was not available, the nuclear fuel overheated.

By March 30, two days after the start of the chain of events, some hydrogen remained within the primary coolant system in the vessel surrounding the reactor, forming a hydrogen bubble above the reactor core. The concern was that if reactor pressure decreased, the hydrogen bubble would expand and thus interfere with the flow of cooling water through the core.

Over the next few days, the bubble was reduced by adjusting air and water pressures. Nevertheless, a significant amount of fuel melted. Radioactivity in the reactor coolant increased dramatically, and there were small leaks in the reactor coolant system, causing high radiation levels in other parts of the plant and small releases into the environment.

Pennsylvania Governor Richard Thornburgh ordered an evacuation of preschool children and pregnant women within a five-mile zone of the plant. Within a few days, however, the reactor had been brought under control, and the evacuees returned to their homes.

As classified documents continue to be released about the Three Mile Island crisis, surprising revelations have emerged. For example, there is a notarized statement from the daughter-in-law of Adm. Hyman C. Rickover indicating that the admiral had persuaded President Jimmy Carter not to publish the

On April 9, 1979, two weeks after the near-meltdown at the Three Mile Island nuclear power plant, demonstrators gather at the Pennsylvania Capitol in Harrisburg.

entire official report on the disaster because it would terrify the public and have a devastating effect on acceptance of nuclear energy.

But the accident did have permanent repercussions. Before March 1979, according to opinion polls, Americans were fairly optimistic about the future role of nuclear energy. After the accident, with new safety measures driving the costs of reactors much higher and with the dangers magnified by the crisis, public opinion cooled. Three Mile Island changed both the nuclear industry and its public acceptance. Thus, for proponents of nuclear power, Three Mile Island was truly a disaster.

Notarized Statement of Jane Rickover, Adm. Hyman Rickover's Daughter-in-law, 1979

In May, 1983, my father-in-law, Admiral Hyman G. Rickover, told me that at the time of the Three Mile Island nuclear reactor accident, a full report was commissioned by President Jimmy Carter. He [my father-in-law] said that the report, if published in its entirety, would have destroyed the civilian nuclear power industry because the accident at Three Mile Island was infinitely more dangerous than was ever made public. He told me that he used his enormous personal influence with President Carter to persuade him to publish the report only in a highly "diluted" form. The President himself had originally wished the full report to be made public.

In November, 1985, my father-in-law told me that he had come to deeply regret his action in persuading President Carter to suppress the most alarming aspects of that report.

[Signed] Jane Rickover
Notarized by William F. Lamson Q.C.
Notary Public for the Province of Ontario
Toronto, this 18th day of July A.D. 1986

ALMOST
TWISTS OF IRONY
HISTORY

Revolt Not Revolution: Washington Denies Seeking Independence—1774

Letter of George Washington to Capt. Robert Mackenzie

O n September 13, 1774, Robert Mackenzie, a former captain of the Virginia Regiment commanded by Washington in the French and Indian War and a man to whom George Washington often confided, wrote from Boston to his friend regarding the escalating protests about British policy and the growing discontent among the populace. A native of Virginia, Mackenzie had taken a commission in the British army and was attached to a regiment stationed in Boston. He called Massachusetts an "unhappy province," one with "their fixed Aim at total independence," and "how necessary it is, that abler Heads and better Hearts should draw a Line for their Guidance." The uprisings in Massachusetts, Mackenzie said, had forced the British to take increasingly stern measures to ensure the peace.

At the first Continental Congress, Washington had appeared as one of the representatives of Virginia. At this time, with the growing notion of independence relatively confined to the Northeast, he assured Mackenzie, on October 9, 1774, that the colonies did not seek independence.

On October 4, 1775, more than a year after the exchange of letters between Washington and Mackenzie, John Adams of Massachusetts, another delegate to the Continental Congress, wrote to his friend William Lee, an American who had been elected as an alderman in London: "We cannot in this country conceive that there are men in England so infatuated as seriously to suspect the Congress, or people here, of a wish to erect ourselves into an independent state. If such an idea really obtains among those at the helm of affairs, one hour's residence in America would eradicate it. I never met one individual so inclined."

Whether John Adams, in the midst of the agitation in Massachusetts province, was being totally honest with William Lee is open to question. The irony, nevertheless, is that both Washington and Adams, two of the individuals later so closely identified with the success of the American Revolution, with strong political influence in the two most prominent colonies, were clearly thinking reform at this time, not rebellion. Washington and Adams, two of the towering Founding Fathers, were not, even at this point, thinking of founding anything.

Letter of George Washington to Capt. Robert Mackenzie, October 9, 1774

Philadelphia, October 9, 1774

Dear Sir: Your letter of the 13th. ultimo from Boston gave me pleasure, as I learnt thereby, that you were well, and might be expected at Mount Vernon in your way to or from James River, in the course of the winter.

When I have said this, permit me with the freedom of a friend (for you know I always esteemed you) to express my sorrow, that fortune should place you in a service, that must fix curses to the latest posterity upon the diabolical contrivers, and, if success (which, by the by, is impossible) accompanies it, execrations upon all those, who have been instrumental in the execution.

I do not mean by this to insinuate, that an officer is not to discharge his duty, even when chance, not choice, has placed him in a disagreeable situation; but I conceive, when you condemn the conduct of the Massachusetts people, you reason from effects, not causes; otherwise you would not wonder at a people, who are every day receiving fresh proofs of a systematic assertion of an arbitrary power, deeply planned to overturn the laws and constitution of their country, and to violate the most essential and valuable rights of mankind, being irritated, and with difficulty restrained from acts of the greatest violence and intemperance. For my own part, I confess to you candidly, that I view things in a very different point of light to the one in which you seem to consider them; and though you are led to believe by venal men, for such I must take the liberty of calling those new-fangled counsellors, which fly to and surround you, and all others, who, for honorary or pecuniary gratifications, will lend their aid to overturn the constitution, and introduce a system of arbitrary government, although you are taught, I say, by discoursing with such men, to believe, that the people of Massachusetts are rebellious, setting up for independency, and what not, give me leave, my good friend, to tell you, that you are abused, grossly abused, and this I advance with a degree of confidence and boldness, which may claim your belief, having better opportunities of knowing the real sentiments of the people you are among, from the leaders of them, in opposition to present measures of the administration, than you have from those whose business it is, not to disclose truths, but to misrepresent facts in order to justify as much as possible to the world their own conduct; for give me leave to add, and I think I can announce it as a fact, that it is not the wish or interest of that government, or any other upon this continent, separately or collectively, to set up for independency; but this you may at the same time rely on, that none of them will ever submit to the loss of those valuable rights and privileges, which are essential to the happiness of every free state, and without which, life, liberty, and property are rendered totally insecure.

These, Sir, being certain consequences, which must naturally result from the late acts of Parliament relative to America in general, and the government of Massachusetts Bay in particular, is it to be wondered at, I repeat, that men, who wish to avert the impending blow, should attempt to oppose it in its progress, or prepare for their defence, if it cannot be diverted? Surely I may be allowed to answer in the negative; and again give me leave to add as my opinion, that more blood will be spilt on this occasion, if the ministry are determined to push matters to extremity, than history has ever yet furnished instances of in the annals of North America, and such a vital wound given to the peace of this great country, as time itself cannot cure, or eradicate the remembrance of.

But I have done. I was involuntarily led into a short discussion of this subject by your remarks on the conduct of the Boston people, and your opinion of their wishes to set up for independency. I am as well satisfied as I can be of my existence that no such thing is desired by any thinking man in all North America; on the contrary, that it is the ardent wish of the warmest advocates for liberty, that peace and tranquility, upon constitutional grounds, may be restored, and the horrors of civil discord prevented. . . .

James Whistler, Failed Soldier and Bureaucrat—1855

Etching by James Whistler, made while employed as a draftsman in the cartographic section of the U.S. Coast Survey

A merican artist James Whistler spent several of his childhood years in Russia, where his father had gone to work as a civil engineer. In 1855, Whistler traveled to Paris, where he studied intermittently under Charles Gleyre and developed an admiration for Japanese print and Oriental art. Through Henri Fantin-Latour, Whistler met Gustave Courbet, whose Realism inspired much of his early work. Whistler had thus become entwined in European artistic circles. Fantin-Latour's "Homage to Delacroix," for example, portrays Whistler alongside Charles Baudelaire, Èdouard Manet, and others.

Whistler settled in London in 1859, but he often returned to France. He became one of the most recognized, celebrated artists of the 19th century.

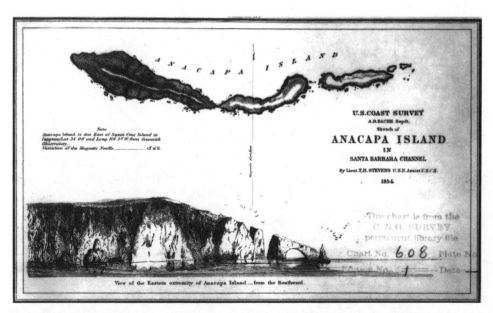

While employed in the cartographic section of the United States Coast Survey in late 1854, James Whistler learned etching. Although his career in the federal government lasted only two months, his "Sketch of Anacapa Island in Santa Barbara Channel" was embellished with flocks of gulls soaring over rocky cliffs.

Flamboyant, witty, a dandy whose friends included Dante Gabriel Rossetti and Oscar Wilde, Whistler, although usually in debt, lived lavishly.

Where did this unconventional, influential figure in the art world get his early training? In the U.S. federal government. In 1851, he entered West Point, from which he was dismissed in 1854, and later that year, at the age of 21, he joined the cartographic section of the U.S. Coast Survey as a draftsman for $1.50 a day. Asked to prepare an official cartographic drawing of Anacapa Island in the Santa Barbara Channel, Whistler did that and more. Thinking the map looked dull, he added two flocks of gulls soaring over the rocky coast.

Whistler's career as a bureaucrat did not work out. His unconventional work habits led to his dismissal on January 9, 1855, and to his search for another career.

More than Mischief: The Cartoon That Did in Boss Tweed   1875

Cartoon by Thomas Nast that led to capture of Boss Tweed in Spain

Thomas Nast's blistering cartoons in Harper's Weekly and other magazines helped turn public opinion and law enforcement against powerful William Marcy Tweed of New York City's Tammany Hall and boss of a political ring that had stayed in power for more than a decade through assiduous, imaginative corruption and a massive bribery network. Nast had caricatured Tweed more than 100 times in his cartoons and the publicity had made the Boss's likeness—a gruff, black visage loaded onto a corpulent frame with an ill-fitting suit—known throughout the United States and even in Europe. Indeed, Tweed had once tried to bribe Nast himself to stop his wicked caricatures, but the cartoonist had turned him down.

In December 1875, Tweed was being held in debtors' prison as the state pursued a major lawsuit against him and his cronies for $6 million. The Boss would be confined, the state authorities said, until he posted $3 million in bail.

Although Tweed could not come up with that kind of cash, his fortune did bring him, it was said, the most sumptuous prison accommodations ever recorded in the state of New York. Tweed was even allowed to leave the prison on occasion to visit his family. On one such excursion, the prisoner failed to return, boarding a ship on the sly to Europe, possibly with the jailer's help, in return for a fee.

Tweed remained in Spain for more than a year. What brought him down? Another of Nast's damnable cartoons. A Spanish official recognized Tweed, portrayed in the cartoon in the act of kidnapping two children, and turned him in to American authorities. Because of the cartoon characterization, the official assumed that Tweed was wanted for kidnapping. The irony was that Tweed, for all his various legal transgressions, had never been accused of that one.

Boss Tweed was never able to escape Thomas Nast's cartoons. This one, in the July l, 1876, Harper's Weekly, *portraying Tweed as a child kidnapper, led to Tweed's arrest in Spain.*

But for Metal Mattress Coils—1881

Invention of Alexander Graham Bell that nearly saved the life of President James Garfield

O n July 2, 1881, President James Garfield was shot by an assassin named Charles J. Guiteau, a lawyer with a history of mental illness and afflicted with religious delusions. One bullet fired by Guiteau merely grazed the president's arm, but a second had lodged inside his body. If the bullet had penetrated an organ, it would mean certain death. If, however, the bullet had not cut into an organ or wasn't lodged tightly against one, removing it by surgery was possible.

Garfield was rushed to the White House, having never lost consciousness. A squad of physicians gathered, all with various ideas on how to treat the seriously injured president. At first, they thought the bullet had penetrated the liver and therefore surgery would be of no help. His fever rose, and he was put on a diet of milk spiked with brandy. The doctors held out little hope. After several days, however, Garfield was still alive.

It was clear that the bullet had not reached the liver. Now, finding the exact location of the bullet quickly was critical—and this at a time when the X ray was yet to be invented. Newspaper accounts detailed the frantic efforts of the physicians as they unsuccessfully conducted several probes into Garfield's wound, operations that very likely caused additional infection.

Alexander Graham Bell, inventor of the telephone, was intrigued by the case, suspecting that certain research in which he was engaged might be helpful. Joining with another scientist, Simon Newcomb, Bell brought to the White House an experimental model of a metal detector. Newcomb had been experimenting with running electricity through wire coils and the effect metal had when placed near the coils. The device that Bell and Newcomb devised, a combination of Newcomb's research and Bell's telephone, emitted a faint hum when placed near metal. It was similar to another invention Bell had constructed to locate the cause of induction interference on telephone lines.

Bell had tested the invention on a number of Civil War survivors residing in the Old Soldiers' Home in Washington, D.C., who had carried bullets in their bodies since the war, mostly in arms, legs, or shoulders. The invention, when placed against their bodies, invariably indicated the location of the bullets.

In the case of the esteemed patient in the White House, however, the device did not work. Why? The inventors were foiled in their efforts by the fact that the president, unknown to them, had been placed on a coil-spring mattress, a relatively new innovation in mattress design. The coils in the mattress interfered with the electrical impulses, and the scientists were unable to discover the exact location of the bullet.

Garfield's condition was growing steadily worse, so the doctors decided to operate again. The bullet was not found. Garfield, suffering internal hemorrhages and heart failure, died on September 19, 1881.

Metal mattress coils, it could be argued, made a successful presidential assassin.

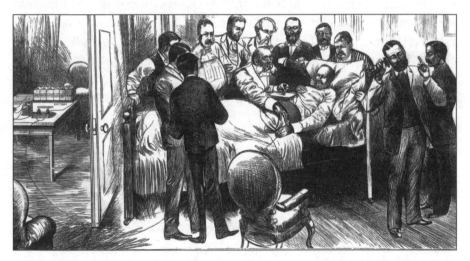

As President James Garfield, victim of an assassin, fought for his life in the late summer of 1881, the press kept the nation informed. Frank Leslie's Illustrated Newspaper *ran an artist's characterization of Alexander Graham Bell's attempt, using a newly invented electrical device, to locate the bullet in the president's body.*

Letter from a Dayton Bicycle Shop—1899

**Letter of Wilbur Wright to the Smithsonian Institution,
headed by Samuel Langley, the foremost researcher on air
flight, asking about available works on the subject**

S amuel Pierpont Langley spent 18 years attempting to become the first to build an airplane. Highly educated, the secretary of the Smithsonian Institution and a man who had developed unmanned aerodromes, Langley managed to convince the War Department and the Smithsonian to contribute $50,000 each toward his work.

Believing a flying machine would be safer over water, Langley spent almost half his funds constructing a houseboat with a catapult that would be capable of launching his new craft. The experimental plane had to go from a dead stop to a 60 m.p.h. flying speed in only 70 feet. Because the stress of the catapult was far greater than the flimsy wood-and-fabric airplane could withstand, his first launch, on October 7, 1903, nearly destroyed the front wing; a reporter quipped that the plane flew "like a handful of mortar."

Things were even worse on the second try on December 9, 1903. When the rear wing and tail completely collapsed during the launch, Langley's pilot, Charles Manley, nearly drowned in the ice-covered Potomac River. A member of the House of Representatives remarked acidly, "You tell Langley for me . . . that the only thing he ever made fly was Government money."

Eight days after the crash in the Potomac River, another airplane, costing about $1,000, struggled into the air in Kitty Hawk, North Carolina. It was probably the most unlikely success story in American scientific history.

In 1899, Orville and Wilbur Wright, bicycle-shop owners in Dayton, Ohio, were experimenting with gliders. On May 30, in an action that seems in hindsight loaded with historical irony, Wilbur Wright wrote Langley's Smithsonian Institution asking for published materials on aeronautics. The Smithsonian sent him four pamphlets and a list of other publications. Thus began the road to Kitty Hawk.

By 1901, Wilbur Wright had published his own technical paper on the ideas of flight in both British and German journals. The brothers experimented with gliders. At first, Wilbur remembered, the work was enormously frustrating: "We doubted that we would ever resume our experiments. . . . At this time, I made the prediction that men would sometime fly, but it would not be in our lifetime."

But they persevered. They built a wind tunnel to conduct their own research on wing surfaces. They discovered the benefits of a movable rudder over a fixed tail. They began designing aircraft propellers. The research was confusing, often contentious. At one point, they discovered that bicycle-tire cement worked well in gluing the sprockets to the shafts.

Then, on December 17, 1903, at 10:35 A.M., Orville Wright made the first powered flight in a fully controllable aircraft capable of sustaining itself in the air. The flight lasted just 12 seconds and stretched only 120 feet. But, in four years, beginning with a few pamphlets obtained from the Smithsonian Institution, the Wright brothers had succeeded. Today, the Wright brothers' aircraft is among the most prized possessions of the Smithsonian Institution.

Letter of Wilbur Wright to the Smithsonian Institution, May 30, 1899

Smithsonian Institution
Washington
May 30, 1899

I have been interested in the problem of mechanical and human flight ever since as a boy I constructed a number of bats of various sizes after the style of Cayley's and Pènaud's machine. My observations since have only convinced me more firmly that human flight is possible and practical. It is only a question of knowledge and skill just as in all acrobatic feats. Birds are the most perfectly trained gymnasts in the world and are specially well fitted for their work, and it may be that man will never equal them, but no one who has watched a bird chase an insect or another bird can doubt that feats are performed that require three or four times the effort required in ordinary flight. I believe that simple flight at least is possible to man and that the experiments and investigations of a large number of independent workers will result in the accumulation of information, knowledge and skill which will finally lead to accomplished flight.

The works on the subject to which I have access are Marey's and Jamieson's books published by Appleton's and various magazines and cyclopaedic articles. I am about to begin a systematic study of the subject in preparation for practical work to which I expect to devote what time I can spare from my regular business. I wish to obtain such papers as the Smithsonian Institution has published on this subject, and if possible a list of other works in print in the English language.

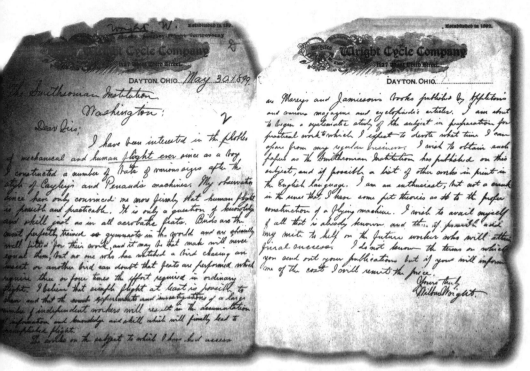

On May 30, 1899, Wilbur Wright, an obscure bicycle mechanic from Dayton, Ohio, wrote this letter to the Smithsonian Institution for information about research that had been done on a possible flying machine. The Smithsonian's director, the scientist Samuel Langley, was already hard at work on the invention. But it would not be Langley's achievement.

I am an enthusiast, but not a crank in the sense that I have some pet theories as to the proper construction of a flying machine. I wish to avail myself of all that is already known, and then if possible add my mite to help on the future worker who will attain final success. I do not know the terms on which you send out your publications but if you will inform me of the cost I will remit the price.

Yours truly,
Wilbur Wright

Richard Nixon, FBI Agent—1937

**Job application of Richard M. Nixon
for employment at the FBI**

These were the days of Dillinger, Baby Face Nelson, Ma Barker, Pretty Boy Floyd, Bonnie and Clyde, and other big-name hoodlums. In Washington in the 1930s, at their new building on Pennsylvania Avenue, Department of Justice officials, especially FBI Director J. Edgar Hoover, were determined to wipe out the menace, the high-profile criminals who had captured the public fancy.

In the 1930s, when Hoover sought to strengthen the power and image of the FBI and of himself and to crush the image of the bandit folk hero, he turned to the tools by which the bandit images had been created. He managed the news, helped authors promote the deeds of lawmen, and helped make movies. Soon after John Dillinger was shot, Hoover worked with Hollywood in sending forth Jimmy Cagney as the "G-Man." Magazines and comic books and 10-cent pulp monthlies praised the FBI; there were even bubble-gum cards featuring pictures of great FBI victories. No longer would G-Men be bunglers; they would now be "Heroes of the Law."

All of this hoopla impressed many young men who now wished to be G-Men. One of those was a recent graduate of the Duke University law school, third in his class, a serious and determined man in search of a career, a man some of his classmates called Gloomy Gus. On April 23, 1937, he sat down and filled out a long application form seeking a job at the FBI. His name was Richard M. Nixon.

His application was rejected. He went back home to Southern California, where his mother helped him get a job at a friend's local law firm. After a stint in the navy during World War II, he entered politics, answering a call in the local newspaper by Republican Party officials seeking someone to run against five-term Democratic Congressman Jerry Voorhis. The rest is history.

If he had become a G-Man . . .

Job application of Richard M. Nixon for Employment at the FBI, April 23, 1937

APPLICATION FOR EMPLOYMENT

DIRECTOR,
FEDERAL BUREAU OF INVESTIGATION
U.S. DEPARTMENT OF JUSTICE
Washington, D.C.

Duke Law School, Durham, N.C.

......April 23,............................, 19..37

Sir:

I hereby make application for appointment to the position indicated by check mark, in the Federal Bureau of Investigation, U.S. Department of Justice, and for your use in this connection submit the following information:

Special Agent............................ ☐
Special Agent (Accountant) ..... ☐
Stenographer............................ ☐
Typist .... ☐
Messenger .... ☐
.... ☐
(Indicate by check.)

(This application should be typewritten if possible)

1. Name in full (please print) ....Nixon   Richard   Milhous......
    (Family Name)   (Given Name)   (Middle Name)

    (a) Female applicants must furnish maiden name ....

2. Legal Residence. 2706 Whittier Blvd.,Whittier, Calif.................................

3. Mail and telegraphic address ..... Duke Law School, Durham, N.C...................

4. Date of Birth Jan. 9, 1913 Weight 160..........Height 5'11".....Color ..White.........

5. Place of birth ..Yorba Linda, Calif...

6. (a) Father's name ....Francis A. Nixon....(b) Father's birthplace...................Ohio........

7. (a) Mother's maiden name ..Hannah Milhous (b) Mother's birthplace...........Indiana.......

8. If you were not born in the United States, how long have you lived here?............................

9. Are you a citizen of the United States? ....Yes..

10. If naturalized, date and place of naturalization ....

11. Are you single, married, widowed, separated, or divorced?......Single...................
    (Specify)

12. If your husband (or wife) is employed, state where employed ....

13. Number of children, if any...........None..

14. Are you entirely dependent on your salary?......Yes...

15. To what extent are you financially indebted to others and to whom? ......None..................

This application is a reconstruction of the original document, which may be viewed in digital form at www.thesmokinggun.com.

16. Education (Please print.)

	NAME AND LOCATION OF SCHOOL	FROM—	TO–	COURSES PURSUED, DIPLOMAS OR DEGREES RECEIVED
(a) Elementary	Yorba Linda School, Yorba Linda, Calif.	1919	1923	
(b) High School Equivalent	Fullerton High School, Fullerton, Calif.	1926–1928		
	Whittier High School, Whittier, Calif.	1928	1930	
(c) College or technical	Whittier College Whittier, Calif.	1930	1934	A.B.
	Duke University School of Law Durham, N.C.	1934	1937	To receive LL. B. in June, 1937
(d) Miscellaneous				

17. Give names of clubs, societies, and other similar organizations of which you are a member:

Pi Gamma Mu, Honorary Social Science Fraternity

18. Are you physically capable of discharging the duties of the position sought? (any physical defects should be fully described) ..... Yes

19. Health record for the past 3 years (give number of days of illness and nature of ailments):

No days of illness; two or three common, slight colds.

20. Experience: (Please print.)

NAME AND ADDRESS OF EMPLOYER	POSITION	FROM–	TO–	ANNUAL SALARY
Individual enterprise	Mgr. of service station	1930, 1931-Summers		
F. A. Nixon, 2706 Whittier Blvd., Whittier, Calif.	Clerk in grocery store	1926 1932- Summers	1930 1934	
William R. Roalfe, ¢ Duke Law School, Durham, N.C.	Library Assistant	1935	1936	$420
H.C. Horack, Dean, Duke Law School, Durham, N.C. (NYA)	Research Assistant	1936	1937	$150

21. Have you ever been arrested? No

22. Have you ever been a defendant in any court action? No

Specify:

22. Give five personal references (not relatives, former employers, fellow employees, or school teachers), more than 30 years of age, who are householders or property owners, business or professional men or women (including your family physician, if you have one) of good standing in the community, and who have known you well during the past 6 or more years. (Please print.)

NAME AND ADDRESS OF EMPLOYER	RESIDENCE ADDRESS	NUMBER OF YEARS ACQUAINTED	BUSINESS ADDRESS
1. H.A. Schuyler	Leffingwell Rancho Whittier, Calif.	12	Same
2. A.U. Ozie	1002 Second Ave., East Whittier, Cal.	12	Same
3. Eseck Perry	537 N. Washington, Whittier, Calif.	12	Same
4. Guy Welch	442 S. Pickering, Whittier, Calif.	8	Whittier Police Dep't
5. Dr. H.C. Thompson	116 E. Beiley, Whittier, Calif.	8	Same

24. List the names of any relatives now in the Government service, with the degree of relationship, and where employed:

........None...

....

....

25. What is the lowest entrance salary you will accept?........Standard for special agents

26. Are you in a position to accept probationary employment at any time, without previous notice, and if notice is required, how much? ......Yes - no notice necessary..

27. In the event of appointment will you be willing to proceed to Washington, D.C., upon 10 days notice and at your own expense? ....Yes...

28. If appointed are you willing and prepared to accept assignment or transfer to any part of the United States where services are required, for either temporary or permanent duration? .....Yes.............

a photograph not larger than 3 by 4 $\frac{1}{4}$ inches. Write your name plainly graph to be taken *not more than 30 days prior to date of application.*

Respectfully,

......*Richard M Nixon*........
(Signature of applicant as usually signed)

NOTE.—If the applicant desires to make any further remarks or statements concerning his qualifications or in answer to any question contained in the application, the same should be made on a separate sheet of paper, numbering the remarks in accordance with the original questions.

rt be subscribed to by all applicants for positions in the Federal Bureau of Investi-

to before me by the above-named applicant, this........[29].....................day

of....[April]................,19[37], at city (or town) of......[Durham]..., county

of......[Durham]........................, and State (or Territory or District) of....[North Carolina]...............

......[Lina E. Wilson]...
(Signature of officer)

[OFFICIAL IMPRESSION SEAL]

......[Notary Public]...
(Official title)

Federal Bureau of Investigation
United States Department of Justice

Los Angeles, California,
July 17th, 1937.

To: The Director, Federal Bureau of Investigation, United
           States Department of Justice, Washington, D. C.

From: Inspector   Special Agent in Charge J. H. Hanson

Subject: Report of Interview with Applicant   RICHARD M. NIXON
           for appointment as Special Agent   2706 E. Whittier Blvd.,
                                                 Whittier, Calif.

1. PERSONAL APPEARANCE:

A.   PERSONAL APPEARANCE AND APPROACH: Excellent. Good. Fair. Poor
B.   DRESS: Neat. Flashy. Poor. Untidy.
C.   FEATURES: Refined. Ordinary. Coarse. Dissipated.
D.   PHYSICAL DEFECTS, if any: None

2. CONDUCT DURING INTERVIEW:

A.   PERSONALITY: Excellent. Good. Fair. Average. Poor.
B.   POISE: Well-poised. Steady. Temperamental. Average
C.   SPEECH: Average. Reticent. Talkative. Boastful.
D.   ASSURANCE: Self-Confident. Fair. Over-Confident. Lacking.
E.   NERVOUSNESS: None. Slight. Very nervous.
F.   FOREIGN ACCENT: None. Slight. Noticeable.
G.   TACT: Tactful. Average. Lacking.

3. GENERAL INTELLIGENCE:

A.   Answers general questions definitely. Quickly. Vaguely.
B.   Has Applicant studied Federal Procedure? No
C.   Any investigative experience? If so, describe - none

D.   Does the Applicant appear to be resourceful? Yes
F.   Does the Applicant appear to have executive ability?   Perhaps
G.   Is he likely to develop? Yes

4. GENERAL INFORMATION:

A.   What are the Applicant's plans for the future?   Legal field if not
                                                        appointed

B.   What are his recreations and tastes? Handball, swimming, movies,
                                           bridge, poker, dancing, reading

5. HEALTH RECORD: Good.

6. GENERAL IMPRESSIONS OF APPLICANT:

Applicant was born January 9, 1913 at Yorba Linda, California. He is
single and resides with his parents. His father is a grocer. He has
two brothers who are students. He has never been arrested or involved
in any kind of trouble, nor have any members of his family. He takes
an occasional social drink of liquor. He typewrites poorly with the
touch system. He has had no training or experience with firearms.
He drives an automobile. He has no relatives in Government service.

Applicant attended public grammar school at Yorba Linda, California,
and high school at Fullerton and Whittier, California, graduating from
the latter school in 1930, thereafter entering the Whittier College where
he was awarded an AB Degree in 1934, having majored in history. He then
enrolled in the law school at Duke University, receiving an LL.B Degree
in June, 1937. He plans to take the California Bar examination commencing
on September 7, 1937.

Applicant's chief employment during his spare time from his studies and
during his vacations has been with his father who operates a grocery store.
He claims, however, that in the Summer of 1931 he worked part time for
the Whittier College, interviewing prospective students. This work was
done under the supervision of the Acting President at that time, a Dr.
Herbert Harris. He claims that in the Summers of 1932 and 1933 he rented
from his father a gasoline filling station at 2708 East Whittier Blvd.,
which he operated on his own account, doing business with the Richfield
Oil Products Co. In the Summers of 1934 and 1935 he assisted his father
in the latter's grocery store. During the school year of 1935 and
Summer of 1936 he worked as assistant in the law library at Duke University. Also during the school year of 1936 and 1937 he did research
work for the Dean of the Law School. He mentioned that at the time
he was awarded his Degree at Duke he was elected to membership in the
Order of Coif, Honorary Legal Fraternity. He also mentioned that he made
the football squad at Whittier, playing on it for four years and did
not receive a letter.

The Applicant learned of this Bureau through a talk made by SAC J. A. Smith
at Duke University. He is not acquainted with any Special Agents of the
Bureau, nor employees of the Department of Justice.

        Result of dictation test: Good. Fair. Poor.
        Bureau test rating   %

7. Do you consider the applicant qualified for the appointment he
    seeks and, if appointed, do you believe he would develop into
    better than an average employee?   YES

                    J. H. HANSON Special
                              Inspector.   Agent in
                                                    Chge.

Richard Nixon.   7-17-37
Page 2.

The results or the fictitious interview given to Applicant are attached hereto. Special Agent J. G. Ross, who was used for this
purpose, advised that applicant had a very good appearance, appeared
to be confident and thorough, commensurate with his inexperience, adding that he reported the information obtained correctly. The applicant also dictated satisfactorily.

The applicant is being recommended. It is believed that he is above
average in intelligence and mental alertness. He appears to be
possessed of sufficient force and aggressiveness; also of good, common
ordinary sense. He expresses his thoughts well and uses good English.
He is manly appearing, possessing a good physique, and it is felt that he
could successfully contact persons of all walks of life and that he
would inspire confidence.

This is to certify that forty minutes were spent in the interview with
this applicant and that the examination and interview were given to
him personally by the interviewing official.

                                    H. HANSON
                                    Special Agent in Charge

The DAR Loses a Member—1939

Letter of Eleanor Roosevelt to the president of the Daughters of the American Revolution, resigning from the organization because of its refusal to allow singer Marian Anderson to perform at Constitution Hall

Her glorious voice was legendary in South Philadelphia. Nevertheless, when she graduated from high school and applied to an all-white music school in Philadelphia, she was turned down. The school did not accept blacks. She began to study privately with world-famous voice teacher Giuseppe Boghetti, who refined her technical skills and expanded her repertoire to include classical songs and arias. Entering a New York Philharmonic voice competition in 1925 with more than 300 competitors, she emerged victorious and debuted with the Philharmonic to rave critical reviews. On December 30, 1928, she made her Carnegie Hall debut. In the early 1930s, she toured Europe. In the late 1930s, the renowned Marian Anderson sang at the White House.

In February 1939, Howard University attempted to rent Constitution Hall in Washington, D.C., for an Anderson performance. Despite her established reputation and admiration from audiences around the world, Anderson was turned down. The hall was owned by the Daughters of the American Revolution, an organization that in 1932 had adopted a rule excluding African-American artists from the Constitution Hall stage following protests about "mixed seating."

Eleanor Roosevelt, first lady of the United States, although not an active member of the DAR, sat on its board. She did not remain on the board long. She resigned her membership in protest over this decision, and other prominent women followed suit. The flap drew enormous publicity, finally leading to Mrs. Roosevelt arranging a concert for Anderson at the Lincoln Memorial, where on Easter Sunday, April 9, 75,000 people gathered for a public recital. Millions more listened to the radio broadcast of the event. The incident gave powerful shape to the issue of racial discrimination.

By its actions in 1939, the DAR had unwittingly created a controversy that embarrassed the organization and dramatized a national cause. Ironically, thanks to the DAR, the forces of racial reform now had a new symbol. Many of those who gathered that Easter against the backdrop of the Lincoln Memorial to hear Anderson may have returned there a quarter of a century later to hear a preacher from Atlanta thunder the words "I have a dream."

When the Daughters of the American Revolution refused to allow the celebrated black singer Marian Anderson to perform at the organization's Constitution Hall in Washington, First Lady Eleanor Roosevelt resigned her membership in February 1939. Mrs. Roosevelt and others then arranged for Anderson's Easter concert at the Lincoln Memorial, which Mrs. Roosevelt attended. The two remained good friends.

Letter of Eleanor Roosevelt to Mrs. Henry N. Robert, DAR President, February 26, 1939

My dear Mrs. Robert:

I am afraid that I have never been a very useful member of the Daughters of the American Revolution, and I know it will make very little difference to you whether I resign, or whether I continue to be a member of your organization.

However, I am in complete disagreement with the attitude taken in refusing Constitution Hall to a great artist. You have set an example which seems to me unfortunate, and I feel obliged to send in to you my resignation. You had an opportunity to lead in an enlightened way and it seems to me that your organization has failed.

I realize that many people will not agree with me, but feeling as I do this seems to me the only proper procedure to follow.

Very sincerely yours,
Eleanor Roosevelt

LBJ: Vietnam Dove—1954

Report of meeting of U.S. Secretary of State and congressional leaders on possible involvement in French Indochina

O n Saturday, April 3, 1954, cherry-blossom time in Washington, D.C., eight congressional leaders met at the State Department with Secretary of State John Foster Dulles, Chairman of the Joint Chiefs of Staff Adm. Arthur Radford, and several other members of the Eisenhower administration. Dulles had called the congressional leadership together at the request of the president, who was at Camp David preparing a speech about the cold war, Russia, and the dangers of an escalating Communist menace. The meeting that morning at the State Department, although about Communism, was concerned with a subject about which few Americans knew anything—Vietnam.

The Eisenhower administration had decided that the United States would use air and naval power to stave off impending French military defeat. The focus of the administration's attention was the French fortress of Dienbienphu, deep in the jungles of Vietnam, which was under siege by troops of the communist-led Viet Minh independence movement. If the fortress fell, the administration believed that all of Indochina and eventually all of Southeast Asia would fall to the communists.

The president wanted congressional support before committing troops. If the congressional leadership could be persuaded of the serious peril that the national prestige and influence would suffer if Communist aggression were not halted in Vietnam, they would, the administration believed, demonstrate a united front to the world. At the State Department meeting on April 3, the leadership was not convinced.

Three days after the meeting, during a National Security Council briefing, Secretary Dulles reported on the misgivings of the senators and congressmen. To get congressional authorization for overt action in Vietnam, the administration would have to meet certain conditions. Intervention must be part of a coalition of other free nations in Southeast Asia; also, the French must not be allowed to pull out their troops and expect the United States to shoulder the principal responsibility for correcting French failure. Dulles told the Joint Chiefs that it would be a hopeless fight to overcome congressional opposition if those conditions were not met.

Dulles did not mention to the Joint Chiefs who among the congressional leadership had been especially demanding, who had shown very little enthusi-

asm about entangling the United States in a dubious venture in Asia that would certainly be long, arduous, and costly in both money and lives.

The vociferous opponent that day in the State Department had been the minority leader of the U.S. Senate, Lyndon B. Johnson of Texas.

The Reporter, September 14, 1954

The Day We Didn't Go to War
By Chalmers Roberts

The atmosphere became serious at once. What was wanted, Dulles said, was a joint resolution by Congress to permit the President to use air and naval power in Indo-China. Dulles hinted that perhaps the mere passage of such a resolution would in itself make its use unnecessary. But the President had asked for its consideration, and, Dulles added, Mr. Eisenhower felt that it was indispensable at this juncture that the leaders of Congress feel as the Administration did on the Indo-China crisis.

Then Radford took over. He said the Administration was deeply concerned over the rapidly deteriorating situation. He used a map of the Pacific to point out the importance of Indo-China. He spoke about the French Union forces then already under siege for three weeks in the fortress of Dienbienphu.

The admiral explained the urgency of American action by declaring that he was not even sure, because of poor communications, whether, in fact, Dienbienphu was still holding out. (The fortress held out for five weeks more.)

Dulles backed up Radford. If Indo-China fell and if its fall led to the loss of all of Southeast Asia, he declared, then the United States might eventually be forced back to Hawaii, as it was before the Second World War. And Dulles was not complimentary about the French. He said he feared they might use some disguised means of getting out of Indo-China if they did not receive help soon.

The eight legislators were silent: Senate Majority Leader Knowland and his G.O.P. colleague Eugene Millikin, Senate Minority Leader Lyndon B. Johnson and his Democratic colleagues Richard B. Russell and Earle C. Clements, House G.O.P. Speaker Joseph Martin and two Democratic House leaders, John W. McCormack and J. Percy Priest.

What to do? Radford offered the plan he had in mind once Congress passed the joint resolution.

Some two hundred planes from the thirty-one-thousand-ton U.S. Navy carriers *Essex* and *Boxer*, then in the South China Sea ostensibly for "training," plus land-based U.S. Air Force planes from bases a thousand miles away in the Philippines, would be used for a single strike to save Dienbienphu.

The legislators stirred, and the questions began.

Radford was asked whether such action would be war. He replied that we would be in the war.

If the strike did not succeed in relieving the fortress, would we follow up? "Yes," said the chairman of the Joint Chiefs of Staff.

Would land forces then also have to be used? Radford did not give a definite answer.

In the early part of the questioning, Knowland showed enthusiasm for the venture, consistent with his public statements that something must be done or Southeast Asia would be lost.

But as the questions kept flowing, largely from Democrats, Knowland lapsed into silence.

Clements asked Radford the first of the two key questions: "Does this plan have the approval of the other members of the Joint Chiefs of Staff?"

No," replied Radford.

"How many of the three agree with you?"

"None."

"How do you account for that?"

"I have spent more time in the Far East than any of them and I understand the situation better."

Lyndon Johnson put the other key question in the form of a little speech. He said that Knowland had been saying publicly that in Korea up to ninety per cent of the men and the money came from the United States. The United States had become sold on the idea that that was bad. Hence in any operation in Indo-China we ought to know first who would put up the men. And so he asked Dulles whether he had consulted nations who might be our allies in intervention.

Dulles said he had not.

The Secretary was asked why he didn't go the United Nations as in the Korean case. He replied that it would take too long, that this was an immediate problem.

There were other questions. Would Red China and the Soviet Union come into the war if the United States took military action? The China question appears to have been sidestepped, though Dulles said he felt the Soviets could handle the Chinese and the United States did not think that Moscow wanted a general war now. Further, he added, if the Communists feel that we mean business, they won't do "any further down there," pointing to the map of Southeast Asia.

John W. McCormack, the House Minority Leader, couldn't resist temptation. He was surprised, he said, that Dulles would look to the "party of treason," as the Democrats had been called by Joe McCarthy in his Lincoln's Birthday speech under G.O.P. auspices, to take the lead in a situation that might end up in a general shooting war. Dulles did not reply.

In the end, all eight members of the Congress, Republicans and Democrats alike, were agreed that Dulles had better first go shopping for allies. Some people who should know say that Dulles was carrying, but did not produce, a draft of the joint resolution the president wanted Congress to consider.

The whole meeting had lasted two hours and ten minutes. As they left, the Hill delegation told waiting reporters they had been briefed on Indo-China. Nothing more.

To Assure Nonviolence:
King on Trial—1968

In 1968, city officials in Memphis were worried about violence. On February 1, two separate incidents there had triggered a labor strike: 22 black sewer workers were laid off without pay at the same time that some of the white supervisors were kept on the job; two black construction workers were crushed to death in an accident many thought could have been prevented. More than 90 percent of Memphis's sanitation workers walked off the job, demanding job safety and higher wages and benefits.

As the tensions between the city and the strikers grew more heated, most of the black religious, fraternal, and political organizations in Memphis rallied to the side of the strikers. They raised money for clothes and food for the strikers and organized demonstrations. One of the most outspoken champions of the sanitation workers was a familiar citizen of Memphis, the Reverend Martin Luther King, Jr.

As head of the Southern Christian Leadership Conference, King was, at the time of the strike, planning a "Poor Peoples' Campaign." Nevertheless, he found time to lend support, speaking at a rally in Memphis on March 18 and promising to lead a large march through the city later in the month.

At that rally, a group of rowdy students broke some windows and looted stores. Before the demonstration was finally dispersed, about 60 people had been injured.

The city retaliated against King, bringing a complaint in the district court. Defendants King, Hosea Williams, James Bevel, Ralph Abernathy, and other well-known figures in the civil rights movement submitted a brief, assuring the court of the peaceful intent of the rally, denying conspiratorial or criminal intent, and pledging to supply the city with a continuing flow of information on future march plans.

Due to the submission of the court brief and the energetic, persuasive negotiation with the city by Andrew Young and other SCLC attorneys, another march was thus arranged, this one scheduled for April 8.

Memphis braced for another sanitation worker march. King and his lieutenants worked hard to ensure that they gained sufficient control to keep the march nonviolent; Memphis police finalized plans for crowd control.

But violence did come to Memphis. It came in a far more menacing shape *than any of the organizers or city authorities could have imagined. It did not come from city sanitation workers or civil rights workers or from the police. It did not come at a rally. It came on the evening of April 4 on a motel balcony, where Martin Luther King, Jr., was assassinated.*

Answer to Plaintiff from *City of Memphis v. Martin Luther King, Jr.*, 1968

IN THE UNITED STATES DISTRICT COURT FOR THE WESTERN DISTRICT OF TENNESSEE WESTERN DIVISION

CITY OF MEMPHIS
A Municipal Corporation,

Complainant
VS
MARTIN LUTHER KING, JR.,
HOSEA WILLIAMS, REVEREND
JAMES BEVEL, REVEREND
JAMES ORANGE, RALPH D. ABERNATHY and
BERNARD LEE, all non-residents of the State of Tennessee,

Defendants

ANSWER

The defendants deny each and every allegation of the complainant except as follows:

The defendant Martin Luther King, Jr. and members of his staff were invited by local ministers to participate in a march held on March 28, 1967. Said march was held under the supervision of local ministers and the responsibility for planning and supervision to maintain order did not rest with these defendants.

The defendant King at the urgent request of local march leaders did leave the scene of disorder. At the same time, local leaders made immediate and successful efforts to turn the march back.

The defendants have organized and conducted in many communities utilizing the principals of non-violence numerous marches, none of which have resulted in civil disturbance. The defendants are not presently and have never been engaged in any conspiracies as alleged in the complaint. Defendants have in no way in their private or public statements sponsored, fermented, encouraged and incited riots, mobs or breaches of the peace as alleged in the complaint.

Defendants further state that they have never refused to furnish information concerning marches or plans as such information became available; that in fact said information has been furnished on a continuing basis to local law enforcement officers; that there is no statute or ordinance requiring the issuance of a parade or march permit by police authorities. However, to the extent that there is any custom or practice of submitting plans for parades or marches to police officials for discussion and review, the defendants have and will continue to do so as soon as practical after said plans have been made.

The defendants utilizing their experience have undertaken the following general steps to insure that the march will be non-violent and under control at all times. Limitations will be placed on the number of marchers in each line; parade marshals will be carefully selected and given training in their duties; liaison will be maintained with local law enforcement officers and the necessary protection and assistance will be requested; all groups in the community have been contacted to insure the parties in the march will participate on a non-violent basis; a route has been tentatively selected, together with tentative starting and ending times for the march and other necessary organizational steps have been and are continuing to be taken to insure a peaceful march. Steps have further been taken to prohibit the use of signs affixed to sticks or any other object which might be utilized in an improper manner.

Defendant, Martin Luther King, Jr., further states: that he has on numerous other occasions received threats or been informed of threats received by others concerning his personal safety; that while due precautions have been taken, there have been no difficulties encountered as a result of such threats.

Defendants respectfully request that the application for an injunction should be denied or in the alternative that the Court permit the march to be held under such reasonable restrictions as may be necessary giving due regard to the defendants and their First Amendment rights.

LUCIUS E. BURCH, JR.
LOUIS R. LUCAS
WALTER BAILEY

W. J. MICHAEL CODY
DAVID E. CAYWOOD
CHARLES F. NEWMAN

Of Counsel:
Jack Greenberg
Mel Zar
10 Columbus Circle
New York, New York

Deporting John Lennon—1972

FBI memorandum on efforts to deport John Lennon

In the eyes of the Nixon administration, John Lennon was not Pat Boone. The British rocker, Nixon's inner circle was convinced, was antireligious, a druggy, and an antiwar zealot. Lennon had trumpeted the case of the Chicago Seven, men such as Jerry Rubin, Dave Dellinger, and Bobby Seale; there was evidence also that Lennon was going to attempt to disrupt the 1972 Republican National Convention with a New Left group in protest against Richard Nixon's policies in Vietnam. Indeed, it was learned that he had contributed money to help pay for some of the organizing activities.

Nixon and his operatives wanted to punish Lennon, wanted him deported. In 1972, they began their attack.

Lennon was in the United States on a temporary visa that was about to expire. He applied for renewal, indicating his intention to become a U.S. citizen.

In May 1972, Lennon, with his wife, Yoko Ono, appeared at the Immigration and Naturalization Service headquarters in New York to face deportation hearings. Lennon, the INS representative contended, must not be allowed to remain in the United States because of 1968 drug convictions in England.

FBI files on John Lennon had been growing thicker by the month as agents tracked his movements and statements, cataloging a variety of allegations, rumors, gossip, and underground suspicions. After Lennon and Ono were seen together with the infamous Rubin in New York, for example, one FBI agent jotted down in large capital letters on a report that was added to Lennon's file, *"ALL EXTREMISTS SHOULD BE CONSIDERED DANGEROUS."*

After five years of lawsuits, trials, convictions, appeals, dismissals, new suits, waivers—a bewildering maze of legal parrying and thrusting—Chief Judge Irving R. Kaufman finally ruled that Lennon's 1968 conviction in London need not be recognized under U.S. immigration law. The judge ordered the INS to adjudicate Lennon's residence case without considering the drug conviction.

Lennon's lawyer, Leon Wilder, then petitioned to allow residence for Lennon and Ono on the grounds of their being "outstanding persons in the arts or sciences whose presence in the United States is deemed by the Attorney General to be in the national interest."

Despite the protests of Senator Strom Thurmond of South Carolina and other like-minded political figures, Lennon won his right to remain in the

United States. He was informed of the judicial decision on the very day that Ono was in the hospital to give birth to their son Sean.

Soon Lennon and Ono moved from their New York apartment on Jane Street to a larger, magnificent residence in the Dakota on Central Park West.

Ironically, if Lennon had not won his deportation case, if the government had been successful in sending him out of the country, it is unlikely that Mark David Chapman, his eventual killer, would have followed.

FBI Memorandum on Efforts to Deport John Lennon, April 23, 1972

April 23, 1972

Honorable H.R. Haldeman
Assistant to the President
The White House
Washington, D.C.

John Winston Lennon is a British citizen and former member of the Beatles singing group. . . .

Despite his apparent ineligibility for a United States visa due to a conviction in London in 1968 for possession of dangerous drugs, Lennon obtained a visa and entered the United States in 1971. During February, 1972, a confidential source who has furnished reliable information in the past, advised that Lennon had contributed $75,000 to a newly organized New Left group formed to disrupt the Republican National Convention. The visas of Lennon and his wife, Yoko Ono, expired on February 29, 1972, and since that time Immigration and Naturalization Service (INS) has been attempting to deport them. During the Lennons most recent deportation hearing at New York, New York, on April 18, 1972, their attorney stated that Lennon felt he was being deported due to his outspoken remarks concerning United States policy in Southeast Asia. The attorney requested a delay in order that character witnesses could testify for Lennon, and he then read into the court records that Lennon had been appointed to the President's Council for Drug Abuse (National Commission on Marijuana and Drug Abuse) and to the faculty of New York University, New York, New York.

If I Were in Your Shoes . . .—1987

Letter of Richard Nixon to Ronald Reagan recommending he stonewall on Iran-Contra

In August 1987, President Ronald Reagan attempted to deal with the stories, leaks, rumors, and embarrassing revelations battering the administration about the Iran-Contra affair. Was the administration sending weapons to the terrorist state of Iran in return for hostages? Were the Contra forces in Nicaragua being illegally supported against specific congressional restriction? What about the document shredding and the lying under oath by Reagan subordinates, some of it already admitted? How much did the president know about the numerous tawdry aspects of the affair?

Ex-president Richard Nixon had some advice for Reagan: "Don't ever comment on the Iran-Contra matter again."

After the grand wallow of Watergate; after all of the books, articles, treatises, charges and countercharges, and jail time spent; after the shame and the attempts at image rehabilitation; after all the tell-all books and autobiographies and hand-wringing from the bizarre cast of characters, from G. Gordon Liddy to John Mitchell; after all the arguments about executive privilege, usurpation of authority, accountability, cover-up, and disclosure; after all of that—here was Richard Nixon advising Ronald Reagan to stonewall on Iran-Contra.

Letter of Richard Nixon to Ronald Reagan, August 13, 1987

Dear Ron,

The speech last night was one of your best. What was even more important than what you said was that you sounded and looked strong. You gave the lie to the crap about your being over-the-hill, discouraged, etc.

If I could be permitted one word of advice: Don't ever comment on the Iran-Contra matter again. Have instructions issued to all White House staffers and Administration spokesmen that they must never answer any question on or off the record about that issue in the future. They should reply to all inquiries by stating firmly and categorically that the President has addressed the subject and that they have nothing to add.

The committee labored for nine months and produced a stillborn midget. Let it rest in peace!

Sincerely,

Dick

ALMOST
PLANS THWARTED
HISTORY

Dousing Confederate Fire:
A Conspiracy Foiled—1864

Telegram of William Henry Seward to mayor of New York on plans of Confederates to set fire to principal cities of the North

Early in 1864, the Confederate government in Richmond formulated plans for terrorizing major cities in the North in an effort to force the Union to sue for peace. Various chapters of the Knights of the Golden Circle, the Order of American Knights, and the Sons of Liberty dispatched sympathizers to New York, Chicago, Detroit, and Cleveland in a conspiracy to set major fires on the day of the presidential election in November 1864.

The major target city was New York. If the elaborate conspiracy worked as planned, a series of fires would erupt at major hotels and other buildings all across the city. The fires, however, were to act only as a diversion. While the city burned, other plotters would seize various federal buildings, municipal offices, and, most important, the police department, most of whose officers, it was assumed, would be dispatched around the city searching for arsonists. A group of conspirators would then free Confederate prisoners from Fort Lafayette and imprison Maj. Gen. John Adams Dix, Army Commander in New York, in his own dungeon. If all went as planned, the Confederate flag would fly over Manhattan, a coup of unmatched dimensions.

But with all the planning, organizing, and communicating that was necessary to pull off such a grand plot, sketchy information was reaching the Lincoln administration. The Washington government at least knew that Southern forces were concocting a terrorist assault in the North. It was at this point that Secretary of State William Henry Seward decided on an overt gambit. He drafted a message to major cities in the North about an imminent attack, warning them to be vigilant in the coming days. Seward's message was published in major newspapers across the country on November 4, 1864.

The Seward message acted not only to warn city officials but also intimidated the plotters who had assumed their conspiracy had, up to this time, been undetected. Seward's strategy worked. When most of the Confederate plotters learned that some of the details were being uncovered, many of them pulled back, deciding to wait until they could achieve complete surprise.

All of the conspirators were not derailed. The leader of one of the terrorist squads in New York, a man named Robert Kennedy, refused to be cowed. Kennedy gathered his comrades at the St. Dennis Hotel to go over details of the firebombing work they had been assigned. Later they distributed among the men small bottles of "Greek fire," a special chemical combination that looked like water but when exposed to air would, after a delay, ignite in flames.

On the evening of November 25, 1864, several fires began. Before the night was over, many major hotels in New York City had been damaged, including the St. Nicholas, St. James, Metropolitan, Hudson River Park, Astor House, and Belmont. There were also fires on the Hudson River docks.

Although Kennedy and his men managed to escape from New York after the arson attacks, he was captured three months later and was hanged on March 25, 1865. Nevertheless, Kennedy, with a few compatriots, had caused much havoc and damage. He and his few men had represented only a fraction of the elaborate scheme of Southern plotters. If it had not been for Secretary of State Seward's savvy move at a critical time, the massive plot might have had far more serious repercussions across the North.

Telegram of William Henry Seward to Mayor of New York, November 2, 1864

Washington, Nov. 2, 1864
The Mayor of the City of New York:

This department has received information from the British Provinces to the effect that there is a conspiracy on foot to set fire to the principal cities in the Northern States on the day of the Presidential election. It is my duty to communicate this information to you.

W. H. SEWARD.

Jefferson Davis, Guerrilla Fighter—1865

Plans of Jefferson Davis to continue military campaign after Appomattox

Before Gen. Robert E. Lee surrendered his exhausted, beleaguered Army of Northern Virginia to Gen. Ulysses S. Grant's equally exhausted forces at Appomattox Courthouse, some of Lee's lieutenants pleaded with their leader to continue fighting, to take a few of his men away from Virginia, establish a guerrilla force of especially intrepid and skilled fighters, and continue the war with a series of hit-and-escape attacks. Lee declined. He was now convinced that there was no reason to continue the killing, that the Southern troops had fought nobly and done everything they could to win but that the situation was hopeless and any further action could lead to no other end than the killing of additional young Americans. He later wrote, "I think it's the duty of every citizen to do all in their power to aid in the restoration of peace and harmony, and in no way oppose the policy of the government."

After Appomattox, Confederate President Jefferson Davis reached a different conclusion. Davis decided to attempt to do what had been proposed to General Lee—to escape to Texas, rearm, and, with a small but active force, continue hostilities. Accompanied by a military escort, along with his wife and several friends and relatives, Davis headed southwest in May 1865.

As they reached Georgia, they were hotly pursued by the 4th Regiment Michigan Cavalry and the 1st Wisconsin Cavalry. One of the members of the Michigan Cavalry, pretending to be a part of Davis's escort, managed to gain information from a citizen that Davis was encamped in the woods about three-fourths of a mile north of Irwinville.

The two regiments, although not working together, charged into the camp at dawn, on May 10, completely surprising Davis and his military escort and also apparently surprising themselves. The two Union forces actually exchanged fire before it was all sorted out.

Davis and the others were first taken to Macon. Along the way, they were taunted by members of the two cavalry units, singing a verse from "John Brown's Body": "We'll hang Jeff Davis from a sour apple tree." From Macon, the prisoners traveled by train through Atlanta to Augusta, where they boarded a steamer for the trip down the Savannah River. On May 16, they sailed from Hilton Head Island toward the North. Davis would be jailed, but his life was spared.

When Confederate president Jefferson Davis attempted to flee to Texas in May 1865 after General Robert E. Lee's Army of Northern Virginia surrendered at Appomattox Courthouse, Davis was captured near Irwinville, Georgia. When Northern troops spread a rumor that Davis tried to escape dressed in his wife's clothing, cartoonists and artists let their imaginations romp, as this music sheet shows.

Although it seemed like a pitiful, ragtag group that was rounded up that morning in Georgia, if he had been able to carry out his plan of continuing guerrilla activity, Davis could have compromised the efforts of Reconstruction. Although any such guerrilla campaign would have had almost no chance of permanently affecting the final outcome of the war, such military strikes could have taken many more lives, continuously exacerbated attempts at compromise, and likely brought even more serious reprisals from a government largely controlled by men who sought every possible justification for revenge.

Jefferson Davis's Message to Brigade Commanders, May 2, 1865

It is time we adopt some definite plan upon which the further prosecution of our struggle shall be conducted. I have summoned you for consultation. I feel that I ought to do nothing now without the advice of my military chiefs . . . even if the troops now with me be all that I can for the present rely on. Three thousand brave men are enough for a nucleus around which the whole people will rally when the panic which now afflicts them has passed away.

A Different Path to Reconciliation—1865

The last public speech of Abraham Lincoln, devoted mainly to his vision of Reconstruction

With the assassination of President Abraham Lincoln and the advent of the presidency of Andrew Johnson, postwar Reconstruction took on an inflammatory cast, with Radical Republicans battling the moderate chief executive from the border state of Tennessee. If Lincoln had lived and set his own Reconstruction agenda, the era might have been far different.

Lincoln's views on Reconstruction had been evolving throughout the war years, as he tried to devise ways to achieve the monumental task not only of "binding the nation's wounds" but of formulating the necessary, specific programs that could enable both sides to work together again under the same government. The task—finding a blend of steps that could moderate cravings of revenge and retribution and emphasize restoration of rights and rebirth of common ground—was daunting.

Although Lincoln would not have compromised national supremacy and would have had no part in restoring the slave-owning aristocracy, his hope was to treat the South more like a lost brother returning home than as a hardened criminal deserving strict punishment. Lincoln had been clear that he intended to act as swiftly as possible to take whatever actions were necessary to get the Southern states "into that proper practical relation" from which they had been separated during the war. For example, a new constitution of Louisiana, although not everything Lincoln might have wanted, was acceptable to him as a first step. It was attacked by Radical Republicans as forsaking the emancipation goals of the war.

It was not so much that Lincoln's ideas for Reconstruction differed from those of his vice president; they were quite similar. But Lincoln's political power in relation to the Radical Republicans in Congress was towering compared to that of Johnson, and he was a deft, skillful political operator. With Lincoln's death, the hope of moderation and conciliation was buried. Ironically, John Wilkes Booth energized the movement for Radical Reconstruction.

Excerpts from the Last Public Speech of Abraham Lincoln, April 11, 1865

By these recent successes the reinauguration of the national authority—reconstruction—which has had a large share of thought from the first, is pressed much more closely upon our attention. It is fraught with great difficulty. Unlike the case of a war between independent nations, there is no authorized organ for us to treat with. No one man has authority to give up the rebellion for any other man. We simply must begin with, and mould from, disorganized and discordant elements. Nor is it a small additional embarrassment that we, the loyal people, differ among ourselves as to the mode, manner, and means of reconstruction.

As a general rule, I abstain from reading the reports of attacks upon myself, wishing not to be provoked by that to which I can not properly offer an answer. In spite of this precaution, however, it comes to my knowledge that I am much censured for some supposed agency in setting up, and seeking to sustain, the new State Government of Louisiana. In this I have done just so much as, and no more than, the public knows. In the Annual Message of Dec. 1863 and accompanying Proclamation, I presented a plan of reconstruction (as the phrase goes) which, I promised, if adopted by any State, should be acceptable to, and sustained by, the Executive government of the nation. I distinctly stated that this was not the only plan which might possibly be acceptable; and I also distinctly protested that the Executive claimed no right to say when, or whether members should be admitted to seats in Congress from such States. This plan was, in advance, submitted to the then Cabinet, and distinctly approved by every member of it. . . . The message went to Congress, and I received many commendations of the plan, written and verbal; and not a single objection to it, from any professed emancipationist, came to my knowledge, until after the news reached Washington that the people of Louisiana had begun to move in accordance with it. . . .

I have been shown a letter on this subject, supposed to be an able one, in which the writer expresses regret that my mind has not seemed to be definitely fixed on the question whether the seceded States, so called, are in the Union or out of it. It would perhaps, add astonishment to his regret, were he to learn that since I have found professed Union men endeavoring to make that question, I have purposely forborne any public expression upon it. As appears to me that question has not been, nor yet is, a practically material one, and that any discussion of it, while it thus remains practically immaterial, could have no effect other than the mischievous one of dividing our friends. As yet, whatever it may hereafter become, that question is bad, as the basis of a controversy, and good for nothing at all—a merely pernicious abstraction.

We all agree that the seceded States, so called, are out of their proper practical relation with the Union; and that the sole object of the government, civil and military, in regard to those States is to again get them into that proper practical relation. I believe it is not only possible, but in fact, easier, to do this, without deciding, or even considering, whether these states have even been out of the Union, than with it. Finding themselves safely at home, it would be utterly immaterial whether they had ever been abroad. Let us all join in doing the acts necessary to restoring the proper practical relations between these states and the Union; and each forever after, innocently indulge his own opinion whether, in doing the acts, he brought the States from without, into the Union, or only gave them proper assistance, they never having been out of it. . . .

Trashing Diplomacy: Japan Rebuffs a Peace Plan—1941

Introduction to the proposed agreement between the United States and Japan prior to Pearl Harbor attack

Throughout the summer of 1941, neutrality was slipping away. Not only was the United States moving closer to war with Nazi Germany, relations with Japan were also deteriorating. In July, the Japanese moved into French Indochina. Immediately, the United States and Great Britain halted all trade with Japan. President Roosevelt mobilized the Philippine armed forces into the service of the United States and appointed Gen. Douglas MacArthur commander of all U.S. and Philippine forces.

In mid-August, shortly after President Roosevelt and Prime Minister Churchill met secretly in Newfoundland to draw up the Atlantic Charter, setting forth mutual political aims in the face of the Axis threat, President Roosevelt warned the Japanese ambassador that further aggression by Japan in the Far East would lead to a U.S. military response. Representatives of the two governments had been carrying on informal discussions and had exchanged proposals in attempting to define various principles and conditions acceptable to both sides. National sovereignty, commercial relations, the reliance on cooperative organizations to settle territorial and commercial disputes—all these issues were central in the discussions surrounding the escalating tensions between the United States and Japan.

In an aggressive move, the Tojo cabinet, on November 5, formulated what it called an "absolutely final proposal," a document stating a number of demands that would involve substantial concessions by the United States. U.S. Ambassador to Japan Joseph C. Grew warned that war with Japan might come with "dramatic and dangerous suddenness."

In responding to the proposal, on November 26, the U.S. State Department turned over to the Japanese ambassador a two-part proposed agreement between the two countries, an "effort to bridge the gap" between the various demands made in the continuing negotiations.

The November 5 document did turn out to be Japan's "absolutely final proposal." Japan's leaders, while making a pretense of continuing the Japanese-American conversations, moved additional troops into southern Indochina. When Roosevelt questioned the moves, the Japanese government claimed, on December 5, that the movements were defensive, protection against an attack by the Chinese.

Two days later, at Pearl Harbor, the Japanese government gave its answer to the latest U.S. attempt at diplomacy.

Introduction to Proposed Agreement between United States and Japan, November 26, 1941

The representatives of the Government of the United States and of the Government of Japan have been carrying on during the past several months informal and exploratory conversations for the purpose of arriving at a settlement if possible of questions relating to the entire Pacific area based upon the principles of peace, law and order and fair dealing among nations. These principles include the principle of inviolability of territorial integrity and sovereignty of each and all nations; the principle of noninterference in the internal affairs of other countries; the principle of equality, including equality of commercial opportunity and treatment; and the principle of reliance upon international cooperation and conciliation for the prevention and pacific settlement of controversies and for improvement of international conditions by peaceful methods and processes.

It is believed that in our discussions some progress has been made in reference to the general principles which constitute the basis of a peaceful settlement covering the entire Pacific area. Recently the Japanese Ambassador has stated that the Japanese Government is desirous of continuing the conversations directed toward a comprehensive and peaceful settlement in the Pacific area; that it would be helpful toward creating an atmosphere favorable to the successful outcome of the conversations if a temporary modus vivendi could be agreed upon to be in effect while the conversations looking to a peaceful settlement in the Pacific were continuing. On November 20 the Japanese Ambassador communicated to the Secretary of State proposals in regard to temporary measures to be taken respectively by the Government of Japan and by the Government of the United States, which measures are understood to have been designed to accomplish the purposes above indicated.

The Government of the United States most earnestly desires to contribute to the promotion and maintenance of peace and stability in the Pacific area, and to afford every opportunity for the continuance of discussions with the Japanese Government directed toward working out a broad-gauge program of peace throughout the Pacific area. The proposals which were presented by the Japanese

Amidst the early-morning horror at Pearl Harbor, December 7, 1941, a soldier managed to take a photograph that has lived as a historical icon.

Ambassador on November 20 contain some features which, in the opinion of this Government, conflict with the fundamental principles which form a part of the general settlement under consideration and to which each Government has declared that it is committed. The Government of the United States believes that the adoption of such proposals would not be likely to contribute to the ultimate objectives of ensuring peace under law, order and justice in the Pacific area, and it suggests that further effort be made to resolve our divergences of views in regard to the practical application of the fundamental principles already mentioned.

With this object in view the Government of the United States offers for the consideration of the Japanese Government a plan of a broad but simple settlement covering the entire Pacific area as one practical exemplification of a program which this Government envisages as something to be worked out during our further conversations.

Avoiding the Quagmire—1963

W as the Kennedy administration about to begin a phased effort to reduce U.S. involvement in the Vietnam conflict at the time of the president's assassination? Historians and public officials have sparred over this question for decades. Kennedy administration memos now available suggest that a reduction of forces was an active option of the administration at the time of the president's death.

In 1963, the administration could see a quagmire developing in South Vietnam. The political situation was unstable. Although there was some progress in making the South Vietnamese an effective fighting force, it was not clear how much U.S. support would be necessary to halt the aggression from the North. The president asked Secretary of Defense Robert McNamara and Chairman of the Joint Chiefs of Staff Gen. Maxwell Taylor also to go to Vietnam and issue a report containing all the data necessary to make final decisions regarding the directions the administration might go in handling the Vietnam situation.

Although McNamara and Taylor reported favorably on the military campaign the South was waging against the North, their report noted serious political tensions in South Vietnam and fears that it might further deteriorate. They recommended a program be established to train Vietnamese so that essential functions being performed by U.S. military personnel could be carried out by Vietnamese by the end of 1965 and the bulk of U.S. personnel withdrawn by that time. And, in accordance with the training program, they recommended that the Defense Department withdraw 1,000 U.S. military personnel by the end of 1963. This would be an initial step in a long-term program to replace U.S. personnel with trained Vietnamese without impairing the war effort.

President Kennedy and his advisors remained convinced that the security of South Vietnam was vital to U.S. security. In an interview after President Kennedy's assassination, Robert Kennedy denied that his brother had become convinced that protecting South Vietnam against the North Vietnamese was any less vital than he first believed. The question was strategic and tactical. How to achieve victory without further immersing the country in the tar pit?

"All planning will be directed towards preparing Republic of Vietnam forces for the withdrawal of all United States special assistance units and personnel *by the end of calendar year 1965," read an October 1963 memorandum drafted by Gen. Maxwell Taylor and discussed by the Joint Chiefs that day. "Execute the plan to withdraw 1,000 United States military personnel by the end of 1963."*

The plan was never carried out. A month later, the president was assassinated. Had he lived, Kennedy, an ardent cold warrior, would, like his successor, have been faced with the prospect of the defeat of South Vietnam by the Viet Cong insurgency, controlled from the North. But the decision on the U.S. reaction would not be his to make, but Lyndon Johnson's. The United States had 16,300 military personnel in special assistance units in South Vietnam at the time of Kennedy's death. By the end of 1968, it had more than 500,000 soldiers in the country.

National Security Action Memorandum No. 263, October 11, 1963

The White House
Washington
October 11, 1963

NATIONAL SECURITY ACTION MEMORANDUM NO. 263

To: Secretary of State
Secretary of Defense
Chairman of the Joint Chief of Staff

SUBJECT: South Vietnam

At a meeting on October 5, 1963, the President considered the recommendations contained in the report of Secretary McNamara and General Taylor on their mission to South Vietnam.

The President approved the military recommendations contained in Section I B (1-3) of the report, but directed that no formal announcement be made of the implementation of plans to withdraw 1,000 U.S. military personnel by the end of 1963.

After discussion of the remaining recommendations of the report, the President approved an instruction to Ambassador Lodge which is set forth in State Department telegram No. 534 to Saigon.

s/McGeorge Bundy

Planning for Cuban Rapprochement—1963

CIA Memorandum on Cuba

D iplomacy often takes simultaneous, divergent paths. If one avenue of approach does not ultimately work, another might. In its tortuous relations with Cuba since the advent of the Castro regime, the United States has attempted assassination against the Communist leader on several occasions, each one embarrassingly inept. It has also made cautious gestures of accommodation.

In 1963, the Kennedy administration and the Castro government undertook communications that might have led to a possible rapprochement, or at least a serious reduction of tension between the two countries. The United States wanted to lure Castro out of the Soviet orbit of influence, using what a National Security Council memorandum described as "the sweet approach." In addition, following the Cuban Missile Crisis, Castro appeared more willing to discuss ways in which U.S. and Cuban interests might converge.

First, in the spring of 1963, a U.S. intermediary, James Donovan, engaged in secret talks with Castro that seemed promising. When Castro asked Donovan how better relations could come from such a current quagmire of tangled and injured relations—how the two countries could actually move toward a new era—Donovan said, "Do you know how porcupines make love?" When Castro said no, Donovan replied, "Very carefully."

The two countries did move carefully. In May 1963, journalist Lisa Howard conducted a lengthy interview with Castro and returned to tell the CIA that he was interested in better relations with the United States. She offered to act as an intermediary in future discussions, in much the same way John Scali, another reporter, had dealt with Soviet diplomats during the Cuban Missile Crisis.

The administration responded positively to Howard's suggestion. In September 1963, Deputy U.S. Ambassador to the United Nations William Attwood proposed in a Memorandum on Cuba a course of action that could lead to "neutralizing Cuba on our terms." Attwood received permission from the administration to make secret contact with Cuba's U.N. Ambassador Carlos Lechuga. Their first discussion took place at Howard's New York apartment.

A few weeks after the meeting, John Kennedy was dead. The groundwork laid by Donovan, Howard, Attwood, and others was flooded with renewed hostility and accusations, and any immediate hope for reconciliation was dashed.

CIA Memorandum, June 5, 1963

Memorandum on Cuba

This memorandum proposes a course of action which, if successful, could remove the Cuban issue from the 1964 campaign.

It does not propose offering Castro a "deal"—which could be more dangerous politically than doing nothing. It does propose a discreet inquiry into the possibility of neutralizing Cuba on our terms.

It is based on the assumption that, short of a change of regime, our principal political objectives in Cuba are:

a. The evacuation of all Soviet bloc military personnel.

b. An end to subversive activities by Cuba in Latin America.

c. Adoption by Cuba of a policy of non-alignment.

This memorandum is also based on the assumption that our present policy of isolating Cuba economically and politically will not overthrow the Castro regime in time to keep Cuba out of the 1964 campaign. So long as he receives Soviet aid and keeps his power base among the peasantry, his position seems secure.

It follows that the effect of our present policy is mainly negative:

a. It aggravates Castro's anti-Americanism and his desire to cause us trouble and embarrassment.

b. In the eyes of a world largely made up of small countries, it freezes us in the unattractive posture of a big country trying to bully a small country.

Since we do not intend to overthrow the Castro regime by military force, is there anything else we can do which might advance U.S. interests without risking charges of appeasement?

According to neutral diplomats and others I have talked to at the U.N. and in Guinea, there is reason to believe that Castro is unhappy about his present dependence on the Soviet bloc; that he does not enjoy being in effect a satellite; that the trade embargo is hurting him—though not enough to endanger his position; and that he would like to establish some official contact with the U.S. and go to some length to obtain normalization of relations with us—even though this would not be welcomed by most of his hard-core Communist entourage, such as Che Guevara.

All of this may or may not be true. But it would seem that we have something to gain and nothing to lose by finding out whether in fact Castro does want to talk and what concessions he would be prepared to make.

The most propitious time and place to find out would be at the U.N. during the present General Assembly. Without appearing to take the initiative for a meeting, we could easily feel out the Cubans as follows:

a. As a former journalist who spent considerable time with Castro in 1959, I could arrange a casual meeting with the Cuban Delegate, Dr. Lechuga. This could be done socially thorough mutual acquaintances.

b. I would refer to my last talk with Castro, at which he stressed his desire to be friends with the U.S., and suggest that, as a journalist, I would be curious to know how he felt today. If Castro is ready to talk, this should provide sufficient reason for Lechuga to come back to me with an invitation.

It would be understood that I would be going as an individual but would of course report to the President before and after the visit.

My reasons for suggesting that I undertake this mission are three-fold:

a. Although Castro did not like my final article in 1959, we got along well and I believe he remembers me as someone he could talk to frankly.

b. I have had considerable experience in the past seventeen years talking with Communist and neutralist leaders on both sides of the iron curtain.

c. I have enough rank to satisfy Castro that this would be a serious conversation. At the same time, I am not so well-known that my departure, arrival or return would be noticed.

Two other points are worth emphasizing:

a. Such a meeting would be purely exploratory. I would make no offers, promises or deals. I would simply sound him out as to whether he would be willing to take the three steps listed in paragraph three, and on what terms. I would report to the President and the decision to pursue negotiations or not could then be taken.

b. The risk that the press would get wind of this project is minimal. For their part, the Cubans would not want it known they had solicited a meeting. On our side, it is of course important that the fewest possible people know of it. But in any case we are on firm ground so long as the invitation comes from the Cubans, since we are always ready to listen to an offer that could advance U.S. interests.

For the moment, all I would like is the authority to make contact with Lechuga. We'll see what happens then.

William Attwood

A Speech Undelivered—1963

Prepared remarks of President John F. Kennedy for delivery at the Trade Mart in Dallas, Texas

Less than a year before his reelection bid, President John F. Kennedy was in Texas on a political fund-raising and fence-mending expedition. It had been a challenging summer of turmoil and growing unrest. The foreign policy clouds over Cuba had not lifted, and the haunting questions of how vigorously the country should support South Vietnam were becoming increasingly burdensome. The president had recently signed a treaty with the Soviet Union and Great Britain to ban all nuclear tests in the atmosphere, in outer space, and underwater and declared that it was "a shaft of light cut into the darkness." But at home, the assassination of Medgar Evers, the Birmingham riots, and the "March on Washington for Jobs and Freedom" had moved Kennedy to propose new civil rights legislation. The trip to Texas would give the president an opportunity to lay out his vision for dealing with these issues in a second term. In Dallas, he would be back on the campaign trail.

On Thursday, November 21, 1963, the president flew to San Antonio, where Vice President Lyndon B. Johnson joined the party. The president dedi-

Dallas, Texas, November 23, 1963. A woman in a crowd of onlookers watching the presidential motorcade snapped this Polaroid photo moments after John F. Kennedy slumped in the arms of his wife.

cated new research facilities at the U.S. Air Force School of Aerospace Medicine and participated in a testimonial dinner in Houston for U.S. Representative Albert Thomas. The group then flew to Fort Worth where, on the morning of November 22, the president spoke at a large breakfast gathering. Late that morning, the entourage arrived at Love Field in Dallas.

Following a motorcade through downtown Dallas and a luncheon speech at the Trade Mart, the president was to fly to Austin for a Democratic fund-raising dinner. From there he was to proceed to the Texas ranch of the vice president. The Dallas motorcade, his advisors hoped, would demonstrate his personal popularity in a city he had lost in the 1960 election.

The motorcade left Love Field shortly after 11:50 A.M. As it proceeded through residential neighborhoods, Kennedy twice asked for the car to stop so he could greet well-wishers. As the president and his friends had hoped, the crowds were friendly.

Excerpts of Prepared Remarks of President John F. Kennedy for Delivery at the Trade Mart in Dallas, Texas, November 22, 1963

November 22, 1963

I am honored to have this invitation to address the annual meeting of the Dallas Citizens Council, joined by the members of the Dallas Assembly—and pleased to have this opportunity to salute the Graduate Research Center of the Southwest. . . .

In a world of complex and continuing problems, in a world full of frustrations and irritations, America's leadership must be guided by the lights of learning and reason or else those who confuse rhetoric with reality and the plausible with the possible will gain the popular ascendancy with their seemingly swift and simple solutions to every world problem.

There will always be dissident voices heard in the land, expressing opposition without alternatives, finding fault but never favor, perceiving gloom on every side and seeking influence without responsibility. Those voices are inevitable.

But today other voices are heard in the land—voices preaching doctrines wholly unrelated to reality, wholly unsuited to the sixties, doctrines which apparently assume that words will suffice without weapons, that vituperation is as good as victory and that peace is a sign of weakness. At a time when the national debt is steadily being reduced in terms of its burden on our economy, they see that debt as the greatest single threat to our security. At a time when we are steadily reducing the number of Federal employees serving every thousand citizens, they fear those supposed hordes of civil servants far more than the actual hordes of opposing armies.

We cannot expect that everyone, to use the phrase of a decade ago, will "talk sense to the American people." But we can hope that fewer people will listen to nonsense. And the notion that this Nation is headed for defeat through deficit, or that strength is but a matter of slogans, is nothing but just plain nonsense.

I want to discuss with you today the status of our strength and our security because this question clearly calls for the most responsible qualities of leadership and the most enlightened products of scholarship. For this Nation's strength and security are not easily or cheaply obtained, nor are they quickly and simply explained. There are many kinds of strength and no one kind will suffice. Overwhelming nuclear strength cannot stop a guerrilla war. Formal pacts of alliance cannot stop internal subversion. Displays of material wealth cannot stop the disillusionment of diplomats subjected to discrimination.

Above all, words alone are not enough. The United States is a peaceful nation. And where our strength and determination are clear, our words need merely to convey conviction, not belligerence. If we are strong, our strength will speak for itself. If we are weak, words will be of no help.

I realize that this Nation often tends to identify turning-points in world affairs with the major addresses which preceded them. But it was not the Monroe Doctrine that kept all Europe away from this hemisphere—it was the strength of the British fleet and the width of the Atlantic Ocean. It was not General Marshall's speech at Harvard which kept communism out of Western Europe—it was the strength and stability made possible by our military and economic assistance.

In this administration also it has been necessary at times to issue specific warnings—warnings that we could not stand by and watch the Communists conquer Laos by force, or intervene in the Congo, or swallow West Berlin, or maintain offensive missiles on Cuba. But while our goals were at least temporarily obtained in these and other instances, our successful defense of freedom was due not to the words we used, but to the strength we stood ready to use on behalf of the principles we stand ready to defend. . . .

It should be clear by now that a nation can be no stronger abroad than she is at home. Only an America which practices what it preaches about equal rights and social justice will be respected by those whose choice affects our future. Only an America which has fully educated its citizens is fully capable of tackling the complex problems and perceiving the hidden dangers of the world in which we live. And only an America which is growing and prospering economically can sustain the worldwide defenses of freedom, while demonstrating to all concerned the opportunities of our system and society. . . .

Our adversaries have not abandoned their ambitions, our dangers have not diminished, our vigilance cannot be relaxed. But now we have the military, the scientific, and the economic strength to do whatever must be done for the preservation and promotion of freedom.

That strength will never be used in pursuit of aggressive ambitions—it will always be used in pursuit of peace. It will never be used to promote provocations—it will always be used to promote the peaceful settlement of disputes.

We in this country, in this generation, are—by destiny rather than choice—the watchmen on the walls of world freedom. We ask, therefore, that we may be worthy of our power and responsibility, that we may exercise our strength with wisdom and restraint, and that we may achieve in our time and for all time the ancient vision of "peace on earth, good will toward men." That must always be our goal, and the righteousness of our cause must always underlie our strength. For as was written long ago: "except the Lord keep the city, the watchman waketh but in vain."

Trying to Take Down the Cuban Roadrunner—1967

Recently released report of inspector general, on CIA plots to assassinate Fidel Castro

T hey tried poisoned cigars and exploding cigars. They tried to booby-trap a beach. They tried lethal pills and even a powder to make his beard fall out. Fidel Castro is still there.

In the early 1960s, there were at least eight separate attempts to assassinate the Cuban leader (Castro has bragged that the number was closer to two dozen), some of which resembled plots from rejected B-movie scripts. If the plotters had been successful, the history of Cuban–U.S. relations would have been dramatically different in the last 40 years of the 20th century. Given the lack of skill demonstrated by those attempting to do the deed, however, that possibility seems in retrospect to have been extremely remote.

In 1967, President Johnson, in response to a Drew Pearson–Jack Anderson newspaper column on assassination attempts against Castro, ordered the CIA inspector general to investigate and report the facts. So explosive were the revelations that the entire report remained classified three decades after its completion.

How badly did the CIA and the Kennedy administration want to get Castro? To the agency, working with mobsters interested in reestablishing gambling, prostitution, and drug monopolies in Cuba was worth the price of ridding the island of its Communist leader. On one occasion, the CIA offered the mob $150,000 to assassinate Castro; the mobsters insisted on taking the job for free. The CIA got what it paid for.

In hindsight, all of the sinister machinations, all of the wheeling and dealing between U.S. government officials and members of the Mafia, take on a peculiarly comic, pathetic cast. After one assassin wanna-be attempted to convert a Paper-Mate pen into a hypodermic syringe with which to go after Castro, one of his contacts remarked that surely they "could come up with something more sophisticated than that."

Excerpts from Report of the Inspector General on CIA Plots to Assassinate Fidel Castro, 1967

Dr. Edward Gunn, Chief, Operations Divisions, Office of Medical Services, has a notation that on 16 August 1960 he received a box of

Cuban cigars to be treated with a lethal material. He understood them to be Fidel's favorite brand, and he thinks they were given to him by Shef Edwards. Edwards does not recall the incident. Gunn has a notation that he contact (deleted) of TSD, on 6 September 1960. (Deleted) remembers experimenting with some cigars and then treating a full box. He cannot now recall whether he was initially given two boxes, experimenting with one and then treating the other; or whether he bought a box for experimentation, after which he treated the box supplied him by Gunn. He does not, in fact, remember Gunn as the supplier of any cigars. He is positive, though, that he did contaminate a full box of fifty cigars with botulinum toxin, a virulent poison that produces a fatal illness some hours after it is ingested. (Deleted) distinctly remembers the flaps-and-seals job he had to do on the box and on each of the wrapped cigars, both to get at the cigars and to erase the evidence of tampering. He kept one of the experimental cigars and still has it. He retested it during our inquiry and found that the toxins still retained 94% of its original effectiveness. The cigars were so heavily contaminated that merely putting one in the mouth would do the job; the intended victim would not actually have to smoke it.

Gunn's notes show that he reported the cigars as being ready for delivery on 7 October 1960. (Deleted) notes do not show actual delivery until 13 February 1961. They do not indicate to whom delivery was made. Gunn states that he took the cigars, at some unspecified time, and kept them in his personal safe. He remembers destroying them within a month of Shef Edwards retirement in June 1963. . . .

November 1963 . . .

Samuel Halpern and (deleted) approached Dr. Gunn for assistance. Although none of the participants specifically so stated, it may be inferred that they were seeking a means of assassination of a sort that Cubela might reasonably have been expected to have devised himself. What they settled upon was Black Leaf 40, a common, easily-obtainable insecticide containing about 40% nicotine sulphate. Nicotine is a deadly poison that may be administered orally, by injection, or by absorption through the skin. It is likely that there also were discussions of means of administering the poison, because Gunn was ready to move when asked.

The plan reached the action stage when Halpern and (deleted) contacted Gunn again on the morning of 20 November 1963 and told him that the device for administering the poison (a ballpoint pen rigged as a hypodermic syringe) had to be ready in time for (deleted) to catch a plane at noon the next day. Gunn says that he went immediately to the FI/D workshop and spent the rest of the day and most of that night fabricating the device. Those in FI/D who worked with him knew what he was trying to make but not for whom it was intended. Eventually, after seven or eight failures, he succeeded in converting a Paper-Mate pen into a hypodermic syringe that worked. He said that the needle was so fine that the victim would hardly feel it when it was inserted - he compared it with the scratch from a shirt with too much starch. He delivered the workable device to (deleted) the following morning and retained two of the later prototypes. He states that they are still in his safe. he does not know what happened to the device he gave (deleted); he does not remember as having been returned to him. He believes he was told that Cubela refused to accept the device. He says it would not now be able to differentiate the final pen from the earlier prototypes that are in his safe.

22 November 1963

(Deleted) arrived in Paris on the morning of 22 November and met with Cubela late that afternoon. (Deleted) states that he showed the pen/syringe to Cubela and explained how it worked. He is not sure, but he believes that Cubela accepted the device but said that he would not take it to Cuba with him. (Deleted) distinctly recalls that Cubela didn't think much of the device. Cubela said that, as a doctor, he knew all about Black Leaf 40 and that we surely could come up with something more sophisticated than that. It should be noted that Gunn and (deleted) agree that the syringe was not loaded. Cubela was expected to supply his own poison; we merely suggested Black Leaf 40 as an effective poison for use in the syringe.

(Deleted) wrote a contract report of the meeting. It makes no mention of a pen or of poison. The following is a summary of the contact report. Cubela said that he was returning to Cuba fully determined to pursue his plans to initiate a coup against Castro. (Deleted) reiterated the assurances given Cubela by FitzGerald of full U.S. support if a real coup against the Castro regime were successful. Cubela asked for the following items to be included in a cache inside Cuba: 20 hand grenades, two high-powered rifles with telescopic sights, and approximately 20 pounds of C-4 explosive and related equipment.

Cubela suggested the best place for the cache was on the finca (farm) managed by his friend, (deleted). Since he was returning to Cuba by way of Prague, he did not want to carry S/W or any other incriminating materials with him. As they were coming out of the meeting, (deleted) and Cubela were informed that President Kennedy had been assassinated. Cubela was visibly moved over the news. He asked, "Why do such things happen to good people." The contact report does not state the time nor the duration of the (deleted) Cubela meeting, but it is likely that at the very moment President Kennedy was shot a CIA officer was meeting with a Cuban agent in Paris and giving him an assassination device for use against Castro.

ALMOST

OPPORTUNITIES MISSED; WARNINGS UNHEEDED

HISTORY

A Young Illinois Congressman Challenges U.S. Imperialism—1847

Abraham Lincoln introduces the Spot Resolutions

On December 22, 1847, a freshman Whig congressman from Illinois named Abraham Lincoln introduced resolutions challenging President James K. Polk's decision to involve the United States in the Mexican War and his extension of the war powers of the executive.

Congress had declared war against Mexico in May 1846 after Polk's contention that Mexicans had fired on American soldiers in U.S. territory. The area itself had been under dispute, and the justification for the war, therefore, was shaky. Although Congress had gone along with Polk's war plans, many legislators on both sides of the aisle remained unconvinced, including several with very different political philosophies and regional interests. For example, Senator John C. Calhoun of South Carolina abstained from voting, worried that the war would aggravate sectional strife. Massachusetts senator Daniel Webster doubted the constitutionality of Polk's actions, believing that the president had failed to consult adequately with Congress.

In December 1847, Lincoln challenged the truth of the contention that Mexicans had attacked Americans in U.S. territory. He introduced a resolution questioning whether the actual spot on which the firing took place belonged to the United States. In another resolution he claimed that the American troops were on that spot in violation of the orders of their commanding officer, Gen. Zachary Taylor. The following month, Lincoln supported a Whig resolution declaring that the Mexican War had been "unnecessarily and unconstitutionally . . . begun by the President."

Although Lincoln's resolutions made little impression either on Congress or on the president, they caused an uproar in Illinois, whose citizens overwhelmingly approved of Polk's actions. Lincoln was soon denounced by his opponents as nothing less than a traitor, and opposition newspapers began to characterize him as "Spotty Lincoln."

He had taken his seat in the Congress on December 6. It had taken him only 16 days to offer a resolution so unpopular that his first term in Congress would likely be his last. The young congressman either woefully lacked political sense or had certain leadership qualities not yet recognized.

Lincoln's resolutions, later known as the Spot Resolutions, were never acted upon by the full Congress; a full debate might have prompted Congress to *define more succinctly its view of executive wartime authority, an issue that has remained in flux throughout the history of the United States.*

Resolution of Abraham Lincoln Before the U.S. House of Representatives, December 22, 1847

Whereas the President of the United States, in his message of May 11, 1846, has declared that "the Mexican Government not only refused to receive him [the envoy of the United States], or listen to his propositions, but, after a long-continued series of menaces, has at last invaded our territory and shed the blood of our fellow-citizens on our own soil:"

And again, in his message of December 8, 1846, that "we had ample cause of war against Mexico long before the breaking out of hostilities; but even then we forbore to take redress into our own hands until Mexico herself became the aggressor, by invading our soil in hostile array, and shedding the blood of our citizens:"

And yet again, in his message of December 7, 1847, that "the Mexican Government refused even to hear the terms of adjustment which he [our minister of peace] was authorized to propose, and finally, under wholly unjustifiable pretexts, involved the two countries in war, by invading the territory of the State of Texas, striking the first blow, and shedding the blood of our citizens on our own soil."

And whereas this House is desirous to obtain a full knowledge of all the facts which go to establish whether the particular spot on which the blood of our citizens was so shed was or was not at that time our own soil: Therefore, Resolved By the House of Representatives, That the President of the United States be respectfully requested to inform this House—

First. Whether the spot of soil on which the blood of our citizens was shed, as in his messages declared, was or was not within the territory of Spain, at least after the treaty of 1819, until the Mexican revolution.

Second. Whether that spot is or is not within the territory which was wrested from Spain by the revolutionary Government of Mexico.

Third. Whether that spot is or is not within a settlement of people, which settlement has existed ever since long before the Texas revolution, and until its inhabitants fled before the approach of the U.S. Army.

Fourth. Whether that settlement is or is not isolated from any and all other settlements by the Gulf of Mexico and the Rio Grande on the south and west, and by wide uninhabited regions on the north and east.

Fifth. Whether the People of that settlement, or a majority of them, or <u>any</u> of them, have ever, previous to the bloodshed mentioned in his message, submitted themselves to the government or laws of Texas or the United States, by <u>consent</u> or <u>compulsion</u>, either by accepting office, or voting at elections, or paying tax, or serving on juries, or having process served upon them, or in <u>any other way</u>.

Sixth. Whether the People of that settlement did or did not flee from the approach of the United States army, leaving unprotected their homes and their growing crops, <u>before</u> the blood was shed, as in the messages stated; and whether the first blood, so shed, was or was not shed within the <u>enclosure</u> of the People, or some of them, who had fled from it.

Seventh. Whether our <u>citizens</u>, whose blood was shed, as in his message declared, were or were not, at that time, <u>armed</u> officers and <u>soldiers</u>, sent into that settlement by the military order of the President, through the Secretary of War, and

Eighth. Whether the military force of the United States including their <u>citizens</u> was or was not sent into that settlement after Genl. Taylor had more than once intimated to the War Department that, in his opinion, no such movement was necessary to the defence or protection of Texas.

A Georgian Olive Branch Rejected—1863

**Remembrances of Alexander Stephens of aborted
Confederate plan to seek terms for an end to
Civil War hostilities**

In early 1863, Confederate Vice President Alexander H. Stephens suggested that a delegation be sent north to negotiate terms for ending Civil War hostilities. The war had ground along indecisively, a grueling, seemingly endless conflict sapping both sides of men and resources. The two armies had suffered grievous losses with no resolution in sight. It was in this atmosphere that Stephens felt he had a chance to fashion a compromise that would end hostilities and possibly lead to a recognition of the Confederacy and some form of Southern independence.

This was before Gettysburg and Vicksburg, before the South had been placed totally on the defensive, before Northern troops and political leaders had gained confidence that a total victory in the war was likely. Much of history, especially in wartime, is shaped by timing—the factors and circumstances surrounding a series of conditions and events. Any chance for negotiation that Stephens saw early in 1863 was lost in the events later that summer and fall.

When Stephens later reflected on that critical time of the war, he did so wistfully, lost in speculation of what might have been. If General Lee had not attempted his northern offensive but had remained on the defensive south of the Rappahannock, Stephens believed, the stalemated war might have ended differently, with a disillusioned and dissatisfied Union army and its leaders realizing the wisdom of ending a seemingly futile quest for victory.

When Stephens looked back, he could see a continuing series of inconclusive battlefield skirmishes, a number of conferences and meetings about a cease-fire, and eventually some kind of Southern independence. "Upon these questions," he wrote, "others must form their own speculative judgments." Indeed.

Remembrances of Alexander Stephens of Confederate Aborted Plan, 1863

The result of wars generally depends quite as much upon diplomacy as upon arms—upon the proper use of the pen as of the sword. There is a time for each. It is a matter of the utmost importance to know when and how to use both. The Confederate armies, officers and men, for two years and upwards, as we have seen, had nobly and gloriously performed their part. With less than five-hundred thousand in all, from the beginning up to this time, they had brought the enemy, numbering more than a million, during the same period, almost to a standstill. Gen. Grant, it is true, was still "pegging away," in his slow approaches upon Vicksburg, but on no other line were any active movements being made. I thought the time had now come, in view of the situation, both politically at the North and militarily at the South, as matters stood in the early part of June, 1863, for our Civil authorities to essay something in their department. . . . The entire propriety and expediency, however, in making this essay, in my judgment, depended upon the *then* military *status*.

In this view, Mr. Davis did not concur. He did not believe that the road to Peace lay in that way. He did not think that anything towards its ultimate obtainment could be effected on this line of external policy, indicated by me. He regarded Mr. Lincoln and his Cabinet as thoroughly representing the fixed principles and sentiments of a majority of the people of the Northern States. He thought, after Mr. Lincoln's conduct towards our first Peace Commissioners, that the surest, if not only means, of securing our rights was the power of our arms. The efficiency of Diplomacy, at the proper time, and in the proper manner, he fully recognized. On these points there was no disagreement between us, except as to time and manner. In this case his opinion was, that Diplomacy and Arms ought to act in conjunction, and that the Commissioner I had suggested ought to go with a victorious and threatening army. The result of my proposed mission, therefore, was the yielding of my views in this particular to his on this occasion, and not of his to mine. . . .

"Ma Bell" Beats "Ma Gray" by a Nose—1876

Patent for the telephone filed by inventor Elisha Gray only hours after Alexander Graham Bell's

History seldom, if ever, rewards second place. At the turn of the century, Samuel Langley, head of the Smithsonian Institution, sought to be the inventor of the airplane. He was beaten out by two brothers who owned a bicycle shop in Ohio. Langley's fame, compared to that of the Wright brothers, was scant.

Three decades earlier, inventor Elisha Gray, like Langley, was considered an eminent professional scientist. He had received his first patent for an automatic telegraph relay in 1867. Later, when Western Union bought his printer translating Morse code into type, he used the profit to form Gray & Barton, a partnership that eventually became Western Electric.

But, in the 1870s, Gray's passion was to create a device to send several simultaneous signals over one telegraph wire. He called it a "multiplex." At the beginning, Gray's notion was to use a different musical tone for each message. The problem was in creating a receiver capable of sorting out the tones. As the research continued, Gray believed that such a receiver could also reproduce the tones of the human voice if an adequate transmitter could be developed. Although he thought he knew the research path that would solve that problem, he wished first to complete the multiplex telegraph.

Meanwhile, a young speech teacher for the deaf named Alexander Graham Bell was doing similar research. To Bell, an amateur inventor, the multiplex telegraph held great promise if it could be adapted for the mechanics of speech. Soon Gray became aware of Bell's work. "Bell seems to be spending all his energies in [the] talking telegraph," Gray wrote to his attorney. "While this is very interesting scientifically, it has no commercial value. . . . I don't want at present to spend my time and money for that which will bring no reward." Nevertheless, on Valentine's Day 1876, Gray filed a description of a new talking telegraph—for "transmitting vocal sounds telegraphically"—with the U.S. Patent Office.

He was too late. Two hours earlier on that very day, unknown to Gray, Bell had already applied for a patent on his own telephone, even though it, too, was not yet perfected. Later research indicated that the device described by Gray would have worked and the one described by Bell would not have. However, Bell held the patent. Despite lengthy court battles, Bell could write to his father,

---

"The whole thing is mine and I am sure of fame, fortune, and success."

He was right. He continued teaching the deaf (Helen Keller became a close friend); he created the audiometer to detect hearing loss, and, as a result of his research, loudness came to be measured in bels or decibels. After his newborn son died of respiratory failure, Bell even developed a "vacuum jacket," a forerunner of the iron lung.

A bitter, combatant Gray spent many of his remaining days trying to prove that he, not Bell, was the inventor of the telephone. If he had been two hours quicker, he would have been.

Although it bears scant resemblance to modern telephones, this was the model for Alexander Graham Bell's Patent No. 174465, submitted on March 7, 1876, the invention to which his name has forever been linked.

No Hurricane Can Make a Left Turn:
How a Killer Storm Defied the Rules and Destroyed a City—1900

Warnings of Cuban weather forecasters of hurricane heading toward Galveston ignored by U.S. Weather Bureau

A century ago a hurricane destroyed Galveston, Texas. It was the deadliest natural disaster in U.S. history. It killed more Americans than the legendary Chicago Fire, the San Francisco earthquake, and the Johnstown flood combined. It killed at least 8,000 people, cut Galveston Island off from the Texas mainland, and submerged it under the sea. It swept away 20,636 homes, nearly half the city's total, and reduced to rubble at least 1,000 more.

"With a raging sea rolling around them," an eyewitness wrote later, "with a wind so terrific none could hope to escape its fury, with roofs being torn away and buildings crumbling . . . men, women and children . . . huddled like rats in the structures. As buildings crumpled and crashed, hundreds were buried under debris, while thousands were thrown into the waters, some to meet instant death, others to struggle for a time in vain, and yet other thousands to escape death in miraculous and marvelous ways."

Born west of the Cape Verde Islands around August 27, 1900, the storm was moving northward over Cuba a week later. By September 5, when it reached the Florida Keys, it was a hurricane.

Nevertheless, at daylight on Saturday morning, most citizens of Galveston were not concerned about the weather. Many were actually on the beach, watching the increasingly thunderous surf smash farther inland. Even when a wall of water damaged several buildings along the coast and destroyed a streetcar trestle, most folks enjoyed the cooling relief from what had been many days of sweltering heat.

But that afternoon, hell hit Galveston. The Gulf of Mexico was suddenly several feet into its streets, breaking up houses, and bridges, submerging the wharves. Fierce winds ripped down telephone poles, tore apart large buildings, and flung humans and horses in all directions.

The awesome physical dimensions of the horror were made even more painful by the fact that there had been warnings that Galveston had not heeded. Forecasters in Cuba had sent a series of messages days earlier notifying the city that they believed the storm would head through the Gulf toward Galveston. The U.S. Weather Bureau experts, however, both in Washington, D.C., and in

---

Galveston, had little faith in Cuban predictions, which they believed were always somewhat exaggerated, if not totally erroneous. Besides, historical data indicated that hurricanes did not make the kind of left turn that would be necessary for the Cuban storm to become a Galveston hurricane. In all probability, the storm would veer north.

Three days earlier, one of the U.S. forecasters was writing a detailed letter assuring his superiors that a comparison of U.S. and Cuban forecasts "will show that the forecasts of this Bureau were verified in every particular; and that the conditions which obtained did not warrant the issuance of a forecast likely to cause any alarms whatsoever." Tragically, he and many others were very wrong.

For residents of Galveston, Texas, in September 1900, the world and this house on Avenue N had tragically tilted.

Dispatch of Cuban Weather Forecaster Father Lorenzo Gangoite, September 10, 1900

At day-break, the sky was an intense red, cirrus clouds were moving from the W by N and NW by N, with a focus at these same points; these are clear indications that the storm had much more intensity and was better defined than when it crossed this island. It is, we think, central in Texas, probably at the WSW of San Antonio and northward of the city of Porfirio Diaz. . . .

Now, some circles have been written saying that the disturbance from the SE had moved by the first quadrant out over the Atlantic; we think, however that we still have it in sight as it passes through the Gulf, and that it is at present in the 4th quadrant, between Abilene and Palestine. . . .

Who is right?

Ice Warnings and the Unsinkable Titanic —1912

Wireless message of the *Mesaba* to the *Titanic*

When the Titanic launched its maiden voyage from Southampton, England, in the spring of 1912 bound for New York City, it was hailed as a triumph of a new world of science and technology. Unmatched in size and grandeur, unparalleled in design, and "unsinkable," the ship, in the eyes of pundits and philosophers alike, was a paean to the coming age of man's dominance over nature. When the glorious ship went down on April 15, never completing even its first voyage, it was testimony to something else entirely, something much simpler and more human—that arrogance, overconfidence, and a failure to heed warnings can lead to disaster.

On the second day of the voyage, the Titanic's wireless operators began receiving ice warnings from other ships in the North American shipping lanes, with several communications reporting that ships had been forced to stop in densely packed ice fields. Despite the messages, the Titanic's 30,000-horse-power engines roared on at full speed.

The warnings, pitted against the general assumption that the enormous ship could not be sunk, were ignored. One message from the Mesaba the evening of April 14 warned of a great number of large icebergs. That warning never reached the Titanic's captain, Edward J. Smith, because it did not contain a vital prefix used by wireless operators to ensure that the captains of ships being contacted be given messages personally. Later that night, another ship, the Californian, mired in the ice a few miles away, attempted to warn the Titanic, only to be told by the doomed ship's operator to "Keep out!"; he was busily attempting to catch up on a backlog of personal messages for the passengers.

The Titanic struck an iceberg at 11:40 P.M., and by 2:20 A.M., Monday, April 15, 1912, it had sunk 12,500 feet beneath the 28° F waters of the Atlantic Ocean. Of the 2,231 passengers on board, two-thirds died, including the captain and two millionaires, John Jacob Astor and Benjamin Guggenheim.

The Titanic's Captain Smith, with 40 years' experience at sea, seemed oblivious to the dangers of the ice fields, especially under the prodding of J. Bruce Ismay, his employer from the White Star Line, who was determined that the Titanic best the Atlantic crossing speed achieved by the slightly older sister ship the Olympic. In addition, Smith had long sailed the Atlantic without *benefit of information from the emerging wireless technology. His own instincts were tried and true. He rode them and his ship to the bottom of the Atlantic.*

In the aftermath of Titanic's *collision with an iceberg in April 1912, survivors in lifeboats struggled to escape from the mammoth sinking ship. But as the artist's conception suggests, there were far too few boats available, one of the several factors that not only caused the tragedy but increased its dimensions.*

Wireless Message of the *Mesaba* to the *Titanic*, April 14, 1912, 7:50 P.M.

In lat 42N to 41.25N long 49W to long 50.30W saw much heavy pack ice and great number of large icebergs also field ice. Weather good, clear.

Advertised in Advance: The Lusitania Disaster—1915

Warnings published in New York newspapers from the German government that American citizens should not board European cruise ships on the day the *Lusitania* was sunk

On a drizzly May Day afternoon in 1915, RMS Lusitania, one of the world's great, glamorous ocean liners, slowly glided from New York's Pier 54, headed on its 202nd Atlantic crossing. The magnificent Lusitania, 745 feet long with regal accommodations and Edwardian-class dining, was also fast—"a greyhound," the London Times called it. In 1908, the ship had broken the existing transatlantic speed record.

More than 1,000 passengers and a crew of 700 plus had set off that day during uncertain times. With war raging in Europe and control of the high seas at stake, the German embassy had actually inserted advertisements in a number of American newspapers warning of the danger to British ships in the waters around the British Isles. The Germans had known that British sailing ships were carrying arms, along with passengers, and the Lusitania was no exception.

Because the warning appeared only on the day of the sailing, not all those who boarded the Lusitania read it. Yet for travelers who did glance at the New York newspapers that morning, there was an alternative. The American Line's New York, with space available, sailed the same day as the Lusitania. The New York, however, required eight days to cross the Atlantic, two more days than the Lusitania. Thus, despite the German embassy warning, the Lusitania's captain, William Turner, laughingly told a reporter just before sailing that "by the look of the pier and the passenger list" the U-boats had not scared away many people.

The Lusitania was not carrying many highbrow celebrities that day. One exception was Alfred Gwynne Vanderbilt, en route to Britain for a meeting of horse breeders. In addition to his enormous inherited wealth and his horses, Vanderbilt had another interesting distinction: three years earlier, he had booked passage on the Titanic's maiden voyage but had missed the fatal cruise because of a change in plans.

The long trip across the Atlantic had been largely uneventful. On May 7, about 375 miles from Liverpool, passengers awoke to the deep blasts of the

German advertisements had warned Americans to stay off British ocean liners. After the sinking of the Lusitania, artist W. A. Rogers published in the New York Herald on August 4, 1915, this pen-and-ink drawing entitled simply "Those Flippant Americans."

liner's foghorn. Because of the fog, the ship reduced its speed from 21 to 18 knots.

That day at Buckingham Palace, Col. Edward House, close advisor to President Woodrow Wilson, was meeting with King George I. In his diary, House later wrote that his conversation with the king had actually turned to the dreaded possibility of a British liner with American passengers on board being sunk, and the name of the Lusitania had been mentioned. That evening, as House dined in the American embassy, he was given a dispatch informing him that at two in the afternoon, a German submarine had torpedoed and sunk the Lusitania.

Almost 1,200 lost their lives. One survivor said that the sinking of the ship *reminded him of the collapse of a great building during a fire. The* Lusitania *had been off the Old Head of Kinsale, which was in sight to port. According to reports, the ship had been warned on two occasions by the Admiralty that there was submarine activity along the south coast of Ireland. Inexplicably, instead of taking evasive action as he entered the war zone, the captain had steered the* Lusitania *straight for Southampton, England. U-boat captain Walter Schwieger could hardly believe his luck as the ship swung directly into his periscope sights.*

The sinking of the Lusitania *was thus a veritable catalog of warnings unheeded, both by passengers and crew.*

As for Alfred Vanderbilt, he reportedly gave up his life vest to a woman who had lost hers and stood by the railing while the Lusitania *dove to the bottom.*

Warnings Sent to New York Newspapers from the German Government, published May 1, 1915

NOTICE!

Travelers intending to embark on the Atlantic voyage are reminded that a state of war exists between Germany and her allies and Great Britain and her allies; that the zone of war includes the waters adjacent to the British Isles; that, in accordance with formal notice given by the Imperial German Government, vessels flying the flag of Great Britain, or any of her allies, are liable to destruction in those waters and that travelers sailing in the war zone on ships of Great Britain or her allies do so at their own risk.

IMPERIAL GERMAN EMBASSY
Washington, D.C., April 22, 1915

Eleven Months' Warning—1941

U.S. Ambassador to Japan Joseph Clark Grew to U.S. State Department, on rumors in Tokyo of plan to attack Pearl Harbor

Some very influential national figures did not foresee Japanese war aims against the United States. Gen. Douglas MacArthur, at a dinner party in Manila on September 27, 1940, said, "Japan will never join the Axis." The next day, Japan joined the Axis. On December 7, 1941, Wendell Wilkie, former Republican candidate for president, predicted, "We won't be at war with Japan within 48 hours, 48 days or 48 years."

Nevertheless, the Pearl Harbor attack did not suddenly occur without warning. Indeed, on January 27, 1941, 11 months prior to the attack, the U.S. Ambassador to Japan, Joseph Clark Grew, warned the State Department that he had heard from many quarters that such an attack against the United States was not only likely but that the target would be Pearl Harbor.

Adm. Isoroku Yamamoto assumed command of Japan's Combined Fleet in August 1939. Sometime between January and March 1940, he devised a plan to destroy the U.S. Navy in Hawaii. With trade sanctions and embargoes creating increasing hostility with the United States and draining Japanese oil reserves throughout 1941, Yamamoto approached other Japanese officials about his ideas of an all-out, massive hit on Pearl Harbor, one that would not only ruin U.S. naval power but also demoralize the American people and its government.

It was from these discussions in early 1941 that Ambassador Grew began hearing leaks of information. No one in Washington seemed particularly concerned. Most senior American military experts believed that if the Japanese launched an attack against the United States, it would be in the Philippines because of its strategic geographic location.

During the spring and summer, additional intelligence, especially gathered by the navy, indicated an imminent move by the Japanese. But, as December 7, 1941, approached, the experts did not see Pearl Harbor as the most likely point of attack. They should have paid attention to Ambassador Grew.

Wire of Ambassador to Japan Joseph Clark Grew to U.S. State Department, January 7, 1941

TOKYO, January 27, 1941 6 p.m. A member of the Embassy was told by my . . . colleague that from many quarters, including a Japanese one, he had heard that a surprise mass attack on Pearl Harbor was planned by the Japanese military forces, in case of "trouble" between Japan and the United States; that the attack would involve the use of all the Japanese military facilities. My colleague said that he was prompted to pass this on because it had come to him from many sources, although the plan seemed fantastic.

GREW

Thomas Jefferson, Woodrow Wilson, and Ho Chi Minh—1945

Ho Chi Minh's Declaration of Independence for Vietnam

O n September 2, 1945, in Hanoi's Ba Dinh Square, Ho Chi Minh announced Vietnamese independence and presented a Declaration of Independence for the Democratic Republic of Vietnam. It began: "All men are created equal. They are endowed by their Creator with certain inalienable rights, among these are Life, Liberty, and the pursuit of Happiness."

It had been a quarter of a century since he had drafted another such declaration of independence. In 1919, he was living in Paris. His name then was Nguyen Ai Quoc. His document at that time was modeled after the 14-point declaration of U.S. president Woodrow Wilson that called for independence for all peoples. Nguyen Ai Quoc wanted an opportunity to present his declaration at the Versailles Peace Conference, and he had asked for a meeting with President Wilson, seeking to win American support for his cause against French colonialist rule. He had not been granted an interview.

Born in Annam in 1890, he left Vietnam on a French merchant ship at the age of 21. After working in London for several years, he moved to France and became active in the Vietnamese community in Paris. After his efforts were ignored at the Versailles conference, he joined the French Communist party and rose rapidly in the Communist movement. For a time, he worked in Moscow and then in Canton, where he organized the Vietnamese Revolutionary Youth. When the Chinese leader Chiang Kai-shek broke with the Communists, Ho (the former Quoc) returned to Moscow. Later, in Hong Kong, he created the Indochinese Communist party, which he headed for the rest of his life.

During World War II, Ho Chi Minh cooperated with American intelligence in Indochina from 1943 through 1945. Although trained in Moscow, he was primarily a nationalist seeking independence for his country. He helped rescue downed American pilots and provided information on Japanese troop movements. Many navy and OSS members expressed admiration for him.

And on V-J Day, he presented his new constitution to Vietnam. He would be Vietnam's Jefferson. He hoped that the document, beginning with the words of Jefferson's Declaration of Independence, would encourage the Americans to see the cause of the Democratic Republic of Vietnam as similar to the founding of the United States and that the United States would aid him in his efforts.

The United States did not respond. The French, with no opposition from the United States, occupied their Indochinese colony. After inconclusive negotia-

tions, military conflict broke out in 1947 between the French and Ho's Viet Minh independence forces.

The United States financed, armed, and advised the French until 1954, when, faced with the reality of French defeat, the Eisenhower administration sought to establish an anticommunist nationalist alternative to Ho Chi Minh. The result was the partition of Vietnam and the planting of the seeds of a new and bigger war. The United States and Ho Chi Minh would take opposite roads to a showdown. The United States had lost opportunities it might have had to play an early role in the direction of Vietnamese independence.

Ho Chi Minh's Declaration of Independence for the Democratic Republic of Vietnam, September 2, 1945

Hanoi

"All men are created equal. They are endowed by their Creator with certain inalienable rights, among these are Life, Liberty, and the pursuit of Happiness."

This immortal statement was made in the Declaration of Independence of the United States of America in 1776. In a broader sense, this means: All the peoples on the earth are equal from birth, all the peoples have a right to live, to be happy and free.

The Declaration of the French Revolution made in 1791 on the Rights of Man and the Citizen also states: "All men are born free and with equal rights, and must always remain free and have equal rights." Those are undeniable truths.

Nevertheless, for more than eight years, the French imperialists, abusing the standard of Liberty, Equality, and Fraternity, have violated our Fatherland and oppressed our fellow-citizens. They have acted contrary to the ideals of humanity and justice.

In the field of politics, they have deprived our people of every democratic liberty.

They have enforced inhuman laws; they have set up three distinct political regimes in the North, the Center and the South of Vietnam in order to wreck our national unity and prevent our people from being united. They have built more prisons than schools. They have mercilessly slain our patriots—they have drowned our uprisings in rivers of blood.

They have fettered public opinion; they have practiced obscurantism against our people.

To weaken our race they have forced us to use opium and alcohol.

Ho Chi Minh's life and career spanned generations of international wars and politics, from his early efforts to enlist the support of President Woodrow Wilson to help Vietnamese independence to the protracted hostilities between Vietnam and the United States decades later. In this New York Times *photo, he is seen walking with his delegation on a French beach.*

In the fields of economics, they have fleeced us to the backbone, impoverished our people, and devastated our land.

They have robbed us of our rice fields, our mines, our forests, and our raw materials. They have monopolized the issuing of banknotes and the export trade.

They have invented numerous unjustifiable taxes and reduced our people, especially our peasantry, to a state of extreme poverty.

They have hampered the prospering of our national bourgeoisie; they have mercilessly exploited our workers.

In the autumn of 1940, when the Japanese Fascists violated Indochina's territory to establish new bases in their fight against the Allies, the French imperialists went down on their bended knees and handed over our country to them.

Thus, from that date, our people were subjected to the double yoke of the French and the Japanese. Their sufferings and miseries increased. The result was that from the end of last year to the beginning of this year, from Quang Tri province to the North of Vietnam, more than two million of our fellow-citizens died from starvation. On March 9, the French troops were disarmed by the Japanese. The French colonialists either fled or surrendered, showing that not only were they incapable of "protecting" us, but that, in the span of five years, they had twice sold our country to the Japanese.

On several occasions before March 9, the Vietminh League urged the French to ally themselves with it against the Japanese. Instead of agreeing to this proposal, the French colonialists so intensified their terrorist activities against the Vietminh members that before fleeing they massacred a great number of our political prisoners detained at Yen Bay and Cao Bang.

Notwithstanding all this, our fellow-citizens have always manifested toward the French a tolerant and humane attitude. Even after the Japanese putsch of March 1945, the Vietminh League helped many Frenchmen to cross the frontier, rescued some of them from Japanese jails, and protected French lives and property.

From the autumn of 1940, our country had in fact ceased to be a French colony and had become a Japanese possession.

After the Japanese had surrendered to the Allies, our whole people rose to regain our national sovereignty and to found the Democratic Republic of Vietnam. The truth is that we have wrested our independence from the Japanese and not from the French.

The French have fled, the Japanese have capitulated, Emperor Bao Dai has abdicated. Our people have broken the chains which for nearly a century have fettered them and have won independence for the Fatherland. Our people at the same time have overthrown the monarchic regime that has reigned supreme for dozens of centuries. In its place has been established the present Democratic Republic.

For these reasons, we, members of the Provisional Government, representing the whole Vietnamese people, declare that from now on we break off all relations of a colonial character with France; we repeal all the international obligation that France has so far subscribed to on behalf of Vietnam and we abolish all the special rights the French have unlawfully acquired in our Fatherland. The whole Vietnamese people, animated by a common purpose, are determined to fight to the bitter end against any attempt by the French colonialists to reconquer their country.

We are convinced that the Allied nations which at Tehran and San Francisco have acknowledged the principles of self-determination and equality of nations, will not refuse to acknowledge the independence of Vietnam.

A people who have courageously opposed French domination for more than eighty years, a people who have fought side by side with the Allies against the Fascists during these last years, such a people must be free and independent.

For these reasons, we, members of the Provisional Government of the Democratic Republic of Vietnam, solemnly declare to the world that Vietnam has the right to be a free and independent country and in fact it is so already. The entire Vietnamese people are determined to mobilize all their physical and mental strength, to sacrifice their lives and property in order to safeguard their independence and liberty.

A Ripsnorting Chance to "Give 'Em Hell" Missed—1950

Telegram of Senator Joseph McCarthy to President Truman, demanding he provide Congress with a full accounting of communist infiltrations, and draft of Truman's response

have in my hand fifty-seven cases of individuals who would appear to be either card-carrying members or certainly loyal to the Communist Party, but who nevertheless are still helping to shape our foreign policy." With a speech in Wheeling, West Virginia, in February 1950, the junior senator from Wisconsin, Joseph McCarthy, launched his personal crusade to weed out Communist infiltration of the U.S. government. Two days later a telegram from McCarthy to President Harry Truman was made public. In the telegram, McCarthy repeated his charge that Truman's State Department was swarming with Communists and Communist sympathizers.

The McCarthy phenomenon exploded at a time of escalating Cold War fears and tensions. Two days before McCarthy's Wheeling speech, the United States had recognized the newly formed anti-Communist state of Vietnam. Meetings of the U.N. Security Council were under way in New York without the participation of representatives of the Soviet Union, who were boycotting the meetings because of the Security Council's refusal to oust Nationalist Chinese representatives. China had fallen to the Communists.

President Truman was a fighter, not one to take shots without a quick counterattack, certainly not one to blithely accept the kind of public attack waged against him and his administration by McCarthy. Truman drafted an intemperate response excoriating McCarthy as unfit to serve in the U.S. government. Whether Truman sent the letter to McCarthy is not certain; what is clear, however, is that he did not make it public.

With anti-Communist rhetoric filling the airways, with the House Un-American Activities Committee and other congressional committees scurrying to call hearings about purging the country of Communist infestation—and with a recent conviction in January of former State Department official Alger Hiss for perjury after he denied engaging in espionage—the freshman senator from Wisconsin was in his ascendancy.

Over the next few years, McCarthy's sweeping, hysterical investigations would escalate until finally destroyed by a Senate resolution of condemnation that said McCarthy had acted "contrary to senatorial ethics and tended to *bring the Senate into dishonor and disrepute, to obstruct the constitutional processes of the Senate, and to impair its dignity."*

Harry Truman had said much the same thing in his letter written in February 1950. If he had made it public, it would have expressed confidence in his administration, offering support of his appointees as well as career diplomats; it would have put McCarthy on notice that he was in for a vigorous fight. It was a chance for Truman to "Give 'Em Hell"; unfortunately, in this case, he did not.

Telegram of Senator Joseph McCarthy to President Harry S. Truman, February 11, 1950

The President
The White House

In a Lincoln Day speech at Wheeling Thursday night I stated that the State Department harbors a nest of communists and communist sympathizers who are helping to shape our foreign policy. I further stated that I have in my possession the names of 57 communists who are in the State Department at present. A State Department spokesman flatly denied this and claimed that there is not a single communist in the department. You can convince yourself of the falsity of the State Department claim very easily. You will recall that you personally appointed a board to screen State Department employees for the purpose of weeding out fellow travelers. Your board did a pains-taking job, and named hundreds which it listed as "dangerous to the security of the nation" because of communistic connections.

While the records are not available to me, I know absolutely that of one group of approximately 300 certified to the secretary for discharge, he actually discharged only approximately 50. I understand that this was done after lengthy consultation with Alger Hiss. I would suggest, therefore, Mr. President, that you simply pick up your phone and ask Mr. Acheson how many of those whom your board had labeled as dangerous, he failed to discharge. The day the House Un-American Activities Committee exposed Alger Hiss as an important link in an inter-national communist spy ring, you signed an order forbidding the State Departments giving to the Congress any information in regard to the disloyalty or the communistic connections of anyone in that department, despite this State Department blackout,

Draft

My dear Senator:

    I read your telegram of February eleventh from Reno, Nevada with a great deal of interest and this is the first time in my experience, and I was ten years in the Senate, that I ever heard of a Senator trying to discredit his own Government before the world. You know that isn't done by honest public officials. Your telegram is not only not true and an insolent approach to a situation that should have been worked out between man and man but it shows conclusively that you are not even fit to have a hand in the operation of the Government of the United States.

    I am very sure that the people of Wisconsin are extremely sorry that they are represented by a person who has as little sense of responsibility as you have.

                    Sincerely yours,

                    [HST]

In early February 1950, Senator Joseph McCarthy, in a blistering speech in West Virginia and then in a letter to President Harry Truman, charged that Communists had, in great numbers, gained positions in the U.S. State Department and that the president had been negligent. In Truman's papers housed in the Truman Library in Independence, Missouri, is this draft letter. There is no evidence it was sent.

we have been able to compile a list of 57 communists in the State Department. This list is available to you, but you can get a much longer list by ordering the Secretary Acheson to give you a list of these whom your own board listed as being disloyal, and who are still working in the State Department. I believe the following is the minimum which can be expected of you in this case.

    (1) That you demand that Acheson give you and the proper congressional committee the names and a complete report on all of those who were placed in the department by Alger Hiss, and all of those still working in the State Department who were listed by your board as bad

security risks because of the communistic connections.

(2) That under no circumstances could a congressional committee obtain any information or help from the executive department in exposing communists.

Failure on your part will label the Democratic Party of being the bed-fellow of inter-national Communism. Certainly this label is not deserved by the hundreds of thousands of loyal American Democrats throughout the nation, and by the sizable number of able loyal Democrats in both the Senate and the House.

Joe McCarthy U.S.S. Wis.

Draft of Truman's Response to McCarthy

My dear Senator:

I read your telegram of February eleventh from Reno, Nevada with a great deal of interest and this is the first time in my experience, and I was ten years in the Senate, that I ever heard of a Senator trying to discredit his own Government before the world. You know that isn't done by honest public officials. Your telegram is not only not true and an insolent approach to a situation that should have been worked out between man and man but it shows conclusively that you are not even fit to have a hand in the operation of the Government of the United States.

I am very sure that the people of Wisconsin are extremely sorry that they are represented by a person who has as little sense of responsibility as you have.

Sincerely yours,

[HST]

Left at the Space Race Starting Gate—1957

Memorandum of conference with President Eisenhower following Soviet launch of *Sputnik*

The Cold War was many things; as much as anything it was a race—a capitalist vs. Communist race for nuclear development and deployment, a propaganda race, a military arms race, a scientific discovery race, an education race, a physical fitness race—all of which permeated the lives of everyday Americans.

In October 1957, the Soviet Union launched the world's first intercontinental ballistic missile, with the first artificial Earth satellite, Sputnik, aboard. On both sides of the Iron Curtain, scientists had been laboring intensely to be the first to achieve this early space conquest. Indeed, in the United States, rivalries between separate armed forces had caused consternation and some delays. If the United States was going to be first in space, then the army must do the job . . . or the navy. The Defense Department had given priority to the navy's Vanguard Program and charged it with deploying America's first satellite. The army's Redstone Program had conducted test flights but had not been allowed to launch satellites ahead of the navy.

And now, the Soviets had that 184-pound little moon up there circling the Earth, equipped with transmitters to broadcast on frequencies at 20 and 40 MHz: beep, beep, beeping every 90 minutes, reminding everyone of what had just happened—the Soviets had beaten the Americans into space.

Americans reacted with predictable anxiety. Politicians and editorialists beat on the U.S. educational system for having fallen behind Soviet schools in the sciences. As a result, engineering colleges were flooded with new students following a new career opportunity and at the same time fulfilling their patriotic obligation to take on the Soviets in the space race.

President Dwight Eisenhower was surprised and annoyed at the Soviet success but not as anxious as everyone else about the military advantages. From U2 spy flights over the Soviet Union, the U.S. government had photographs of the Soviet launch facilities. Eisenhower and his advisors knew that the Sputnik achievement did not mean that the United States was suddenly vulnerable as never before. Nevertheless, the administration would now be stuck with the "Missile Gap" problem—the need to catch up with the Soviets in that particular race.

According to American scientists, they could have put the first satellite in *orbit in 1956 with a Jupiter rocket that reached 700 miles altitude and was just 1,000 m.p.h. short of orbital speed. A number of issues, nevertheless, discouraged the administration, including the embarrassment over the U2 shootdown. A new satellite would have been labeled as another violation of Soviet air space. And with the separate military services each having its own preference of how to deploy space vehicles, the lack of coordination crippled development.*

When Eisenhower met with his advisors shortly after the launch of Sputnik, it had become apparent that the satellite had become a major propaganda defeat. If he could have foreseen the national and international hype over the Soviet success and the consternation and embarrassment felt by Americans, Eisenhower probably would have placed greater emphasis on launching a satellite. And the United States had been in a position to beat the Soviets to it.

Memorandum of Conference with President Eisenhower following Soviet Launch of *Sputnik*, October 8, 1957

Others Present:

Secretary Quarles
Dr. Waterman
Mr. Hagen
Mr. Holaday
Governor Adams
General Parsons
Mr. Hagerty
Governor Pyle
Mr. Harlow
General Cutler
General Goodpaster

Secretary Quarles began by reviewing a memorandum prepared in Defense for the President on the subject of the earth satellite (dated October 7, 1957). He left a copy with the President. He reported that the Soviet launching on October 4th had apparently been highly successful.

The President asked Secretary Quarles about the report that had come to his attention to the effect that the Redstone could have been used and could have placed a satellite in orbit many months ago. Secretary Quarles said there was no doubt that the Redstone, had it been used, could have orbited a satellite a year or more ago. The Science Advisory Committee had felt, however, that it was better to have the earth satellite proceed separately from military development. One reason was to stress the peaceful character of the effort, and a second was to avoid the inclusion of material, to which foreign scientists might be given access, which is used in our own military rockets. He said that the Army feels it could erect a satellite four months from now if given the order—this would still be one month prior to the estimated date for the Vanguard. The President said that when this information reaches the Congress, they are bound to ask why this action was not taken. He recalled, however, that timing was never given too much importance in our own program, which was tied to the IGY and confirmed that, in order for all scientists to be able to look at the instrument, it had to be kept away from military secrets. Secretary Quarles pointed out that the Army plan would require some modifications of the instrumentation in the missile.

He went on to add that the Russians have in fact done us a good turn, unintentionally, in establishing the concept of freedom of international space—this seems to be generally accepted as orbital space, in which the missile is making an inoffensive passage.

The President asked what kind of information could be conveyed by the signals reaching us from the Russian satellite. Secretary Quarles said the Soviets say that it is simply a pulse to permit location of the missile through radar direction finders. Following the meeting, Dr. Waterman indicated that there is some kind of modulation on the signals, which may mean that some coding is being done, although it might conceivably be accidental.

The President asked the group to look ahead five years, and asked about a reconnaissance vehicle. Secretary Quarles said the Air Force has a research program in this area and gave a general description of the project.

Governor Adams recalled that Dr. Pusey had said that we had never thought of this as a crash program, as the Russians apparently did. We were working simply to develop and transmit scientific knowledge. The President thought that to make a sudden shift in our approach now would be to belie the attitude we have had all along. Secretary Quarles said that such a shift would create service tensions in the Pentagon. Mr. Holaday said he planned to study with the Army the back up of the Navy program with the Redstone, adapting it to the instrumentation.

There was some discussion concerning the Soviet request as to whether we would like to put instruments of ours aboard one of their satellites. He said our instruments would be ready for this. Several present pointed out that our instruments contain parts which, if made available to the Russians, would give them substantial technological information.

A. J. Goodpaster
Brigadier General, USA

Genocide Alert Ignored—1994

Coded cable to United Nations from Maj. Gen. Roméo Dallaire, U.N. Force Commander in Rwanda, warning of imminent genocide, and the United Nations' response

There were a number of warnings. Most compelling was a January 11, 1994, telegram from U.N. Force Commander Maj. Gen. Roméo Dallaire, head of a peacekeeping force in Rwanda, urgently requesting protection for an informant who had revealed to him grisly Hutu plans to exterminate the Tutsi. The informant had also told of plans to slaughter Belgian troops to hasten Belgium's withdrawal from Rwanda. There had been earlier reports of guns being delivered to civilians at secret meetings designed to incite the grimmest violence imaginable. There had been many extremist radio broadcasts and press editorials calling for uprising. As early as 1993, the Human Rights Watch and other organizations made available to government officials in the United States and to the United Nations a litany of warning signs: selective executions, the formations of armed militia by extremist political parties, the drawing up of lists of enemies, and the stockpiling of weapons. The country was on the verge of a heinous outbreak of racial cleansing.

At the United Nations, the sense of urgency did not match the gravity of the crisis. When the Security Council took up the issue, they complained about the lack of specific information. Members talked in generalizations about the "confusion" and the "chaotic" nature of the situation. Despite mounting evidence that a massive ethnic slaughter was imminent, the Security Council made only small increases in troop deployment.

From the first hours after the killings began, it became clear that the violence was a systematic genocide of the Tutsi. Nevertheless, officials in Washington, reluctant to become involved in the affairs of the obscure African nation, continued to downplay the horror that was unfolding. They actually cautioned officials to avoid the word "genocide" in describing the violence, most likely because of the moral and legal imperatives to such a designation. Instead, policy makers referred to the killing as a "tribal conflict" or "tribal warfare" and to Rwanda as a "failed state." A columnist for the New York Times used the two terms in a single sentence.

A number of years after the slaughter, President Bill Clinton told a group of survivors that the United States should have been more vigilant, more responsive to "the most intensive slaughter in this blood-filled century we are

about to leave. . . . All over the world," he said, "there were people like me sit-
ting in offices who did not fully appreciate the depth and the speed with which
you were being engulfed by this unimaginable terror."

Hutu extremists killed between 500,000 and one million people. It was the worst genocide since the Nazis killed six million Jews in World War II.

If the United States had acted swiftly to investigate and corroborate Dallaire's information; if the information and the need for dramatic and imme-diate action had been communicated to policy makers in the United States and the United Nations; if the United States had sponsored an emergency diplo-matic meeting of governments with influence on Rwanda, especially its neigh-bors, and demanded an immediate accounting by Hutu extremists of its arms caches on the threat of massive retaliation; if, based on Dallaire's messages and others, the United Nations had provided him with the resources he requested to combat the imminent violence—if these actions had been taken, several hundred thousand lives might have been saved.

Coded Cable to United Nations from Maj. Gen. Roméo Dallaire, U.N. Force Commander in Rwanda, January 11, 1994

TO: BARIL/DPKO/UNATIONS NEW YORK
FROM: DALLAIRE/UNAMIR/KIGALI
FAX NO: MOST IMMEDIATE-CODE CABLE-212-xxx-xxxx

INMARSAT:
FAX NO: 011-xxx-xxxxx
SUBJECT: REQUEST FOR PROTECTION OF INFORMANT
ATTN: MGEN BARIL ROOM NO: 2052
TOTAL NUMBER OF TRANSMITTED PAGES
INCLUDING THIS ONE: 2

1. Force commander put in contact with informant by very important government politician. Informant is a top level trainer in the cadre of interhamwe-armed militia of MRND.

2. He informed us he was in charge of last Saturdays demonstra-tions which aims were to target deputies of opposition parties coming to ceremonies and Belgian soldiers. They hoped to provoke the RPF BN to engage (being fired upon) the demonstrators and provoke a civil war. Deputies were to be assassinated upon entry or exit from Parliament. Belgian troops were to be provoked and if Belgians sol-

diers restored to force a number of them were to be killed and thus guarantee Belgian withdrawal from Rwanda.

3. Informant confirmed 48 RGF PARA CDO and a few members of the gendarmerie participated in demonstrations in plain clothes. Also at least one Minister of the MRND and the sous-prefect of Kigali were in the demonstration. RGF and Interhamwe provided radio communications.

4. Informant is a former security member of the president. He also stated he is paid RF150,000 per month by the MRND party to train Interhamwe. Direct link is to chief of staff RGF and president of the MRND for financial and material support.

5. Interhamwe has trained 1700 men in RGF military camps outside the capital. The 1700 are scattered in groups of 40 throughout Kigali. Since UNAMIR deployed he has trained 300 personnel in three week training sessions at RGF camps. Training focus was discipline, weapons, explosives, close combat and tactics.

6. Principal aim of Interhamwe in the past was to protect Kigali from RPF. Since UNAMIR mandate he has been ordered to register all Tutsi in Kigali. He suspects it is for their extermination. Example he gave was that in 20 minutes his personnel could kill up to 1000 Tutsis.

7. Informant states he disagrees with anti-Tutsi extermination. He supports opposition to RPF but cannot support killing of innocent persons. He also stated that he believes the president does not have full control over all elements of his old party/faction.

8. Informant is prepared to provide location of major weapons cache with at least 135 weapons. He already has distributed 110 weapons including 35 with ammunition and can give us details of their location. Type of weapons are G3 and AK47 provided by RGF. He was ready to go to the arms cache tonight—if we gave him the following guarantee. He requests that he and his family (his wife and four children) be placed under our protection.

9. It is our intention to take action within the next 36 hours with a possible H HR of Wednesday at dawn (local). Informant states that hostilities may commence again if political deadlock ends.Violence could take place day of the ceremonies or the day after. Therefore Wednesday will give greatest chance of success and also be most timely to provide significant input to ongoing political negotiations.

10. It is recommended that informant be granted protection and evacuated out of Rwanda. This HQ does not have previous UN experience in such matters and urgently requests guidance. No contact has as yet been made to any embassy in order to inquire if they are prepared to protect him for a period of time by granting diplomatic immunity in their embassy in Kigali before moving him and his family out of the country.

11. Force commander will be meeting with the very very important political person tomorrow morning in order to ensure that this individual is conscious of all parameters of his involvement. Force commander does have certain reservations on the suddenness of the change of heart of the informant to come clean with this information. Recce of armed cache and detailed planning of raid to go on late tomorrow. Possibility of a trap not fully excluded, as this may be a set-up against this very very important political person. Force commander to inform SRSG first thing in morning to ensure his support.

U.N. Response to Dallaire's Cable, January 11, 1994

TO: BOOH-BOOH/DALLAIRE, UNAMIR ONLY
NO DISTRIBUTION
FROM: ANNAN, UNATIONS, NEW YORK
NUMBER: UNAMIR: 100
SUBJECT: Contacts with Informant

1. We have carefully reviewed the situation in the light of your MIR-79. We cannot agree to the operation contemplated in paragraph 7 of your cable, as it clearly goes beyond the mandate entrusted to UNAMIR under resolution 872 (1993).

2. However, on the assumption that you are convinced that the information provided by the informant is absolutely reliable, we request you to undertake the initiatives described in the following paragraphs.

3. SRSG and FC should request urgent meeting with the President. At that meeting you should inform the President that you have received apparently reliable information concerning the activities of the Interhamwe militia which represents a clear threat to the peace process. You should inform him that these activities include the training and deployment of subversive groups in Kigali as well as the storage and distribution of weapons to these groups.

4. You should inform him that these activities constitute a clear violation of the provisions of the Arusha peace agreement and of the Kigali weapons-secure area. You should assume that he is not aware of

these activities, but insist that he must ensure that these subversive activities are immediately discontinued and inform you within 48 hours of the measures taken in this regard, including the recovery of the arms which have been distributed.

5. You should advise the President that, if any violence occurs in Kigali, you would have to immediately bring to the attention of the Security Council the information you have received on the activities of the militia, undertake investigations to determine who is responsible and make appropriate recommendations to the Security Council.

6. Before meeting with the President you should inform the Ambassadors of Belgium, France and the United States of your intentions and suggest to them that they may wish to consider making a similar démarche.

7. For security considerations, we leave it to your discretion to decide whether to inform the PM(D) of your plans before or after the meeting with the President. When you meet with the PM(D), you should explain to him the limits of your mandate. You should also assure him that, while the mandate of UNAMIR does not allow you to extend protection to the informant, his identity and your contacts with him will not be repeat not be revealed.

8. If you have major problems with the guidance provided above, you may consult us further. We wish to stress, however, that the overriding consideration is the need to avoid entering into a course of action that might lead to the use of force and unanticipated repercussions.

Regards,

For Lack of a Ferret: Aldrich Ames and the CIA Fiasco—1985–94

1997 report of inspector general of the Department of Justice on the FBI's performance in uncovering espionage activities of Aldrich Ames

On February 21, 1994, FBI agents arrived at the Arlington, Virginia, home of a 52-year-old employee of the CIA. They were there to take Aldrich H. Ames and his wife, Maria del Rosario Casas Ames, into custody for espionage activities on behalf of the Soviet Union. The agents had arrived years late.

Ames, a 31-year veteran of the CIA, had been a career officer in the agency's clandestine service, responsible for collecting secret intelligence through a spy network.

After his arrest, Ames admitted that he had engaged in espionage for nine years, from the spring of 1985 until his arrest in February 1994, that he had compromised "virtually all Soviet agents of the CIA and other American and foreign services known to me" and had provided a "huge quantity of information on United States foreign, defense and security policies."

Ames had turned over a wealth of classified information to the KGB that resulted in the exposure of a number of CIA and FBI intelligence sources and led to their executions. Ames was the first active-duty CIA clandestine service officer to be caught spying for the Soviet Union. His actions virtually destroyed the CIA's human intelligence network in the Soviet Union.

The motive? Money. Several million dollars. At the time of his arrest, Ames owned a new Jaguar and a $540,000 home that he had paid for in cash. The enormous incongruity of a middle-level federal employee accumulating all these trappings of wealth failed to arouse significant suspicions among his superiors. Although Ames was a poor performer and a known alcohol abuser, his professional and personal derelictions were overlooked and covered up because he was a member of what was considered to be an elite corps of intelligence professionals. As part of their plea agreements, both defendants agreed to cooperate with the government to explain the nature and extent of their espionage activities. Both signed agreements forfeiting the proceeds of their espionage activities to the U.S. government. In April 1994, Ames was sentenced to life in prison; his wife was later given 63 months.

In 1997, the inspector general released a report on the Ames affair. There were serious suspicions; there were warnings, all of which went relatively unheeded.

Counterintelligence experts, the report said, were convinced by 1988 that the deaths of agents in 1985 and 1986 had likely been caused by "human penetration" and that there was probably a mole who had "across-the-board access to sensitive Soviet operations." It took the FBI and CIA another six years to find him—the Jaguar-driving, fast-living, cash-paying snoop right there in Arlington.

Excerpts from Report of Inspector General of the Department of Justice on the FBI's Performance in Uncovering Espionage Activities of Aldrich Ames, April 21, 1997

Our review revealed that throughout nearly the entire nine-year period of Ames' espionage, FBI management devoted inadequate attention to determining the cause of the sudden, unprecedented, and catastrophic losses suffered by both the FBI and the CIA in their Soviet intelligence programs. Indeed, FBI's senior management was almost entirely unaware of the scope and significance of the mid-1980s losses and of the FBI's limited efforts to determine their cause. FBI senior management's lack of knowledge concerning the intelligence losses contributed to the FBI's failure to devote priority attention to this matter, particularly after 1987. Moreover, the FBI never showed any sustained interest, prior to mid-1991, in investigating the enormous intelligence losses suffered by the CIA. Even when a joint effort was initiated in mid-1991, that effort suffered from inadequate management attention as well as insufficient resources.

The inadequate briefing of senior FBI managers also led to the FBI's failure to fulfill its statutory obligation under Section 502 of the National Security Act of 1947 (50 United States Code, Section 413(a)) to notify the Congressional intelligence committees of "any significant intelligence failure[s]." Clearly, the entire scope of the losses sustained by the FBI and CIA in 1985 and 1986 falls within the meaning of the statute's notice provision. The FBI's senior managers never understood the scope and significance of these losses, however, and therefore were in no position even to consider briefing Congress on this matter.

A. Findings Concerning the FBI's Performance during the 1985 to September 1987 Period

In 1986, the FBI learned that two of its most important Soviet assets had been compromised. The FBI quickly formed a task force of six agents, code-named ANLACE, to determine how these critical assets had been compromised.

The ANLACE Task Force soon encountered serious obstacles in attempting to determine how the FBI's assets were compromised. When agents attempted to construct an access list showing the FBI personnel who had knowledge of the assets, they determined that as many as 250 FBI employees at the FBI's Washington Field Office alone likely had knowledge of these cases. Given this fact, the ANLACE team made no effort to determine whether any FBI employee with knowledge of the cases had any special vulnerabilities, such as unreported contacts with Soviets, alcohol or drug dependency, or a sudden and unexplained increase in wealth. Instead, once the task force had completed its examination of the operational details of the compromised cases, the investigation of their compromise turned largely to potential explanations outside the FBI, and primarily at the CIA, about which the ANLACE team knew very little.

Ultimately, the ANLACE Task Force issued a final report in September 1987 that failed to resolve the cause or causes of the FBI's recent losses. While the report stated that the ANLACE team had found no evidence of a current penetration of the FBI, the report did not reveal that the team had essentially conducted no investigation of FBI personnel with access to the compromised cases. In addition, the ANLACE report failed to disclose that the CIA, which had access to information concerning the FBI's compromised cases, was simultaneously suffering unprecedented asset losses in its Soviet program.

As a result of the information Ames delivered to the Soviets in June 1985, the CIA had suffered major losses in its Soviet asset pool. Those losses were reported to ANLACE team members and to their FBI Headquarters supervisors at a series of joint FBI/CIA conferences between December 1986 and December 1988. By early 1987, CIA personnel attending these joint conferences had reported to the FBI that the CIA's Soviet program had rapidly suffered unprecedented losses of its most significant assets at the same time the FBI was experiencing its asset losses. The ANLACE team did not disclose this fact in the ANLACE report, however, and our investigation revealed that senior FBI managers at that time, including the FBI Director and the Assistant Director-in-Charge of the Intelligence Division, never gained a true understanding of the scope and significance of the CIA's asset losses in 1985 and 1986.

In sum, between 1986 and September 1987, the FBI was a passive recipient of information concerning the serious losses suffered by the CIA in its Soviet program. Senior FBI managers were unaware of the CIA's losses, while mid-level FBI supervisors and FBI line personnel appear to have believed that receipt of this information imposed no responsibility on the FBI.

Although the events of 1985 and 1986 strongly suggested that the CIA and FBI asset losses were related, the FBI made little effort to convince the CIA to embark on a joint investigation of this problem. Numerous FBI and CIA personnel whom we interviewed agreed that the FBI and the CIA should have pursued a joint investigation of the 1985–86 compromises once the scope of the losses became clear. The FBI's failure to press for a joint investigation with the CIA stemmed primarily from the inadequate briefing of the FBI's most senior management and from the FBI's understanding, at this time, that the CIA would resist sharing sensitive intelligence information.

If the FBI and the CIA had initiated a joint investigation of these losses in 1987 or 1988, there is reason to believe that Ames would have emerged as a mole suspect. Access lists developed after mid-1991, but which could have been prepared earlier, showed that Ames was one of only about forty CIA employees with across-the-board access to the assets compromised in 1985 and 1986. If certain investigative steps were undertaken with respect to these individuals, such as determining whether any had unreported contacts with Soviets, or had suddenly evidenced unexplained wealth, Ames would have come under suspicion. Indeed, the most compelling circumstantial evidence against Ames—the correlation between several meetings he had in 1985 and 1986 with a Soviet diplomat and large cash deposits that he had made to his bank accounts the next business day following those meetings—was available in record form in 1987 and 1988. However, because there was no joint investigation at this time and because the necessary investigative steps were not taken, this information was not requested by either CIA or FBI investigators until the summer of 1992.

ALMOST
VAGARIES OF WAR
HISTORY

British Frustration and the Saratoga Debacle—1777

I t was early in the war. Gen. George Washington had successfully engaged the British forces in the New York City area in early January 1777. In March, Congress met in Philadelphia to discuss ways to enlist foreign aid in the conflict, especially from France.

For their part, the British groped for a strategy to crush the rebellion in its infancy. In September 1776, Gen. William Howe occupied New York City, defeating Washington's army in the process but failing to destroy it. Meanwhile, in London, Gen. John "Gentleman Johnny" Burgoyne proposed cutting the rebellious colonies in half and isolating the center of resistance, New England, by a thrust under his command down the Hudson Valley in New York to link up with Howe's troops advancing north from New York City.

Burgoyne began his campaign in mid-June 1777 but soon became bogged down in the roadless wilderness and fell under attack by American rebel forces around Saratoga. A foray to obtain supplies for his hungry troops was decisively stopped at Bennington, Vermont, in August. Burgoyne needed reinforcements or faced the prospect of a military defeat that would not only blacken his military reputation but also galvanize American resistance.

Gentleman Johnny, however, was facing not only American troops; he was facing the folly of a jealous rival on his own side, Gen. William Howe, a man of strong ego who was not convinced that Burgoyne needed reinforcements and was not eager to lend a hand to his rival even if he did. With Burgoyne's men on half rations, many sick, and supplies dwindling daily, Howe decided not to head to northern New York but to take his own army, three times the size of Burgoyne's, south to attack Philadelphia.

On August 10, 1777, in a coded message to Burgoyne, Sir William Clinton, British military commander in New York City who had tried to persuade Howe to send reinforcements to Burgoyne, wrote to his beleaguered friend now encamped near Saratoga, New York, that Howe's actions had been "the worst he could take." Indeed.

Howe's failure to reinforce Burgoyne, as much a personal rebuff to Burgoyne as a considered military decision, led to Gentleman Johnny's capitulation in October 1777. Under the terms of the Saratoga Convention, the remains of Burgoyne's defeated army laid down its arms, was marched to Boston and shipped to England with the understanding that the men were not to fight again in the war against the colonies.

At this stage of the American Revolution, the defeat at Saratoga was a devastating blow to the British. The defeat convinced the French that the Americans could win the war and led to increasing contributions of French money and guns to the American cause. It also convinced the Americans themselves that the rebellion could not be crushed. Because of Howe's monumental ego and his blundering decision in 1777, the American Revolution continued. In only one way did Howe succeed in August 1777: Gentleman Johnny Burgoyne would not be the British hero who brought down the Americans.

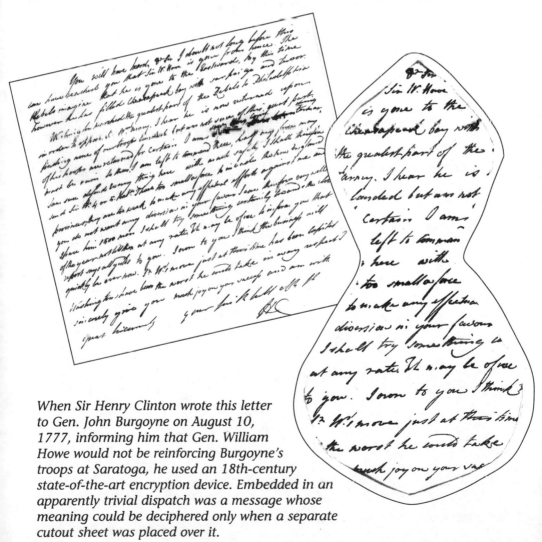

When Sir Henry Clinton wrote this letter to Gen. John Burgoyne on August 10, 1777, informing him that Gen. William Howe would not be reinforcing Burgoyne's troops at Saratoga, he used an 18th-century state-of-the-art encryption device. Embedded in an apparently trivial dispatch was a message whose meaning could be deciphered only when a separate cutout sheet was placed over it.

Letter from Sir William Clinton to Gen. John Burgoyne, August 10, 1777

Sir. W. Howe is gone to the Chesapeak bay with the greatest part of the army. I hear he is landed but am not certain. I am left to command here with too small a force to make any effectual diversion in your favour. I shall try something at any rate. It may be of use to you. I own to you I think Sr W's move just at this time the worst he could take. Much joy on your success.

Establishing a Second Europe: The American Revolution Truce Plan—1781

French plan for truce and settlement of the American Revolution

In February 1781, during the height of hostilities during the American Revolution, with the ultimate resolution of the conflict still uncertain, French Foreign Minister Charles Gravier, Comte de Vergennes, encouraged the Americans to accept a truce and settlement based on lands held by the respective armies at that time. Under the plan, the Americans would gain their independence, but the armistice would allow foreign troops to remain in America, would secure to France—America's ally in the war—a large share in the North Atlantic fisheries, and would establish the western boundary with the Spanish in control.

American negotiator John Adams dealt closely with Vergennes, working under an order from Congress to "undertake nothing in the negotiation of a peace, or truce, without their knowledge and concurrence." Doggedly and to the consternation of Vergennes, Adams refused to continue the negotiations under the terms laid out by the French. Although the American troops had not secured victory in the field by early 1781, Adams refused to carry on discussions that would, in effect, lead to a divided America, with European powers holding significant land areas.

On July 13, 1781, Adams rejected the plan. Three months later, on October 19, Lord Cornwallis surrendered at Yorktown. The American negotiators working for a final peace treaty in Paris would now be working from a position of much greater strength.

When the Americans did sign a peace agreement with Britain in Paris, the details were not shared with Vergennes until after the agreement had been consummated. Vergennes was irked. The peace commissioners, he believed, had acted discourteously toward their ally, France. The American plenipotentiaries, he told an associate, "have cautiously kept themselves at a distance from me" and handled the negotiation, as far as the French were concerned, with "little delicacy. . . . I think it proper that the most influential members of Congress should be informed of the very irregular conduct, of their commissioners in regard to us."

That the peace commissioners had acted out the last of the treaty arrangements with a guarded, suspicious attitude toward the French was not surprising, considering the treaty arrangements that Vergennes himself had earlier encouraged the Americans to accept.

If the plan presented by Vergennes had been accepted by Adams and his fellow negotiators, the land would have been divided between the European powers and the Americans, creating what could have been something like a second Europe.

Memoir of Comte de Vergennes, February 1781

(translation from the French)
February 1781.

In summarizing the details into which we have just entered, we find the following propositions:

1st It is up to the King of England, author of the war, to make Sacrifices to obtain peace.

2nd The first of the Sacrifices to make is the independence of North America.

3rd This independence can be assured by a definitive Treaty or by a Truce.

4th The King of England, whatever form may be adopted, may treat directly with the Americans with the intervention of the two Mediating Powers.

5th The Truce will be for many years, such as 20, 25, 30 years, &c. The United States will be treated as independent in fact, and there will be no restriction placed on the exercise of the rights of Sovereignty.

6th It would be desirable that the *Status Quo* may be avoided; but in case it cannot, it will be proper to limit it to South Carolina and to Georgia, and to stipulate the evacuation of New-York.

7th The proposal of the Truce cannot be made to Congress by the King, if it must be linked to that of the *Status quo*; but by isolating these two proposals His Majesty can take it upon himself to persuade Congress to subscribe to the Truce if he has the secret assurance that New-York will be excepted.

8th In the event of a Truce, the King will propose to the Americans, if there is need, a new Convention the object of which will be to reassure them against attacks by England after the expiration of the Truce.

We think we should conclude the present memoir with the following remark. It is by necessity and not by choice that the King is making War on Great Britain; His Majesty has made, up to now, the greatest efforts to sustain the weight of it: would he wish to lose the fruit of such expenditures by yielding on the principal subject of the Contest? Such a Sacrifice could only be justified by the greatest reverses and by the impossibility of repairing them. If it were the fruit of weakness or of inconstancy, it would tarnish forever the glory and the reputation of His Majesty.

England's means are ready to be exhausted; she is without an ally, her forces are inferior to those of the House of Bourbon; in this state of affairs we can ask the King to be magnanimous; but his condescensions should undermine neither his dignity nor his interest.

SOS from the Alamo—1836

Letter of Col. William Travis appealing for help at the Alamo

With his tiny force of less than 200 men trapped in the Alamo mission in San Antonio, on February 24, 1836, Col. William Travis wrote a letter appealing for help for the besieged Texans. The passionate, alarming appeal of Colonel Travis was carried out of the Alamo through the massing Mexican troops under Antonio López de Santa Anna. A small band of around 30 rangers from Gonzales, Texas, responded to the call and managed to charge through the Mexican siege lines and enter the mission a week later. Could this be the beginning of a wave of reinforcements that could stave off impending disaster for the Texans inside?

Ever since the 26-year-old Travis and his "Legion of Cavalry," a formidable-sounding unit but with only about 30 troops, had been sent to the Alamo and ordered to hold it against the advancing Mexican army until the arrival of reinforcements, he had been pleading with his superiors for additional troops and arms. Threatening to resign his commission, Travis had sent an urgent message asking for reconsideration: "I am unwilling to risk my reputation (which is ever dear to a soldier) by going off into the enemy's country with such little means, and with them so badly equipped." In the end, he obeyed his orders and made his way toward the Alamo, arriving on February 3, 1836. Although additional troops had gradually made their way to help Travis, including a group of volunteers headed by Davy Crockett, the number was still woefully inadequate to hold off several thousand approaching Mexican troops.

Travis and James Bowie, a volunteer colonel, divided the command authorities, Bowie handling the volunteers and Travis the regulars. On February 23, when the two learned that Santa Anna's army had reached the Rio Grande, Travis dispatched a hastily scribbled note to be sent by courier to Gonzales, about 76 miles from the Alamo, with instructions that it be sent on to San Felipe and Goliad and other locations, that the word be spread quickly that several thousand Mexican troops were about to overrun the defenders of the Alamo.

Travis grew increasingly bitter that his fellow Texans seemed deaf to his appeals. In a letter to a friend, Travis revealed his frustration: "If my countrymen do not rally to my relief, I am determined to perish in the defense of this place, and my bones shall reproach my country for her neglect."

As his troops began surrounding the Alamo, Santa Anna sent a courier to demand surrender. Although realizing the cause was hopeless, Travis refused and ordered a cannonball fired into the Mexican forces. Mexican artillerymen responded in a crescendo of fire and began to pound the walls of the Alamo with a sustained barrage.

On February 24, Travis sent his eloquent appeal for help to "people of Texas & all Americans in the world." Pledging that he would "never surrender or retreat," Travis, in the letter written in his own hand, swore "Victory or Death."

The letter never reached the number of Texans who might have been able to respond if they had learned of the desperate situation. On March 6, Santa Anna's army stormed the Alamo, massacring Travis and his men.

If the message had reached the main Texas forces farther removed from the Alamo than Gonzales, and if they had been able to reach the Alamo in time to help its defense, perhaps the Battle of the Alamo would have been a historic confrontation of two major armies instead of a slaughter. On the other hand, the stand at the Alamo did delay Santa Anna's eastward move and gave other Texans time to organize both strategically and politically. "Remember the Alamo" became a rallying cry.

But even though the Battle of San Jacinto and the defeat of Santa Anna on April 21 was the Texans' answer to the Alamo disaster, Travis, Bowie, Crockett, and the others had died in an isolated outpost, with too few men, provisions, and arms. That Travis's message did not bring reinforcements testified to the vulnerable, hopeless position into which they had been placed.

Letter of Col. William Travis, February 24, 1836

Commandancy of the Alamo, Bexar, Fby. 24th, 1836

To the People of Texas & all Americans in the world
Fellow Citizens & Compatriots

I am besieged by a thousand or more of the Mexicans under Santa Anna. I have sustained a continual bombardment & cannonade for 24 hours & have not lost a man. The enemy has demanded a surrender at discretion, otherwise the garrison are to be put to the sword if the fort is taken. I have answered the demand with a cannon shot, and our flag still waves proudly from the walls. <u>I shall never surrender nor retreat.</u>

Then, I call on you in the name of Liberty, of patriotism, & of everything dear to the American character, to come to our aid with all dispatch. The enemy is receiving reinforcements daily & will no doubt increase to three or four thousand in four or five days.

If this call is neglected, I am determined to sustain myself as long as possible & die like a soldier who never forgets what is due to his own honor & that of his country.

Victory or Death
William Barret Travis
Lt. Col. Comdt.

P. S. The Lord is on our side. When the enemy appeared in sight we had not three bushels of corn. We have since found in deserted houses 80 or 90 bushels & got into the walls 20 or 30 head of Beeves. Travis

Some Thought It Lunacy: Pickett's Charge Questioned—1863

Exchange of battlefield notes between James Longstreet and E. P. Alexander at Gettysburg, prior to Pickett's charge

Before the Battle of Gettysburg in July 1863, Confederate general James Longstreet appealed to Gen. Robert E. Lee not to attempt a brazen crossing of open land in assaulting Federal troops. Lee was not persuaded by Longstreet's arguments. Shortly before Gen. George Pickett was ordered to charge the Yankee fortifications, Longstreet and Col. E. P. Alexander exchanged battlefield notes about the futility and likelihood of decimation that faced the Confederates. But the plan went forward.

Lt. Col. Arthur J. L. Fremantle, a British military observer who accompanied Longstreet during the Gettysburg campaign, noted that a close, almost "touching" relationship existed between Longstreet and Lee. "It is impossible to please Longstreet more," said Fremantle, "than by praising Lee. I believe these two generals to be as little ambitious and as thoroughly unselfish as any men in the world." Prior to the Battle of Gettysburg, however, the two men saw the imminent battle from very different perspectives. Longstreet tried hard to dissuade Lee from a massive frontal assault that would expose a large portion of the Southern army to withering fire. But even Longstreet, his close friend, could not convince Lee of the folly of the plan.

Since early June, encouraged by Confederate successes, especially at Chancellorsville, Lee directed his army up the Shenandoah Valley toward Pennsylvania. This would be the great Confederate invasion of the North, the strike that would convince Europeans of the South's chances to win the war and lead to formal recognition and support.

In June, President Lincoln, aware of the strategic vulnerability of Union forces, called up an additional 100,000 volunteers. Both sides sensed that the war was about to reach a critical period.

On July 2, Longstreet, who had been up most of the night reconnoitering the Gettysburg terrain, reported that his scouts had found a route around the left flank of the Union army that would enable him to attack the Round Tops. Lee refused to change the original plan. E. P. Alexander later told his father that Longstreet opposed the attack because the "enemy's position was so powerful, entirely sweeping the 1200 yards over which we had to advance, that it was of doubtful success." Nevertheless, Longstreet, despite confessing his doubts not only to Lee but to Alexander, attempted to carry out the order.

In preparation for the frontal assault, the Confederate artillery battered the Union defenses. Alexander had the responsibility to advise Gen. Pickett when the necessary damage had been inflicted for the charge to begin. But at noon, one of Longstreet's notes to Alexander left the colonel confused. Longstreet said, "If the artillery fire does not have the effect to drive off the enemy or greatly demoralize him, so as to make our effort pretty certain, I would prefer that you should not advise Pickett to make the charge."

Suddenly, Alexander saw his job as not only to tell Pickett when to charge but whether to charge at all. After conferring with other officers and again with Longstreet, Alexander visited Pickett, "who seemed to feel very sanguine of success in the charge, and was only congratulating himself on the opportunity." In his last message to Longstreet, Alexander said that when "our artillery fire is at its best, I will advise Gen Pickett to advance."

Shortly after the Confederate batteries opened at 1:00 P.M., the Union artillery responded. Longstreet, after riding along the lines to both Alexander and Pickett, gave the order to Pickett to begin the assault.

In a letter to his uncle written several weeks after the fateful battle, Longstreet said, "General Lee chose the plan adopted, and he is the person appointed to choose and to order. I consider it a part of my duty to express my views to the commanding general. If he approves and adopts them it is well; if he does not, it is my duty to adopt his views, and to execute his orders as faithfully as if they were my own." The South's great incursion into the North was thus routed at Gettysburg.

E. P. Alexander's Memoirs on His Exchange of Battlefield Notes with James Longstreet at Gettysburg Prior to Pickett's Charge, July 3, 1863

Some half-hour or more before the cannonade began, I was startled by the receipt of a note from Longstreet as follows:—

"Colonel: If the artillery fire does not have the effect to drive off the enemy or greatly demoralize him, so as to make our effort pretty certain, I would prefer that you should not advise Pickett to make the charge. I shall rely a great deal upon your judgment to determine the matter and shall expect you to let Gen. Pickett know when the moment offers."

Until that moment, though I fully recognized the strength of the enemy's position, I had not doubted that we would carry it, in my confidence that Lee was ordering it. But here was a proposition that I

Photographer Timothy O'Sullivan's shot of the grotesquely shredded body of a Confederate soldier on the Gettysburg battlefield, July 5, 1863, captured, perhaps as no other photograph, the brutality and terror of the war.

should decide the question. Overwhelming reasons against the assault at once seemed to stare me in the face. Gen. Wright of Anderson's division was standing with me. I showed him the letter and expressed my views. He advised me to write them to Longstreet, which I did as follows:—

"General: I will only be able to judge of the effect of our fire on the enemy by his return fire, as his infantry is little exposed to view and the smoke will obscure the field. If, as I infer from your note, there is any alternative to this attack, it should be carefully considered before opening our fire, for it will take all the artillery ammunition we have left to test this one, and if result is unfavorable we will have none left for another effort. And even if this is entirely successful, it can only be so at a very bloody cost..."

I failed to fully appreciate all that this might mean. The question seemed merely one of support, which was peculiarly the province of General Lee. I had seen several of Hill's brigades forming to support Pickett, and had heard a rumor that Lee had spoken of a united attack by the whole army. I determined to see Pickett and get an idea of his feelings. I did so, and finding him both cheerful and sanguine, I felt that if the artillery fire opened, Pickett must make the charge but that Longstreet should know my views, so I wrote him as follows:—

"General: When our fire is at its best, I will advise Gen. Pickett to advance."

It must have been with bitter disappointment that Longstreet saw the failure of his hope to avert a useless slaughter, for he was fully convinced of its hopelessness. Yet even he could have scarcely realized, until the event showed, how entirely unprepared were Hill and Ewell to render aid to his assault and to take prompt advantage of even temporary success. None of their guns had been posted with a view to cooperative fire, nor to follow the charge, and much of their ammunition had been prematurely wasted. And although Pickett's assault, when made, actually carried the enemy's guns, nowhere was there the slightest preparation to come to his assistance. The burden of the whole task fell upon the 10 brigades employed. The other 27 brigades and 56 fresh guns were but widely scattered spectators. . . .

There was a decided falling off in the enemy's fire, and as I watched I saw other guns limbered up and withdrawn. We frequently withdrew from fighting Federal guns in order to save our ammunition for their infantry. The enemy had never heretofore practiced such economy. After waiting a few minutes and seeing that no fresh guns replaced those withdrawn, I felt sure that the enemy was feeling the punishment, and at 1:40 I sent a note to Pickett as follows:—"For God's sake come quick. The 18 guns have gone. Come quick or my ammunition will not let me support you properly."

I afterward learned what had followed the sending of my first note. It reached Pickett in Longstreet's presence. He read it and handed it to Longstreet. Longstreet read and stood silent. Pickett said, "General, shall I advance?" Longstreet knew that it must be done, but was unwilling to speak the words. He turned in his saddle and looked away. Pickett saluted and said, "I am going to move forward, sir," and galloped off.

Longstreet, leaving his staff, rode out alone and joined me on the left flank of the guns. It was doubtless 1:50 or later, but I did not look at my watch again. I had grown very impatient to see Pickett, fearing ammunition would run short, when Longstreet joined me. I explained the situation. He spoke sharply,—"Go and stop Pickett where he is and replenish your ammunition." I answered: "We can't do that, sir. The train has but little. It would take an hour to distribute it, and meanwhile the enemy would improve the time."

Longstreet seemed to stand irresolute (we were both dismounted) and then spoke slowly and with great emotion: "I do not want to make this charge. I do not see how it can succeed. I would not make it now but that General Lee has ordered it and is expecting it."

I felt that he was inviting a word of acquiescence on my part and that if given he would again order [to stop Pickett]. But I was too conscious of my own youth and inexperience to express any opinion not directly asked. So I remained silent while Longstreet fought his battle out alone and obeyed his orders.

A Question of Guilt: Custer and His Orders—1876

Orders of Brig. Gen. Albert Terry to Gen. George Custer before the Battle of Little Big Horn

It has been perhaps the most analyzed battle ever to occur on American soil, a clash of cultures and of renowned military figures, an event shrouded in mystery and romance and embellished in legend and history's hype. On June 22, 1876, in the Rosebud–Little Big Horn region of Montana, Crazy Horse met Custer, red met white, and manifest destiny temporarily stalled.

On the evening of June 21, Brig. Gen. Alfred H. Terry, Col. John Gibbon, Maj. James Brisbin, and Gen. George Custer met to develop a plan of attack against hostile Sioux. The next morning, General Terry, as a follow-up to the meeting, directed Capt. E. W. Smith, one of his subordinates, to send orders to Custer concerning the plan of approaching the Little Big Horn. That afternoon, Custer rode with his 264 men into the terrible pincers of a massive force of Sioux warriors. They were slaughtered.

Courts of inquiry, oral histories of Sioux warriors, the speculations of military strategists, the marshaling of documentary evidence—the sum of it all over the years has not bequeathed to us a final truth. Custer still has his defenders and his critics. Was he leading a daring offensive only to suffer betrayal by Reno and other troops who failed to back up his move? Or did he recklessly sacrifice himself and his men?

So compelling has this debate become over the years that it has even spawned moot courts. At the Indiana University School of Law, the Honorable Ruth Bader Ginsburg, Associate Justice of the U.S. Supreme Court, recently presided over Custer's court-martial on charges of negligent conduct, disobedience of orders, and neglect of duty to the prejudice of good order and discipline. The moot court found Custer guilty of two of the charges; he was exonerated on the charge of disobeying orders.

Shortly after the battle, Terry sent a letter to Gens. William T. Sherman and Philip Sheridan in which he implied that Custer had disobeyed his orders of June 22 in moving his troops into such a vulnerable position. The moot court found that the orders were ambiguous and left room for Custer's discretion. Because they were written shortly before the battle, it is possible that Custer never saw the orders. It is possible that he saw them and did not understand precisely the intentions of Reno, as described in the memorandum by Smith. It *is also possible that Custer received the instructions, understood them perfectly, and went his own reckless way into history.*

Orders of Brig. Gen. Albert Terry to Gen. George Custer, June 22, 1876

Headquarters of the Department of Dakota (In the Field)
Camp at Mouth of Rosebud River, Montana Territory June 22nd, 1876

Lieutenant-Colonel Custer,
7th Calvary

Colonel: The Brigadier-General Commanding directs that, as soon as your regiment can be made ready for the march, you will proceed up the Rosebud in pursuit of the Indians whose trail was discovered by Major Reno a few days since. It is impossible to give you any definite instructions in regard to this movement, and were it not impossible to do so the Department Commander places too much confidence in your zeal, energy, and ability to wish to impose upon you precise orders which might hamper your action when nearly in contact with the enemy. He will, however, indicate to you his own views of what your action should be, and he desires that you should conform to them unless you shall see sufficient reason for departing from them. He thinks that you should proceed up the Rosebud until you ascertain definitely the direction in which the trail above spoken of leads. Should it be found (as it appears almost certain that it will be found) to turn towards the Little Bighorn, he thinks that you should still proceed

In 1879, three years after the Battle of Little Big Horn, at the desolate Montana site, these two soldiers joined others to rebury the remains of army troops.

southward, perhaps as far as the headwaters of the Tongue, and then turn toward the Little Horn, feeling constantly, however, to your left, so as to preclude the escape of the Indians passing around your left flank.

The column of Colonel Gibbon is now in motion for the mouth of the Big Horn. As soon as it reaches that point will cross the Yellowstone and move up at least as far as the forks of the Big and Little Horns. Of course its future movements must be controlled by circumstances as they arise, but it is hoped that the Indians, if upon the Little Horn, may be so nearly inclosed by the two columns that their escape will be impossible. The Department Commander desires that on your way up the Rosebud you should thoroughly examine the upper part of Tullock's Creek, and that you should endeavor to send a scout through to Colonel Gibbon's command.

The supply-steamer will be pushed up the Big Horn as far as the forks of the river is found to be navigable for that distance, and the Department Commander, who will accompany the column of Colonel Gibbon, desires you to report to him there not later than the expiration of the time for which your troops are rationed, unless in the mean time you receive further orders.

Very respectfully, Your obedient servant,
E. W. Smith, Captain, 18th Infantry A. A. J. G.

Japanese Americans:
Evidence to the Contrary—1941

**Evidence from suppressed Munson Report,
debunking fears of treachery and treason by
Japanese living in the United States**

I n the fall of 1941, stirred by increasing hostilities with Japan, President
Franklin Roosevelt ordered a secret investigation of persons of Japanese
origin residing in America. The work was done by Special Representative of the
State Department Curtis B. Munson. His principal goal was to evaluate the loyalty of the Japanese population to the United States. Would Japanese
Americans be likely to incite violence or terrorist activity if the United States and
Japan were engaged in war; would they fully cooperate with U.S. officials; or
would their divided loyalties or partisan feelings toward their Japanese heritage
compromise their activities during wartime?

The report clearly stated that "the vast majority [of the Japanese in the
United States] were loyal to America." Especially important, the report empha-
sized, was that most of those who belonged to the highly patriotic Japanese
American Citizens League appeared especially eager to demonstrate their loyalty.

Munson's findings contradicted the assertions of most military and political leaders, as well as civic and social spokespeople for those western states
within whose boundaries most Japanese Americans resided: California,
Oregon, Washington, and Arizona. For example, Walter Lippman, one of the
nation's most influential political columnists, urged the government to "recognize the Western combat zone as territory quite different from the rest of the
country" and to set up in that zone a government force that would relocate all
people of Japanese ancestry, both alien residents and U.S. citizens.

Given the prevailing attitudes, the Munson Report was not likely to play
well with the country or its government leaders. Thus, the specific investigation
requested by President Roosevelt into the question about how to deal with the
Japanese American population in case of war—the report that stated that the
possibility of treachery from Japanese Americans was scant—was suppressed
from the general review of the public until 1946. Despite strong evidence to the
contrary, the Roosevelt administration implemented its own program of concentration camps.

At the time of the bombing of Pearl Harbor, about 127,000 persons of
Japanese origin resided in the mainland United States. On February 19, 1942,
10 weeks after Pearl Harbor, President Franklin D. Roosevelt signed Executive

A Japanese American youngster, an identification tag hanging from a shirt button, waits with his family for a train in southern California that will take them to a relocation camp. The haunting shot was taken by famed photographer Russell Lee in April 1942.

Order 9066, authorizing the removal of these persons from specially designated areas in order to provide security against sabotage and espionage. The army took charge of implementing Roosevelt's order by removing all Japanese residents from the West Coast of the United States and placing them into camps in desolate areas of the country. The American government claimed that the confinement was necessary to prevent subversive actions in time of war.

Altogether, some 110,000 persons of Japanese origin, regardless of their individual circumstances, were uprooted from their homes in the Pacific states and herded at gunpoint into detention camps located mostly in deserts. No formal charges were brought against any of the internees: there were no trials; there were no opportunities to test individual loyalties. The policy was motivated by racism and fear. Although upheld by the Supreme Court in 1941, the policy was later called "our worst wartime mistake" by law professor Eugene Rostow. If President Roosevelt and his advisors had taken the findings and recommendations of the Munson Report to heart, the United States would have found another policy to deal with Japanese Americans and would have avoided one of the most shameful episodes in American history.

Excerpts from the Munson Report, November 11, 1941

1. The ISSEI—First generation of Japanese. Entire cultural background Japanese. Probably loyal romantically to Japan. They must be considered, however, as other races. They have made this their home. They have brought up children here, their wealth accumulated by hard labor is here, and many would have become American citizens had they been allowed to do so. They are for the most part simple people. Their age group is largely 55 to 65, fairly old for a hard-working Japanese.

The Issei, or first generation, is considerably weakened in their loyalty to Japan by the fact that they have chosen to make this their home and have brought up their children here. They expect to die here. They are quite fearful of being put in a concentration camp. Many would take out American citizenship if allowed to do so. The haste of this report does not allow us to go into this more fully. The Issei have to break with their religion, their god and Emperor, their family, their ancestors and their after-life in order to be loyal to the United States. They are also still legally Japanese. Yet they do break, and send their boys off to the Army with pride and tears. They are good neighbors. They are old men fifty-five to sixty-five, for the most part simple and dignified. Roughly they were Japanese lower middle class, about analogous to the pilgrim fathers.

2. The NISEI—Second generation who have received their whole education in the United States and usually, in spite of discrimination against them and a certain amount of insults accumulated through the years from irresponsible elements, show a pathetic eagerness to be Americans. They are in constant conflict with the orthodox, well disciplined family life of their elders. Age group—1 to 30 years.

There are still Japanese in the United States who will tie dynamite around their waist and make a human bomb out of themselves. We grant this, but today they are few. Many things indicate that very many joints in the Japanese set-up show age, and many elements are not what they used to be. The weakest from a Japanese standpoint are the Nisei. They are universally estimated from 90 to 98 percent loyal to the United States if the Japanese-educated element of the Kibei is excluded. The Nisei are pathetically eager to show this loyalty. They are not Japanese in culture. They are foreigners to Japan. Though American citizens they are not accepted by Americans, largely because they look differently and can be easily recognized. The Japanese

American Citizens League should be encouraged, the while an eye is kept open, to see that Tokyo does not get its finger in this pie—which it has in a few cases attempted to do. The loyal Nisei hardly knows where to turn. Some gesture of protection or wholehearted acceptance of this group would go a long way to swinging them away from any last romantic hankering after old Japan. They are not oriental or mysterious, they are very American and are of a proud, self-respecting race suffering from a little inferiority complex and a lack of contact with the white boys they went to school with. They are eager for this contact and to work alongside them.

3. The KIBEI—This is an important division of the NISEI. This is the term used by the Japanese to signify those American born Japanese who received part or all of their education in Japan. In any consideration of the KIBEI they should be again divided into two classes, i.e. those who received their education in Japan from childhood to about 17 years of age and those who received their early formative education in the United States and returned to Japan for four or five years Japanese education. The Kibei are considered the most dangerous element and closer to the Issei with special reference to those who received their early education in Japan. It must be noted, however, that many of those who visited Japan subsequent to their early American education come back with added loyalty to the United States. In fact it is a saying that all a Nisei needs is a trip to Japan to make a loyal American out of him. The American educated Japanese is a boor in Japan and treated as a foreigner. . . .

4. The SANSEI—The third generation of Japanese is a baby and may be disregarded for the purpose of our survey. . . . The Hawaiian Japanese does not suffer from the same inferiority complex or feel the same mistrust of the whites that he does on the mainland. While it is seldom on the mainland that you find even a college-educated Japanese-American citizen who talks to you wholly openly until you have gained his confidence, this is far from the case in Hawaii. Many young Japanese there are fully as open and frank and at ease with a white as white boys are. In a word, Hawaii is more of a melting pot because there are more brown skins to melt—Japanese, Hawaiian, Chinese and Filipino. It is interesting to note that there has been absolutely no bad feeling between the Japanese and the Chinese in the islands due to the Japanese-Chinese war. Why should they be any worse toward us?

Due to the preponderance of Japanese in the population of the

Islands, a much greater proportion of Japanese have been called to the draft than on the mainland. As on the mainland they are inclined to enlist before being drafted. The Army is extremely high in its praise of them as recruits. . . . They are beginning to feel that they are going to get a square deal and some of them are really almost pathetically exuberant.

The story was all the same. There is no Japanese problem on the Coast. There will be no armed uprising of Japanese. There will undoubtedly be some sabotage financed by Japan and executed largely by imported agents . . . In each Naval District there are about 250 to 300 suspects under surveillance. It is easy to get on the suspect list, merely a speech in favor of Japan at some banquet being sufficient to land one there. The Intelligence Services are generous with the title of suspect and are taking no chances. Privately, they believe that only 50 or 60 in each district can be classed as really dangerous. The Japanese are hampered as saboteurs because of their easily recognized physical appearance. It will be hard for them to get near anything to blow up if it is guarded. There is far more danger from Communists and people of the Bridges type on the Coast than there is from Japanese. The Japanese here is almost exclusively a farmer, a fisherman or a small businessman. He has no entree to plants or intricate machinery.

In case we have not made it apparent, the aim of this report is that all Japanese Nationals in the continental United States and property owned and operated by them within the country be immediately placed under absolute Federal control. The aim of this will be to squeeze control from the hands of the Japanese Nationals into the hands of the loyal Nisei who are American citizens. . . . It is the aim that the Nisei should police themselves, and as a result police their parents.

ALMOST HISTORY

CODE-BREAKING CONSEQUENCES

A Decoded Note and the End of Neutrality—1917

The Zimmerman Note, proposing a Mexican-German alliance and adding to American sentiment to join the Allies

I n January 1917, the unfolding events of World War I began to ensnarl relations between the United States and Mexico. Faced with the prospect of war with Germany, the United States was finally considering whether to order Gen. John J. Pershing to discontinue his pursuit of Francisco "Pancho" Villa and his raiders who had been attacking in New Mexico and Texas. Villa and his guerrillas had embarrassed the United States, but the effort to catch him, President Wilson felt, was too expensive. The United States would wait until after elections in Mexico and the adoption of a new Mexican constitution to continue negotiations with the Mexican government.

Meanwhile, by the spring of 1917, German submarine warfare had killed nearly 200 Americans. In February, Wilson had broken diplomatic relations with Germany in response to the German decision to begin unrestricted submarine warfare. Tension between Germany and the United States was mounting.

And then the American public was hit with the infamous Zimmerman Note. A telegram from the German Foreign Minister, Arthur Zimmerman, to the German envoy in Mexico was intercepted and decoded by the British, who turned over the text to American Ambassador Walter Hines Page in London on February 24. Steps were taken to make tracing the British action impossible.

In the note, Zimmerman proposed a Mexican-German alliance. Perhaps the Germans could take advantage of the United States' difficulties with Villa and his band and further complicate U.S. diplomacy with Mexico. In return for Mexican support in the war, the Germans would aid Mexico in retaking former Mexican territories of Arizona, Texas, and New Mexico.

When the note was made public on March 1, it inflamed U.S. public opinion against Germany, particularly in the West and Southwest. It also inflamed President Wilson, who was given the text on February 26, 1917. Shocked by the threat to American security, he proposed to Congress the arming of U.S. ships against German attacks. On April 2, just a month after the Zimmerman document appeared in the press, President Wilson asked Congress to declare war against Germany and the Central Powers; on April 6, 1917, Congress complied.

The German government was not attempting, through the Zimmerman Note, to provoke war with the United States. Indeed, the note was supposed to *have remained secret. It was an attempt by the German government at contingency planning, preparing for the possibility that if America did enter the war, it would be further hampered by its neighbor to the south.*

The discovery and public display of the document, however, was powerful ammunition for the Wilson administration as it prepared America for war.

Note from German Foreign Minister Arthur Zimmerman to the German minister in Mexico, January 19, 1917

On the first of February we intend to begin submarine warfare unrestricted. In spite of this, it is our intention to endeavor to keep neutral the United States of America.

If this attempt is not successful, we propose an alliance on the following basis with Mexico: That we shall make war together and together make peace. We shall give general financial support, and it is understood that Mexico is to reconquer the lost territory in New Mexico, Texas, and Arizona. The details are left to you for settlement....

You are instructed to inform the President of Mexico of the above in the greatest confidence as soon as it is certain that there will be an outbreak of war with the United States and suggest that the President of Mexico, on his own initiative, should communicate with Japan suggesting adherence at once to this plan; at the same time, offer to mediate between Germany and Japan.

Please call to the attention of the President of Mexico that the employment of ruthless submarine warfare now promises to compel England to make peace in a few months.

Zimmerman
(Secretary of State)

Herbert Yardley's American Black Chamber and the Arms Conference—1921

Decryptions by the American Black Chamber allowing Secretary of State Charles Evans Hughes to know Japan's negotiating position during the Washington Naval Conference

Secretary of State Charles Evans Hughes was a distinguished political figure and diplomat. At the Washington Naval Conference of 1921, as he negotiated with a number of foreign dignitaries, especially over matters dealing directly with Japanese military power, he seemed dazzling, a genius. Each time the Japanese diplomatic team attempted to move into a more favorable bargaining position, Hughes would deftly counter and bring the discussions invariably back to U.S. favor. It seemed as if the man were a clairvoyant. Or did he have an edge?

The representatives of nine nations who gathered at Constitution Hall on November 12, 1921, were there to begin discussions of the naval arms race that threatened to emerge among major victorious nations after World War I. The talks centered on the Japanese who, because of serious economic problems at home, were in a complicated position. Ideally, they wished to negotiate the right to build warships up to 70 percent of the British and American total; their leaders, however, feared pushing the United States too far and would be willing, in the end, to settle for less. The United States had called the conference to clarify the relative alliances between Britain, Japan, France, Italy, and itself and to advance a desire among the nations to limit armaments by mutual agreement.

After 12 weeks of negotiations, the five nations signed a five-power treaty that placed a moratorium on naval construction, placed limitations on the size of ships, and agreed on the dismantling of 70 vessels. The treaty was the first major agreement in history in which the signatory nations voluntarily agreed to cut back, and not merely to control, their armaments. One British observer concluded that Hughes had sunk more ships "than all the admirals of the world have sunk in a cycle of centuries."

For Hughes, the conference had been a diplomatic triumph. It had also been a triumph for the great code breaker Herbert O. Yardley, head of the highly secret MI-8, or the Black Chamber. During the Naval Conference, Yardley's

MI-8 first penetrated the Japanese code system on a large scale. Even before the conference opened, he and the Black Chamber were already breaking the codes used for Japan's diplomatic signals.

Yardley began feeding daily decrypts to Hughes, improving the secretary's diplomatic position almost hourly. He appeared to be outsmarting the Japanese at every turn. On November 28, for example, one such decrypt informed the United States that the Japanese were going to attempt to maintain a "middle attitude," that their position was as yet not as flexible as the American negotiators might have wished. The Americans waited. By December 10, another decoded signal from Tokyo indicated that the Japanese were willing to settle at a lower level. When the United States, Great Britian, France, Italy, and Japan signed a treaty on February 6, 1922, to promote peace and reduce the burdens of competition in armaments, United States diplomats came away from the conference feeling that they had achieved a major diplomatic triumph.

Without the decrypts, Hughes, although a skilled negotiator, would not have held all the cards.

Decryptions by the American Black Chamber, November 28, 1921

From Tokio
To Washington.

Conference No. 13. November 28, 1921.
SECRET.

Referring to your conference cablegram No. 74, we are of your opinion that *it is necessary to avoid any clash with Great Britain and America, particularly America, in regard to the armament limitation question.* You will to the utmost maintain a middle attitude and *redouble your efforts to carry out our policy. In case of inevitable necessity you will work to establish your second proposal of 10 to 6.5.* If, in spite of your utmost efforts it *becomes necessary* in view of the situation and in the interests of general policy *to fall back on your proposal No. 3,* you will *endeavor to limit* the power of concentration and maneuver of the Pacific by a *guarantee to reduce or at least to maintain the status quo of Pacific defenses* and to make an adequate reservation which will make clear that [this is] our intention in agreeing to a 10 to 6 ratio.

No. 4 is to be avoided as far as possible

Breaking the Code and Winning Midway—1942

Report of navy code breakers on Japanese plans to attack the Midway Islands

With the infamy of Pearl Harbor a not-too-distant memory, the U.S. Pacific Fleet, in early June 1942, faced an enormous fleet of 88 Japanese warships. The numerically inferior American naval force of 28 warships, in a brilliant flanking attack, sank 4 Japanese aircraft carriers and destroyed about 275 planes in the crucial Battle of Midway. The Japanese had planned to seize the Midway Islands as a base for attacking Hawaii and the United States. Midway was the first major defeat of the modern Japanese navy and significantly turned the fortunes of the naval war in the Pacific.

It could have been otherwise. The Japanese had the numbers, the strategic advantage, and the momentum to rout the Americans at Midway. Most military observers believed at first that Commander in Chief of the Combined Fleet Adm. Isoroklu Yamamoto would follow the Pearl Harbor attack with a second attack on Hawaii. Others believed that the Aleutians were the next target; still others feared that the Japanese were headed for the American West Coast to launch air strikes against aircraft factories in Southern California.

That the United States, despite its vulnerable position, warded off the Japanese threat was largely attributable to the U.S. Navy's advance knowledge of Japanese plans. Midway became not only a victory for U.S. battle forces; it was victory by cryptologists. Shortly before Yamamoto moved his naval force toward Midway, U.S. naval intelligence had uncovered the Japanese navy's plans, strength, and dispositions. The outflanking movement orchestrated by Adm. Chester Nimitz was a brilliant tactical achievement. But perhaps even more important was his own assessment that the information given to him by the code breakers was on the mark, despite the feelings of most of his subordinates that the information was dubious or erroneous.

If naval intelligence had not broken the code and read Yamamoto's intentions correctly or if Admiral Nimitz had not accepted the information as fact, the results in the Pacific would have been far different.

A Japanese victory at Midway would have eliminated American naval power in the Pacific. A Midway catastrophe would have opened the way for capture of the Hawaiian Islands and the menacing of the U.S. West Coast, the Aleutians, and Alaska. The situation would have drastically altered America's war plans. It could have meant postponing the Allied invasion of French terri-

*tories in northwest Africa, a delay in the opening of a second front in Europe,
and possibly the refocusing of American strategy and redirection of American
resources to the Pacific.*

*Defeating the Japanese at Midway gave the United States a better chance
ultimately to defeat not only the Japanese but also the Germans.*

Report of Navy Code Breakers on Japanese Plans to Attack Midway Islands; from Diary of Lt. Burdick Brittin, May 30, 1942

We have history in the palm of our hands during the next week or
so. If we are able to keep our presence unknown to the enemy and sur
prise them with a vicious attack on their carriers, the U.S. Navy
should once more be supreme in the Pacific. But if the Japs see us first
and attack us with their overwhelming number of planes, knock us
out of the picture, and then walk in to take Midway, Pearl will be
almost neutralized and in dire danger—I can say no more—there is too
much tension within me—the fate of our nation is in our hands.

*A Japanese heavy cruiser is hit by U.S. carrier-based naval aircraft near
Midway Island in June 1942. Taken by a U.S. Navy photographer, the
image of the explosion is reportedly the first photograph of the Battle of
Midway.*

ALMOST
SLIPPERY TRUTH
HISTORY

Plots, Forgeries, and the Assassination of Jefferson Davis—1864

The winter of 1863–1864 was particularly bitter—the numbing cold, the military impasse that had the armies of George Meade and Robert E. Lee wintering across the Rapidan River from each other trying to keep warm, the rumors of freezing and starving prisoners. At the White House, President Lincoln, especially concerned about the fate of Union soldiers held in Confederate jails in Richmond, just 100 miles from Washington, approved a bold, midwinter guerrilla action. Its mission: freeing the prisoners on Belle Isle and at Libby, severing Confederate communications, and distributing a presidential amnesty proclamation.

Led by Brig. Gen. Judson Kilpatrick, a dashing if unpredictable commander, and Col. Ulric Dahlgren, a young amputee who had lost a leg at the Battle of Gettysburg, the party of a few hundred troops secretly prepared to enter Richmond to liberate prisoners and accomplish the other aspects of the mission. Dahlgren wrote to his father, a distinguished Union admiral: "There is a grand raid to be made, and I am to have a very important command. If successful, it will be the grandest thing on record; and if it fails, many of us will 'go up' . . . but it is an undertaking that if I were not in, I should be ashamed to show my face again."

The raid was an ignominious failure, and Dahlgren was killed. But the story did not end with this ill-advised military venture. On young Dahlgren's body, Southerners found several papers—two folded documents and a pocket notebook containing other loose items inserted between the leaves. The materials were sent to Gen. Robert E. Lee who took them to Confederate president Jefferson Davis. In the president's office, Lee read some of them aloud. One of the instructions said, "Once in the City it must be destroyed & Jeff. Davis and Cabinet killed."

Davis ordered the documents published. Here was smoking evidence of the Lincoln administration's agenda of arson and murder. Here was firsthand proof of the evils of Washington and its president who had authorized the assassination of another leader.

The Richmond newspapers and Confederate commanders used the papers to rally citizens and troops alike. The Richmond Dispatch headline screamed:

"The Last Raid of the Infernals: Their Plans Unveiled." The story talked of the raiders' diabolical cravings of blood and booty.

For the Confederate government, this find was a public-relations godsend. This was evidence of the black perfidy and barbarism of the Union, of their war without quarter, their war fought under rules only of their own making. The orders not only appeared across the country in newspapers; Confederate leaders also printed and circulated broadsides of the material. They sent copies to England and other European powers claiming that the papers attested to the desperate and malevolent aims of their northern enemy.

But were the documents real? The explanation from Washington was that no orders for assassination had been authorized, not by the president or Secretary of War Edwin Stanton, or any of his subordinates. There were claims, especially by Dahlgren's father, that the Southerners had forged or altered the documents. Most evidence suggests that it is highly unlikely that the documents were forged or that there would have been time for the Confederates to alter some of the language in them. It is more likely that the documents were genuine.

This may have been a commando raid engineered by the hot-tempered Judson Kilpatrick and his companion Dahlgren, who had enhanced their mission somewhat beyond what Washington had in mind. Or perhaps Stanton had a secret agenda. We know that Kilpatrick met with Stanton shortly before his move on Richmond. There is, however, no hard evidence that Stanton authorized such a move and no evidence that Lincoln had assassination as one of the goals of the mission.

Whatever the origins of the Dahlgren Papers and the plot they described, the aborted raid on Richmond was perhaps the most damaging embarrassment for the Union during the Civil War. It is even possible that the legacy of assassination it planted in the minds of readers of the documents across the country could have led other intense partisans on similar missions of murder. John Wilkes Booth, for example, was an avid reader of newspapers.

Extracts from the Dahlgren Papers, 1864

HEADQUARTERS THIRD DIVISION, CAVALRY CORPS, 1864

Officers and Men:
You have been selected from brigades and regiments as a picked command to attempt a desperate undertaking—an undertaking

which, if successful, will write your names on the hearts of your countrymen in letters that can never be erased, and which will cause the prayers of our fellow-soldiers now confined in loathsome prisons to follow you and yours wherever you may go. We hope to release the prisoners from Belle Island first, and having seen them fairly started, we will cross the James River into Richmond, destroying the bridges after us and exhorting the released prisoners to destroy and burn the hateful city; and do not allow the rebel leader Davis and traitorous crew to escape. The prisoners must render great assistance, as you cannot leave your ranks too far or become too much scattered, or you will be lost. Do not allow any personal gain to lead you off, which would only bring you to an ignominious death at the hands of citizens. Keep well together and obey orders strictly and all will be well; but on no account scatter too far, for in union there is strength. With strict obedience to orders and fearlessness in the execution you will be sure to succeed. We will join the main force on the other side of the city, or perhaps meet them inside. Many of you may fall; but if there is any man here not willing to sacrifice his life in such a great and glorious undertaking, or who does not feel capable of meeting the enemy in such a desperate fight as will follow, let him step out, and he may go hence to the arms of his sweetheart and read of the braves who swept through the city of Richmond. We want no man who cannot feel sure of success in such a holy cause. We will have a desperate fight, but stand up to it when it does come and all will be well. Ask the blessing of the Almighty and do not fear the enemy.

U. DAHLGREN
Colonel, Commanding

HEADQUARTERS THIRD DIVISION, CAVALRY CORPS
1864

Guides, pioneers (with oakum, turpentine, and torpedoes), signal officer, quartermaster, commissary, scouts, and picked men in rebel uniform. Men will remain on the north bank and move down with the force on south bank, not getting ahead of them, and if the communication can be kept up without giving an alarm it must be done; but everything depends upon a surprise, and no one must be allowed to pass ahead of the column. Information must be gathered in regard to the crossings of the river, so that should we be repulsed on the

Dashing 21-year-old Col. Ulric Dahlgren led a contingent of raiders in an ill-conceived, hapless, and for him fatal attempt to free Union prisoners in Richmond and perhaps to murder Confederate president Jefferson Davis.

south side we will know where to recross at the nearest point. All mills must be burned and the canal destroyed; and also everything which can be used by the rebels must be destroyed, including the boats on the river. Should a ferry-boat be seized and can be worked have it moved down. Keep the force on the south side posted of any important movement of the enemy, and in case of danger some of the scouts must swim the river and bring us information. As we approach the city the party must take great care that they do not get ahead of the other party on the south side, and must conceal themselves and watch our movements. We will try and secure the bridge to the city, 1 mile below Belle Island, and release the prisoners at the same time. If we do not succeed they must then dash down, and we will try and carry the bridge from each side. When necessary, the men must be filed through the woods and along the river bank. The bridges once secured, and the prisoners loose and over the river, the bridges will be secured and the city destroyed. The men must keep together and well in hand, and once in the city it must be destroyed and Jeff. Davis and cabinet killed. Pioneers will go along with combustible material. The officer must use his discretion about the time of assisting us. Horses and cattle which we do not need immediately must be shot rather than left. Everything on the canal and elsewhere of service to the rebels must be destroyed. As General Custer may follow me, be careful not to give a false alarm.

Horror Concealed: Vignettes of an American Army Nurse—1916

Suppressed account of World War I atrocities and suffering

Ellen La Motte was one of the first American nurses to serve in a French field hospital during World War I. In 1916, she wrote a series of 14 vignettes published in a compendium as The Backlash of War. The book appeared before American entry into the war.

The sketches were written a few miles behind the lines in Belgium. For long periods of time, those lines would shift slightly, uprooting the field hospital and other encampments. But mostly it was the grueling succession of days and nights, an endless time of treating the wounded and dying and knowing that the sum of their efforts would be a few, precious shifting miles. The deeds of valor and courage, the genius of tactical maneuvering, the strategies and counterstrategies all amounted to an ugly, dreary deadlock, a "stagnant place," as she called it. Behind the lines, through the eyes of La Motte, there was little to support patriotism or grand causes.

By 1917, with the United States being inexorably drawn deeper and deeper into the European conflict, especially on the high seas, La Motte's sketches were quickly becoming a liability for a government intent on justifying a moral cause for war. When members of the Senate and House of Representatives were about to vote on entering the war and when the public was about to be asked to sacrifice, the government did not want those sketches out there for ready reading.

La Motte remembered that she was given no notice from the government that the book had been banned. After she asked the publisher why the book had suddenly been taken off the market, she was told that government censors had complained about its reality.

The government knew that La Motte's writings could have compromised efforts to stir patriotic fervor and war enthusiasm. Too much reality most certainly would have been detrimental to those aims.

Excerpts from *The Backlash of War*
by Ellen La Motte, 1916

THIS is how it was. It is pretty much always like this in a field hospital. Just ambulances rolling in, and dirty, dying men, and the guns off there in the distance! Very monotonous, and the same, day after day, till one gets so tired and bored. Big things may be going on over

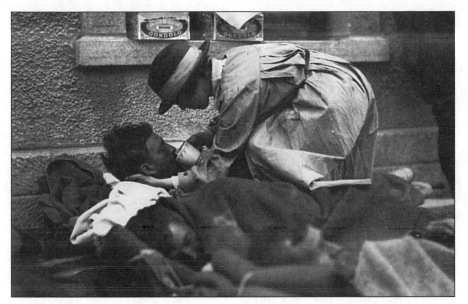

On the platform of a railroad station in Montmirail, France, on May 31, 1918, an American Red Cross nurse named Mrs. Hammond gives a cup of water to a wounded British soldier.

there, on the other side of the captive balloons that we can see from a distance, but we are always here, on this side of them, and here, on this side of them, it is always the same. The weariness of it—the sameness of it! The same ambulances, and dirty men, and groans, or silence. The same hot operating rooms, the same beds, always full, in the wards. This is war. But it goes on and on, over and over, day after day, till it seems like life. Life in peace time. It might be life in a big city hospital, so alike is the routine. Only the city hospitals are bigger, and better equipped, and the ambulances are smarter, and the patients don't always come in ambulances—they walk in sometimes, or come in street cars, or in limousines, and they are of both sexes, men and women, and have ever so many things the matter with them—the hospitals of peace time are not nearly so stupid, so monotonous, as the hospitals of war. Bah! War's humane compared to peace! More spectacular, I grant you, more acute,—that's what interests us,—but for the sheer agony of life—oh, peace is way ahead!

War is so clean. Peace is so dirty. There are so many foul diseases in peace times. They drag on over so many years, too. No, war's clean! I'd rather see a man die in prime of life, in war time, than see him doddering along in peace time, broken hearted, broken spirited, life broken, and very weary, having suffered many things,—to die at last, at a good, ripe age! How they have suffered, those who drive up to our city hospitals in limousines, in peace time. What's been saved them, those who die young, and clean and swiftly, here behind the guns. In the long run it dots up just the same. Only war's spectacular, that's all.

Well, he came in like the rest, only older than most of them. A shock of iron-gray hair, a mane of it, above heavy, black brows, and the brows were contracted in pain. Shot, as usual, in the abdomen. He spent three hours on the table after admission—the operating table—and when he came over to the ward, they said, not a dog's chance for him. No more had he. When he came out of ether, he said he didn't want to die. He said he wanted to live. Very much. He said he wanted to see his wife again and his children. Over and over he insisted on this, insisted on getting well. He caught hold of the doctor's hand and said he must get well, that the doctor must get him well. Then the doctor drew away his slim fingers from the rough, imploring grasp, and told him to be good and patient.

"Be good! Be patient!" said the doctor, and that was all he could say, for he was honest. What else could he say, knowing that there were eighteen little holes, cut by the bullet, leaking poison into that gashed, distended abdomen? When these little holes, that the doctor could not stop, had leaked enough poison into his system, he would die. Not today, no, but day after tomorrow. Three days more . . .

Harry Truman's Puzzling Diary Entry—1945

Diary entry of Harry S. Truman, indicating that new atomic bomb will not be used on civilian populations

He made one of the most awesome decisions in history. He did it, he said, to end the war and to save American lives. He did it with characteristic firmness. And, as his diary reflects, he had great personal misgivings. But Harry Truman's diary indicates something else. We may never know the entire story.

On July 16, 1945, President Truman, in Potsdam, Germany, at a conference with Allied leaders Winston Churchill and Joseph Stalin, was notified that the atomic bomb had been tested and "exceeded expectations." Stalin had confided to Truman that the Soviets would be sending forces against the Japanese in August. In a letter to his wife, Bess, Truman rejoiced, "I've gotten what I came for. . . . I'll say that we'll end the war a year sooner now, and think of the kids who won't be killed! That is the important thing."

When Truman dined with Churchill the following day, they discussed the atomic bomb test. Truman later confided that he had decided to tell Stalin. A week later, the president casually mentioned to Stalin that the United States now had a new weapon of exceptionally destructive force, but he did not call it an atomic bomb. He didn't have to. Although Truman did not realize it, Stalin already had intelligence information that the Americans did, indeed, have a new atomic weapon. He ordered a speed-up of work on a Soviet counterpart.

On July 25, President Truman met in the morning with Britain's Lord Mountbatten, the Allied commander in Southeast Asia, and Chief of Staff George C. Marshall, and they undoubtedly discussed the ramifications of the weapon. He also met with Secretary of War Henry Stimson. That night, he wrote a long diary entry musing about the decision that lay ahead. He talked about the weapon in biblical terms, a force of fire that would rain destruction as prophesied "in the Euphrates Valley Era."

He had learned the specifics—an explosion visible for more than 200 miles, a crater more than 1,000 feet in diameter. He wrote that the weapon would be used between then and August 10 and that he had told Stimson that it was to be used only against military targets, not women and children, and when used it would be with a warning, giving the enemy the chance to surrender to save lives.

On August 6, 1945, the atomic bomb was dropped on Hiroshima. President Truman issued a public statement that described Hiroshima as a military target. "The world will note that the first atomic bomb was dropped on Hiroshima, a military base. That was because we wished in this first attack to avoid, insofar as possible, the killing of civilians. But that attack is only a warning of things to come. If Japan does not surrender, bombs will have to be dropped on her war industries and, unfortunately, thousands of civilian lives will be lost.

"Having found the bomb we have used it. We have used it against those who attacked us without warning at Pearl Harbor, against those who have starved and beaten and executed American prisoners of war, against those who have abandoned all pretense of obeying international laws of warfare. We have used it in order to shorten the agony of war, in order to save the lives of thousands and thousands of young Americans.

"We shall continue to use it until we completely destroy Japan's power to make war. Only a Japanese surrender will stop us."

When President Truman had written his diary entry on July 25, he had said that the bomb would not be unleashed on civilian populations. Hiroshima had a civilian population. Was President Truman unaware that Hiroshima was primarily a city of civilians and that they would be the bomb's main victims? His public statement indicates that he thought the United States had just hit a "military base." Or, between July 25 and August 8, had the president changed his mind? Did he now believe that the righteous end, to save American lives, justified the means to hit a civilian population?

In a letter to Senator Richard Russell on August 9, Truman wrote, "I know that Japan is a terribly cruel and uncivilized nation in warfare but I can't bring myself to believe that, because they are beasts, we should ourselves act in the same manner." That very day, another atomic bomb was dropped on Japan, this one on Nagasaki.

If President Truman had followed the policy he described in his diary entry of July 25, 1945, the populations of Hiroshima and Nagasaki would have been spared the horrors that history has recorded all too well. The war, then, would have been extended to include other horrors. But the diary entry, far from being revealing, remains strangely opaque, Truman's own refutation of a policy option that, less than two weeks later, became fact.

Diary entry of Harry S. Truman, July 25, 1945

We have discovered the most terrible bomb in the history of the world. It may be the fire destruction prophesied in the Euphrates Valley Era, after Noah and his fabulous Ark.

Anyway we "think" we have found the way to cause a disintegra-

One mile southeast of Ground Zero, Nagasaki, Japan, August 10, 1945, a mother and son each hold boiled rice balls given to them by an emergency relief organization.

tion of the atom. An experiment in the New Mexico desert was startling—to put it mildly. Thirteen pounds of the explosive caused the complete disintegration of a steel tower 60 feet high, created a crater 6 feet deep and 1,200 feet in diameter, knocked over a steel tower ½ mile away and knocked men down 10,000 yards away. The explosion was visible for more than 200 miles and audible for 40 miles and more.

This weapon is to be used against Japan between now and August 10th. I have told the Sec. of War, Mr. Stimson, to use it so that military objectives and soldiers and sailors are the target and not women and children. Even if the Japs are savages, ruthless, merciless and fanatic, we as the leader of the world for the common welfare cannot drop that terrible bomb on the old capital or the new.

He and I are in accord. The target will be a purely military one and we will issue a warning statement asking the Japs to surrender and save lives. I'm sure they will not do that, but we will have given them the chance. It is certainly a good thing for the world that Hitler's crowd or Stalin's did not discover this atomic bomb. It seems to be the most terrible thing ever discovered, but it can be made the most useful. . . .

Human Guinea Pig Research and the Tragic Death of Dr. Frank Olson—1963

Memorandum of CIA Official Richard Helms

At the beginning of the Cold War, U.S. intelligence agencies were concerned that the Soviet Union, the People's Republic of China, and other Communist nations were developing chemical and biological weapons that could seriously threaten American security. The United States, they believed, needed a defensive program to investigate the possible threats posed by such weapons.

Thus, in the 1950s, was born within the CIA a program called MKULTRA, unknown to other government agencies or the American public. The brainchild of Richard Helms, deputy director for plans, the program was run by a small unit within the CIA known as the Technical Services Staff. In gaining information about the effects of certain chemicals, MKULTRA would use unwitting American citizens as guinea pigs.

One CIA auditor wrote of MKULTRA, "Precautions must be taken not only to protect operations from exposure to enemy forces but also to conceal these activities from the American public in general. The knowledge that the agency is engaging in unethical and illicit activities would have serious repercussions in political and diplomatic circles."

Although many of the MKULTRA records were destroyed by the CIA in 1972, some of them have made it into the public domain, and they tell a grisly, disturbing story. The most notorious MKULTRA experiments were on the drug called lysergic acid diethylamide (LSD). Hoping that the drug could be used clandestinely to manipulate enemy targets, even foreign leaders (Fidel Castro was at the top of the list), the CIA engaged in a determined quest for its own Manchurian Candidate *solution: a magical brainwashing potion. To find out whether LSD or other similar drugs would do the trick, the CIA needed to test it out.*

In its efforts to find subjects, the CIA most often used prisoners. But the program managers were often more inventive; they even set up brothels run by the agency, in which patrons would be given LSD and then observed through two-way mirrors.

On November 19, 1953, an army scientist and germ-warfare specialist named Frank Olson, who was himself working on an MKULTRA project, was slipped a dose of LSD in his drink. After spending eight days in a paranoid, hallucinatory state, he jumped to his death from a New York City hotel room. His widow wrote an affidavit that included the following: "In 1953 my husband was a distinguished biochemist working as a civilian employee of the United States Army at Camp Detrick, Maryland. My husband and three of his colleagues were given LSD, without warning, by CIA officials Sidney Gottlieb, Chief of CIA's TSS Chemical Division and his Deputy, Robert Lashbrook, as part of the CIA experimental brainwashing program designated as MKULTRA and operating under the direction of Richard Helms, Chief of Staff of CIA's Clandestine Services. Gottlieb and Lashbrook fed the LSD to my husband and the others in their after-dinner liqueur without telling them that there was LSD in the cointreau glass, nor that they were the subject of CIA experiments."

When the CIA's acid experiments were made public in the mid-1970s, a Senate committee report declared: "From its beginning in the early 1950s until its termination in 1963, the program of surreptitious administration of LSD to unwitting non-volunteer human subjects demonstrates a failure of the CIA's leadership to pay adequate attention to the rights of individuals and to provide effective guidance to CIA employees. Though it was known that the testing was dangerous, the lives of subjects were placed in jeopardy and were ignored. . . . Although it was clear that the laws of the United States were being violated, the testing continued."

Revelations of the CIA's misconduct opened the door to revelations of similar activities by other federal agencies. In the 1990s, the Energy Department began to reveal some of the horrors carried out by its predecessor, the Atomic Energy Commission, among them the use of human guinea pigs in radiation experiments and the release of radiation in populated areas.

In all these revelations, there is always the countervailing explanation that the knowledge gained justified the activity; one researcher referred to the phenomenon as "the Buchenwald Touch." If not for the failed cover-ups, if the false testimony of Richard Helms and others involved in these activities had not been exposed, how much further would these brazen violations of law and human rights have extended?

Memorandum of CIA Official Richard Helms, December 17, 1963

Most of our difficulty stems from the fact that the individuals subjected to testing must be unwitting. . . . In the circumstances of potential operational use of this technique, it is virtually certain that the target will be unwitting. Any testing program which does not attempt to approximate this real situation will result in a false sense of accomplishment and readiness. . . .

It goes without saying that whatever testing arrangement we adopt must afford maximum safeguards for the protection of the Agency's role in this activity. . . .

In considering possible alternatives to our present arrangement with the Bureau of Narcotics, we have considered contact with . . . police departments and prisons or prison hospitals. We have attempted several times in the past ten years to establish a testing program in an overseas setting, using indigenous subjects. In every case the necessity of making foreign nationals aware of our role in this very sensitive activity has made such options undesirable on security grounds. . . .

While I share your uneasiness for any program which intrudes on an individual's private and legal prerogatives, I believe it is necessary that the Agency maintain a central role in this activity, keep current on enemy capabilities in the manipulation of human behavior, and maintain an offensive capability. I therefore recommend your approval for continuation of this testing program with the Bureau of Narcotics.

ALMOST
URBAN LEGENDS
HISTORY

Milking Chicago's Urban Cow Legend: Mrs. O'Leary's Cow or a Terrorist?—1871

Official report on Great Chicago Fire

On October 9, 1871, a great fire consumed much of the city of Chicago. The cause of the inferno has traditionally been attributed to Mrs. Catherine "Kate" O'Leary, owner of a barn in the vicinity of where the fire erupted, and her cow, Daisy or Gwendolyn, or was it Adeline? As a folksong relates:

> Late one night, when we were all in bed,
> Mrs. O'Leary lit a lantern in the shed.
> Her cow kicked it over,
> Then winked her eye and said,
> "There'll be a hot time in the old town tonight!"

Did Mrs. O'Leary's cow start the Great Chicago Fire, or did generations have it all wrong about this tragic event in the city's history? Certainly the blaze began in the vicinity of the barn where Mrs. O'Leary's five cows produced a middling local dairy business. An apparently guilt-ridden Kate herself is supposed to have said to several individuals following the fire that her cow had kicked over a lantern, igniting wood shavings and hay that the family had stocked for the winter ahead.

Mrs. O'Leary's confession gained currency. In songs, poetry, cartoons, novels, history books, and nursery rhymes, the story lives:

> . . . For those who had left their Homes so cheery,
> Wrapped in the flames from that Hovel dreary,
> That sheltered the famous Mrs. O'Leary,
> That milked the cow forlorn and weary,
> That kicked the Lamp, that started the
> Fire, that burned the City.
> (Anna Matson, "The City That a Cow Kicked Over,"
> 1881)

Even Norman Rockwell, in 1935, captured on canvas a hearty Mrs. O'Leary milking the cow, that kicked the lantern, that . . .

But is the story as simple as that? Was Mrs. O'Leary and Daisy or

Gwendolyn or Adeline to blame? On the 40th anniversary of the fire, a police reporter named Michael Ahern boasted that he and two cronies had made up the whole thing. Also, an unnamed member of a terrorist organization with ties to the 1871 Paris Commune even became a suspect. A New York newspaper published a short poem that was his "confession."

Confession of a Terrorist

Did out of [Paris's] ashes arise
This bird with a flaming crest,
That over the ocean unhindered flies,
With a scourge for the Queen of the West?

There is even the theory that spontaneous combustion started the Great Chicago Fire, caused by a fiery meteor that split into pieces, igniting not only Chicago but parts of Peshtigo, Wisconsin.

In Frank Leslie's Illustrated Newspaper, *October 1871, artists' sketches portray the Great Chicago Fire and include this scene on Wells Street in front of the Briggs House, which has just burst into flames.*

Guilty or not, Mrs. O'Leary's cow remains the prime suspect, even though a special board of inquiry assembled by the city did not specifically lay the blame entirely in her barn. Leave it to an advertiser to provide another scenario of history.

Chicago's fire probably never would have happened, said Sidney Wanzer & Sons, Inc., a milk company, if only Mrs. O'Leary had "switched to the country milk Sidney Wanzer introduced!"

Excerpt from the Official Report on the Great Chicago Fire, 1871

Whether it originated from a spark blown from a chimney on that windy night, or was set on fire by human agency, we are unable to determine. The Board find that the fire originated in a two-story barn in the rear of No. 137 DeKoven Street, the premises being owned by Patrick O'Leary. The fire was first discovered by a drayman by the name of Daniel [Dennis] Sullivan, who saw it while sitting on the sidewalk on the south side of DeKoven Street, and nearly opposite O'Leary's premises. He fixes the time at not more than twenty or twenty-five minutes past nine o'clock when he first noticed the flames coming out of the barn. There is no proof that any person had been in the barn after nightfall that evening.

Mr. O'Leary and all his family prove to have been in bed and asleep at the time. There was a small party in the front part of O'Leary's house, which was occupied by Mr. McLaughlin and wife. But we fail to find any evidence that anybody from McLaughlin's part of the house went near the barn that night.

Giving the Country a Bath—1917

H. L. Mencken's account of the history of the bathtub in America

O n December 28, 1917, H. L. Mencken published in the New York Evening Mail an account of the history of the bathtub in America, replete with scholarly references and quotations. In the article, Mencken lamented that the country had failed to honor one of the great scientific achievements and marks of social progress in the 19th century: the invention of the modern bathtub.

The American invention was the brainchild of a cotton dealer and merchant named Adam Thompson, who adapted it from bathtubs in England, Mencken declared. But it was not until President Millard Fillmore installed the first bathtub in the White House, in 1851, that bathing became popular in the United States. Before that time, according to Mencken, experts in the medical community had debated the possible health risks of using a bathtub. "Boston, very early in 1845, made bathing unlawful except upon medical advice," Mencken claimed, "but the ordinance was never enforced and in 1862 it was repealed."

Very little Mencken wrote in the story, which he entitled "A Neglected Anniversary," was true, but the author skillfully employed scholarly apparatus, including bogus statistics and references to sources that did not exist. But all of it left little reason for average readers to question its authenticity. Indeed, even though the story made claims that ranged from the improbable to the ludicrous, experts in a number of fields who should have known better believed it was true. Reprinted in journals and other newspapers, it gained increased credibility and even made it into works of scholarship and textbooks. It remains in a few to this day.

Mencken later wrote that as the hoax continued to gain currency as history he became more and more astonished. Not only newspapers accepted the blarney as fact; so did medical journals. "It had, of course, no truth in it whatsoever," wrote Mencken, "and I more than once confessed publicly that it was only a jocosity. . . . Scarcely a month goes by that I do not find the substance of it reprinted, not as foolishness but as fact, and not only in newspapers but in official documents and other works of the highest pretensions."

The confusion raised by Mencken's article, however, was not a totally innocent result of comedy run amok. It was a purposeful, satiric shot taken by the author at the journalistic profession and the public who lapped up every false-hood fed to it. And it all had to do with the escalating war in Europe. At a time of increasing anti-German World War I hysteria, the pro-German Mencken resented the popular portrayal of the German people as Huns and deeply resented the refusal of publishers to print any of his articles exhibiting pro-German sympathies.

Through his hoax, Mencken was giving example to his claims that little of what the American reading public accepts as fact is true, that people would believe any absurdity if it appealed to their emotions or titillated their imaginations.

In 1926, now annoyed as well as astonished at the extent of the hoax's reach, Mencken published an article entitled "Melancholy Reflections" in the Chicago Tribune. None of this tripe about the bathtub was true, Mencken said; he had made it all up. But even this "confession" did not turn things around; indeed, they went from bad to worse. Many readers now thought that the second article was the hoax.

And so, in history books sitting on libraries shelves across America, you can discover that one of the most eventful occurrences in the presidency of Millard Fillmore was the introduction into the White House of the bathtub. What if H. L. Mencken had not enlightened the country about this historical fact? What then would the books say about the invention of the bathtub and its evolution and the nation's dirty past prior to its appearance? Who knows!

New York Evening Mail, December 28, 1917

A Neglected Anniversary
by H. L. Mencken

On December 20 there flitted past us, absolutely without public notice, one of the most important profane anniversaries in American history, to wit, the seventy-fifth anniversary of the introduction of the bathtub into These States. Not a plumber fired a salute or hung out a flag. Not a governor proclaimed a day of prayer. Not a newspaper called attention to the day.

True enough, it was not entirely forgotten. Eight or nine months ago one of the younger surgeons connected with the Public Health Service in Washington happened upon the facts while looking into the early history of public hygiene, and at his suggestion a committee was formed to celebrate the anniversary with a banquet. But before the plan was perfected Washington went dry, and so the banquet had to be abandoned. As it was, the day passed wholly unmarked, even in the capital of the nation. (This was war-time Prohibition, preliminary to the main catastrophe. — HLM)

Bathtubs are so common today that it is almost impossible to imagine a world without them. They are familiar to nearly everyone in all incorporated towns; in most of the large cities it is unlawful to build a dwelling house without putting them in; even on the farm they have begun to come into use. And yet the first American bathtub was installed and dedicated so recently as December 20, 1842, and, for all I know to the contrary, it may still be in existence and in use.

Curiously enough, the scene of its setting up was Cincinnati, then a squalid frontier town, and even today surely no leader in culture. But Cincinnati, in those days as in these, contained many enterprising merchants, and one of them was a man named Adam Thompson, a dealer in cotton and grain. Thompson shipped his grain by steamboat down the Ohio and Mississippi to New Orleans, and from there sent it to England in sailing vessels. This trade frequently took him to England, and in that country, during the '30s, he acquired the habit of bathing.

The bathtub was then still a novelty in England. It had been introduced in 1828 by Lord John Russell and its use was yet confined to a small class of enthusiasts. Moreover, the English bathtub, then as now, was a puny and inconvenient contrivance—little more, in fact, than a glorified dishpan—and filling and emptying it required the attendance of a servant. Taking a bath, indeed, was a rather heavy ceremony, and Lord John in 1835 was said to be the only man in England who had yet come to doing it every day.

Thompson, who was of inventive fancy—he later devised the machine that is still used for bagging hams and bacon—conceived the notion that the English bathtub would be much improved if it were made large enough to admit the whole body of an adult man, and if its supply of water, instead of being hauled to the scene by a maid, were admitted by pipes from a central reservoir and run off by the same means. Accordingly, early in 1842 he set about building the first modern bathroom in his Cincinnati home—a large house with Doric pillars, standing near what is now the corner of Monastery and Orleans streets.

There was then, of course, no city water supply, at least in that part of the city, but Thompson had a large well in his garden, and he installed a pump to lift its water to the house. This pump, which was operated by six Negroes, much like an old-time fire engine, was connected by a pipe with a cypress tank in the garret of the house, and here the water was stored until needed. From the tank two other pipes ran to the bathroom. One, carrying cold water, was a direct line. The other, designed to provide warm water, ran down the great chimney of the kitchen, and was coiled inside it like a giant spring.

The tub itself was of new design, and became the grandfather of all the bathtubs of today. Thompson had it made by James Cullness, the leading Cincinnati cabinetmaker of those days, and its material was Nicaragua mahogany. It was nearly seven feet long and fully four feet wide. To make it water-tight, the interior was lined with sheet lead, carefully soldered at the joints. The whole contraption weighed about 1,750 pounds, and the floor of the room in which it was placed had to be reinforced to support it. The exterior was elaborately polished.

In this luxurious tub Thompson took two baths on December 20, 1842—a cold one at 8 a.m. and a warm one some time during the afternoon. The warm water, heated by the kitchen fire, reached a temperature of 105 degrees. On Christmas day, having a party of gentlemen to dinner, he exhibited the new marvel to them and gave an exhibition of its use, and four of them, including a French visitor, Col. Duchanel, risked plunges into it. The next day all Cincinnati—then a town of about 100,000 people—had heard of it, and the local newspapers described it at length and opened their columns to violent discussions of it.

The thing, in fact, became a public matter, and before long there was bitter and double-headed opposition to the new invention, which had been promptly imitated by several other wealthy Cincinnatians. On the one hand it was denounced as an epicurean and obnoxious toy from England, designed to corrupt the democratic simplicity of the Republic, and on the other hand it was attacked by the medical faculty as dangerous to health and a certain inviter of "phthisic, rheumatic fevers, inflammation of the lungs and the whole category of zymotic diseases." (I quote from the *Western Medical Repository* of April 23, 1843.)

The noise of the controversy soon reached other cities, and in more than one place medical opposition reached such strength that it was reflected in legislation. Late in 1843, for example, the Philadelphia Common Council considered an ordinance prohibiting bathing between November 1 and March 15, and it failed of passage by but two votes. During the same year the legislature of Virginia laid a tax of $30 a year on all bathtubs that might be set up, and in Hartford, Providence, Charleston and Wilmington (Del.) special and very heavy water rates were levied upon those who had them. Boston, very early in 1845, made bathing unlawful except upon medical advice, but the ordinance was never enforced and in 1862 it was repealed.

This legislation, I suspect, had some class feeling in it, for the Thompson bathtub was plainly too expensive to be owned by any save the wealthy; indeed, the common price for installing one in New York in 1845 was $500. Thus the low caste politicians of the time made capital by fulminating against it, and there is even some suspicion of political bias in many of the early medical denunciations. But the invention of the common pine bathtub, lined with zinc, in 1847, cut off this line of attack, and thereafter the bathtub made steady progress.

The zinc tub was devised by John F. Simpson, a Brooklyn plumber, and his efforts to protect it by a patent occupied the courts until 1855. But the decisions were steadily against him, and after 1848 all the plumbers of New York were equipped for putting in bathtubs. According to a writer in the *Christian Register* for July 17, 1857, the first one in New York was opened for traffic on September 12, 1847, and by the beginning of 1850 there were already nearly 1,000 in use in the big town.

After this medical opposition began to collapse, and among other eminent physicians Dr. Oliver Wendell Holmes declared for the bathtub, and vigorously opposed the lingering movement against it in Boston. The American Medical Association held its annual meeting in Boston in 1849, and a poll of the members in attendance showed that nearly 55 per cent of them now regarded bathing as harmless, and that more than 20 per cent advocated it as beneficial. At its meeting in 1850 a resolution was formally passed giving the imprimatur of the faculty to the bathtub. The homeopaths followed with a like resolution in 1853.

But it was the example of President Millard Fillmore that, even more than the grudging medical approval, gave the bathtub recognition and respectability in the United States. While he was still Vice-President, in March, 1850, he visited Cincinnati on a stumping tour, and inspected the original Thompson tub. Thompson himself was now dead, but his bathroom was preserved by the gentlemen who had bought his house from the estate. Fillmore was entertained in this house and, according to Chamberlain, his biographer, took a bath in the tub. Experiencing no ill effects, he became an ardent advocate of the new invention, and on succeeding to the Presidency at Taylor's death, July 9, 1850, he instructed his secretary of war, Gen. Charles M. Conrad, to invite tenders for the construction of a bathtub in the White House.

This action, for a moment, revived the old controversy, and its opponents made much of the fact that there was no bathtub at Mount Vernon, or at Monticello, and that all the Presidents and other magnificoes of the past had got along without any such monarchical luxuries. The elder Bennett, in the New York *Herald*, charged that Fillmore really aspired to buy and install in the White House a porphyry and alabaster bath that had been used by Louis Philippe at Versailles. But Conrad, disregarding all this clamor, duly called for bids, and the contract was presently awarded to Harper & Gillespie, a firm of Philadelphia engineers, who proposed to furnish a tub of thin cast iron, capable of floating the largest man.

This was installed early in 1851, and remained in service in the White House until the first Cleveland administration, when the present enameled tub was substituted. The example of the President soon broke down all that remained of the old opposition, and by 1860, according to the newspaper advertisements of the time, every hotel in New York had a bathtub, and some had two and even three. In 1862 bathing was introduced into the Army by Gen. McClellan, and in 1870 the first prison bathtub was set up at Moyamensing Prison, in Philadelphia.

So much for the history of the bathtub in America. One is astonished, on looking into it, to find that so little of it has been recorded. The literature, in fact, is almost nil. But perhaps this brief sketch will encourage other inquirers and so lay the foundation for an adequate celebration of the centennial in 1942.

The Advent of the Bambino's Curse—1920

Babe Ruth's claim that he would play only with the Boston Red Sox

New York City, 1986, Game 6 of the World Series, the Boston Red Sox and the New York Mets. To many in Boston, the last inning of the game remains riveted in their memories, moments frozen in a morbid abyss, each second there to be lived and relived. Talk to many Bostonians and the names and the nightmare are on their tongues as if the action had occurred seconds before—a two-run lead in the bottom of the tenth, the champagne corks poised for popping, and the scoreboard operator preparing the message: "Congratulations, Boston Red Sox." The Red Sox had not won the series for 68 years. And then . . . young Calvin Schiraldi, one strike away from victory, gives up a single, another single, and then another for a run, and then a new pitcher, Bob Stanley, and then a wild pitch to tie the score, and then a ground ball through the legs of first baseman Bill Buckner for the run that lost the game. The champagne corks remain unpopped; Game 7 the next day seemed like a foregone conclusion. Of course the Red Sox would lose. Who was to blame? Babe Ruth and his damnable curse.

Babe Ruth played for the Red Sox from 1914 to 1919. He was mostly a pitcher, a very good one. But after a few years, it became clear that Ruth was an even better hitter. He became the first genuine home-run slugger in the game, hitting a record 29 home runs in one year at a time when few players reached double digits. It was clear that his own future and that of his team, the Red Sox, was exceptionally bright.

Nevertheless, on January 6, 1920, a day that will live in Boston infamy, Ruth was sold to the New York Yankees for $100,000. Harry Frazee, the owner of the Sox at the time, was a financially strapped entrepreneur looking for a way out. To an astonished and quickly angered citizenry, stories in the Boston press talked of the imminent sale of the Big Guy. When contacted by reporters, Babe himself denied it was about to happen. Despite this temporary reassurance to Boston fans from the slugger, the sale went through.

In addition to the $100,000 he paid for Ruth, Jake Ruppert of the Yankees took a $350,000 mortgage on Fenway Park so that Frazee could pay off some of his debts. The Red Sox manager, Ed Barrow, who had fought very hard against the deal, was furious, along with the press and the fans. And so were the gods. . . .

Since Ruth's sale to the Yankees, the Red Sox have not won a World Series. The closest was in 1986, but there have been numerous times when the team seemed ready to break through. In Boston they will tell you that the "Curse of the Bambino" is palpable, stalking the team through the years, refusing to let go. As surely as the ignominy of the Red Sox world championship drought, they say, the curse lives.

Boston Globe, January 6, 1920

Ruth Says Sale to the New York Club Doesn't Go

Johnny Igoe, Ruth's business manager, who is in Boston, having recently returned from the Pacific Coast, notified Ruth last evening by telegraph of his sale to the New York club, and at 11:30 received the following telegram from "Babe":

"Will not play anywhere but Boston. Will leave for the East Monday."

Igoe gave as a reason for Ruth's objection to playing with any club other than the Red Sox, that the big fellow had invested his money in the cigar business in Boston and that he wished to be here as much as possible to look after his business. Also, that because of his associations here he preferred to play with the Boston club rather than any other.

Notwithstanding the Ruth telegram, Miller Huggins declared in a statement made at Los Angeles last night that he had actually signed the great slugger. Papers were exchanged, Huggins said.

The great Bambino before the curse. The Boston Red Sox pitching staff, including Babe Ruth (second from right), are pictured in October 1915.

ALMOST
LOUSY PREDICTIONS
HISTORY

What About Radial Tires?—1909

Report by *Scientific American* that the automobile has been nearly fully developed

Today in America, the automobile has assumed a dominating cultural niche. It is a metaphoric symbol of freedom and mobility, a near icon of worship. It was not always so. The inventors and industry leaders who first tinkered with the product saw it merely as an extension of the carriage and bicycle, an over-ground vehicle reliable enough to get somewhere and back under its own power, not the power of an animal or a human.

Originating from a diverse collection of electric, steam, and combustion ideas and manufactured from a variety of parts, the automobile of the 1890s was a curiosity, mostly for the rich. It was not, almost everyone would have agreed, the beginning of a revolution. In 1908, the first Model T Ford was introduced. The development was so unspectacular that Scientific American, *the magazine that gauged the nation's developmental pulse, looked back over the recent year and declared that the automobile had just about reached its limits.*

In the history of ludicrous predictions, it could be argued that the forecasters for Scientific American *in 1909 set an almost incomparable standard. The editors looked ahead and did not see:*

- First moving assembly line: Ford produces 1,000 cars in one day, 1913
- An automobile that could accumulate more than 25,000 miles before its demise, 1920
- A time when an average American could purchase an automobile (three cars are registered for every four Americans); motorists have stop signs, paved roads, and installment financing, 1930
- Automatic transmission, 1940
- Power brakes, power steering, air-conditioning, 1950s

And on and on and on . . .

Scientific American, January 2, 1909

That the automobile has practically reached the limit of its development is suggested by the fact that during the past year no improvements of a radical character have been introduced. The six-cylinder

In 1909 Scientific American *magazine ventured the opinion that little was left to improve on the automobile. This is a Buick, vintage 1907.*

machine grows slowly in favor; but there is no indication that it will become the prevailing type. There has been a great increase in popularity of the moderate-priced, medium-sized car, of 24 to 30 horse-power, and costing from $1,200 to $1,800. There is cause for congratulation in the fact that both in racing and touring cars the later American models show a decided improvement in durability; and it can be said without much fear of contradiction that the output of the leading builders of this country is at last fully comparable to the best of the foreign makes. The Glidden tour, that supreme test of reliability, bears out the truth of the above statement. It was run this year over a 1,700-mile course, through Buffalo, Pittsburgh, New York, Albany, Maine, the White Mountains, and Saratoga. Although the conditions of the whole trip were exceedingly trying, the machines made an average speed of 20 miles an hour, and this in spite of the fact that no repairs were allowed in the garages. Of the forty-five machines that started twenty-eight finished with a perfect score, nine of them making up three three-car teams, fourteen others being touring cars, and five runabouts.

Who Is This Guy, Jules Verne?—1920

New York Times **editorial ridiculing**
Robert Goddard's rocket research

When the scientist Robert Goddard convinced the Smithsonian Institution in 1917 that his ideas about developing a rocket capable of probing the high atmosphere were worth supporting with a grant of $5,000, his rocketry career was launched. He worked for a while on military rockets during World War I and, by 1920, his infant research and determination to construct a rocket that could function in space were becoming fairly widely known, especially through an article he published in early 1920 entitled "A Method of Reaching Extreme Altitudes." A number of journalists approached Goddard and printed articles suggesting that he actually believed a device could someday reach the moon.

Goddard may have convinced the Smithsonian that his work held great promise, but he had not convinced the editorial pundits who saw no chance that the spindly devices with which the young scientist was working would ever reach the height of the some of New York's tall buildings, much less outer space. The New York Times *lampooned Goddard's claim that rockets could fly through the vacuum and cruelly charged that the scientist himself seemed "to lack the knowledge ladled out daily in high schools"—that rocket thrust would not be effective beyond the Earth's atmosphere. Goddard responded that "every vision is a joke until the first man accomplishes it; once realized, it becomes commonplace." To those with a more scholarly bent far beyond the high school classroom, he published in* Scientific American *an article entitled "That Moon Rocket Proposition: Refutation of Some Popular Fallacies," debunking some popular misconceptions about the properties of space and the promise of rocketry.*

But the skeptics would hold the high ground until the scientist actually delivered on some of his claims. On March 16, 1926, Goddard flight-tested his first liquid-fuel rocket, a construction with the rocket mounted ahead of a fuel tank shielded from the flame by a metal cone and the lines for fuel and oxygen pulling it behind the rocket. The design worked. At his aunt Effie's farm in Auburn, Massachusetts, Goddard carefully set up the newly designed rocket. Although it burned only about 20 seconds before reaching sufficient thrust for taking off and although it reached only a height of about 41 feet, Goddard had achieved the first flight of a rocket using liquid propellants.

It took many years before The New York Times *finally dined on crow. In its July 17, 1969, edition, three days before a human first set foot on the moon, the* Times *editors printed "A Correction" to their editorial of 1920. "It is now definitely established," the editors said, "that a rocket can function in a vacuum as well as in an atmosphere. The* Times *regrets the error."*

If Goddard and other scientists in his field had been deterred by the ridicule or intimidated by the skeptics, the achievements of 1969 and beyond would have been jokes and not visions. He and they paid little heed.

New York Times, January 13, 1920

A Severe Strain on Credulity

As a method of sending a missile to the higher, and even to the highest part of the earth's atmospheric envelope, Professor Goddard's multiple-charge rocket is a practicable, and therefore promising, device. Such a rocket, too, might carry self-recording instruments to be released at the limit of its flight, and conceivably parachutes would bring them safely to the ground. It is not obvious, however, that the instruments would return to the point of departure; indeed, it is obvious that they would not, for parachutes drift exactly as balloons do. And the rocket, or what was left of it after the last explosion, would have to be aimed with amazing skill and in a dead calm, to fall on the spot whence it started.

But that is a slight inconvenience at least from the scientific standpoint, though it might be serious enough from that of the always innocent bystander a few hundred or thousand yards away from the firing line. It is when one considers the multiple-charge rocket as a traveler to the moon that one begins to doubt and looks again, to see if the dispatch announcing the professor's purposes and hopes says that he is working under the auspices of the Smithsonian Institution. It does say so, and therefore the impulse to do more than doubt the practicability of such a device for such a purpose must be—well, controlled. Still, to be filled with uneasy wonder and to express it will be safe enough, for after the rocket quits our air and really starts on its longer journey, its flight would be neither accelerated nor maintained by the explosion of the charges it then might have left. To claim that it would be is to deny a fundamental law of dynamics, and only Dr. Einstein and his chosen dozen, so few and fit, are licensed to do that.

Undeterred by mocking criticism from several quarters, especially The New York Times, *Professor Robert Goddard continued his rocket research, convinced of theories thought fanciful by his critics. He would later be known as "The Father of Rocketry."*

His Plan Is Not Original

That Professor Goddard with his "chair" in Clark College and the countenancing of the Smithsonian Institution, does not know the relation of action to reaction, and of the need to have something better than a vacuum against which to react—to say that would be absurd. Of course he only seems to lack the knowledge ladled out daily in high schools.

But there are such things as intentional mistakes or oversights, and, as it happens, Jules Verne, who also knew a thing or two in assorted sciences—and had, besides, a surprising amount of prophetic power—deliberately seemed to make the same mistake that Professor Goddard seems to make. For the Frenchman, having got his travelers to or toward the moon into the desperate fix of riding a tiny satellite of the satellite, saved them from circling it forever by means of an explosion, rocket fashion, where an explosion would not have had in the slightest degree the effect of releasing them from their dreadful slavery. That was one of Verne's few scientific slips, or else it was a deliberate step aside from scientific accuracy, pardonable enough in him as a romancer, but its like is not so easily explained when made by a savant who isn't writing a novel of adventure.

All the same, if Professor Goddard's rocket attains sufficient speed before it passes out of our atmosphere—which is a thinkable possibility—and if its aiming takes into account all of the many defective forces that will affect its flight, it may reach the moon. That the rocket could carry enough explosive to make on impact a flash large and bright enough to be seen from the earth by the biggest of our telescopes—that will be believed when it is done.

Some Got It Right—1948

Poll results clearly showing the 1948 election was turning in Truman's favor

O ne of the most recognized photographs in American political history is that of President Harry Truman holding aloft the front-page headline in the Chicago Tribune *declaring that Thomas Dewey had won the presidential election of 1948. The election had been such a foregone conclusion that the* Tribune, *in one of the most celebrated gaffes in American journalistic history, took the early returns on election night, extrapolated those results to coincide with their preconceived notions, and announced a narrow Dewey victory. The article was convincing, statistically accurate in reporting on the early returns, but embarrassingly wrong in its banner announcement.*

The political pollsters took the heat: Elmer Roper, George Gallup, Archibald M. Crossley. All of them had confidently predicted a relatively easy Dewey victory. The polls predicted a Dewey margin of between 5 and 15 points, with Roper on a limb with the largest gap. The Gallup organization later explained that it had stopped polling too early, assuming that significant changes do not occur in the last two weeks of a campaign. Gallup's final prediction, published the day before the election, was actually based on two national samples gathered in mid-October. The other major pollsters also had stopped polling. Crossley's final forecast had been derived from a combination of state surveys taken between August and October, and Roper's final estimate, the greatest of the bloopers, had come from data his organization had collected in August.

Roper later explained that organized labor, fearful of a Republican ascendancy, rallied its troops as never before in the last days of the campaign, and that many Republicans, reading those polls, failed to go to the voting booths and played golf instead.

The "experts" also had not counted on Truman's frenzied, nonstop campaigning. Those large, enthusiastic crowds that showed up behind the president's train car and at Truman rallies began to belie those statistics. But even then, observers passed off the hearty receptions as the result of public curiosity, that folks were gathering merely to watch a celebrity.

The New York Star *had the rare distinction of being able to boast that two of its writers, columnists Jennings Perry and Gerald Johnson, had predicted that the election would be close. In September, Robert Bendiner, a writer for the* Nation, *had the audacity to proclaim "Don't Count Truman Out." And,*

In one of the most recognizable photographs in American political history, President Harry Truman holds aloft a copy of the Chicago Daily Tribune *declaring Thomas Dewey the victor in the 1948 presidential election.*

unknown to much of the media and the public, there were some local and regional polls to which the candidates had access. In the final days of the campaign, Truman's managers received extraordinarily encouraging figures from several polls that showed the president actually pulling ahead in several major states.

Unknown to the press, to the major pollsters, to almost all Americans, and especially to the Chicago Tribune was the fact that the election of 1948 was not going to be, at least to a few in the know, a surprise at all.

Poll Results in Possession of Truman's Campaign, 1948

Speaking of polls, here are the results of the Lyons Poll of 3 Middle Western States. The two checks were made 30 days apart and covered a cross-section of 6700 people in each state, scientifically done in the best poll manner.

	30 Days Ago	Today
NORTH DAKOTA	Dewey 46	Dewey 44
	Truman 36	Truman 43
	Wallace 8	Wallace 5
	Undecided 10	Undecided 8
SOUTH DAKOTA	Dewey 48	Dewey 46
	Truman 37	Truman 45
ILLINOIS	Dewey 44.5	Dewey 44
	Truman 37.5	Truman 45.5
	Wallace 8	Wallace 3.5
	Undecided 10	Undecided 7

A Laptop for a Large Lap—1949

***Popular Mechanics* predicts that someday a computer might weigh as little as a ton and a half**

In 1944, Howard A. Aiken, a Harvard engineer working with IBM, succeeded in producing the Harvard-IBM Automatic Sequence Controlled Calculator, or Mark I. Spurred by research surrounding the war effort, the Mark I was principally used to create ballistic charts for the U.S. Navy. Using electromagnetic signals to move mechanical parts, the machine could make a calculation in as little as three seconds. It was about half as long as a football field and contained about 500 miles of wiring.

Another computer that grew out of the war effort was the Electronic Numerical Integrator and Computer (ENIAC), produced at the University of Pennsylvania. ENIAC's first test runs involved millions of discrete calculations associated with top-secret studies of thermonuclear chain reactions, research relating to the hydrogen bomb. Although less than the size of half a football field, ENIAC had inside its massive frame 18,000 vacuum tubes, 70,000 resistors, and five million soldered joints. It was such a enormous piece of equip-

Thirty feet by fifty feet, filled with 18,000 vacuum tubes, 1,500 relays, and 6,000 switches, this ENIAC computer weighed thirty tons.

ment that it consumed 160 kilowatts of electrical power, enough energy to dim the lights in an entire section of Philadelphia. ENIAC computed at a speed 1,000 times faster than Mark I. It was thus smaller and faster.

With these spectacular developments, the days of first-generation computers would soon be over; hence, the bold predictions of yet smaller machines by Popular Mechanics, machines that weighed less even than a ton and a half. Gone would be the days of huge vacuum tubes and magnetic drums. Gone would be the skepticism not only of society at large but among the scientific community that computers would have very limited, specific use. After all, Lord Kelvin had once observed that radio had no future, and Harry Warner had seen little public acceptance ahead for talking movies.

What Popular Mechanics had in mind was a visionary look at the future, a glimpse into things that were not yet history, but Almost History. But in this case, as often occurs, history took them that far and much farther.

Popular Mechanics, March 1949

Brains that Click

The latest model "thinking machine" that scientists and mathematicians drool over is the electronic-type calculator. Such computers use vacuum tubes and literally figure with the speed of lightning, rather than by any ingenious system of wheels or gears. The Army, the Navy and the U.S. Bureau of Standards have spent several million dollars on such machines.

The Navy has sponsored the work of Dr. Howard Aiken at Harvard who has developed three calculators: Mark I, a mechanical type using counter wheels; Mark II, an electric-relay type which recently was moved to the U.S. Naval Proving Grounds, Dahlgren, VA.; and Mark III, a hush-hush electronic computer which has not yet been completed.

The Army has backed the scientific team of Dr. J. Presper Eckert, Jr., and Dr. John Mauchly, formerly of the University of Pennsylvania. They developed the ENIAC (Electronic Numerical Integrator and Calculator) which has been moved to the Army's Aberdeen Proving Grounds, Aberdeen, MD. The ENIAC is the only all-electronic computer in operation today. It is not a machine in the usual sense—the only moving parts are devices to feed numbers in and print numbers out.

Not long ago Eckert and Mauchly set up their own company in

Philadelphia and are now working on the UNIVAC, the BINAC and other types of computers. The UNIVAC, the only large computer designed to manipulate alphabetic information, will soon be made available to business and industry. The BINAC, two models of which have been built, is a smaller, simpler and lower-priced calculator—almost a "pocket" edition—which is only five feet high, four feet long, and one foot wide.

The Army is also financing the work of Dr. John von Neumann at the Institute for Advanced Study, Princeton, N.J. He's developing a calculator of an advanced type which, it is jokingly said, may be called the MANIAC (Mechanical and Numerical Integrator and Calculator).

The U.S. Bureau of Standards has a four-part program under way. In Washington, D.C. it is setting up a Computation Laboratory, A Statistical Engineering Laboratory, and a Machine Development Laboratory. In Los Angeles, it has organized an Institute for Numerical Analysis on the U.C.L.A. campus to serve Western research and industry.

Engineers and mathematicians are like airplane designers. Models in use are already long outmoded by those on the drawing boards. Where a calculator like the ENIAC today is equipped with 18,000 vacuum tubes and weighs 30 tons, computers in the future may have only 1000 vacuum tubes and perhaps weigh only 1 ½ tons. . . .

Document Sources

PLANNING FOR THE WORST

Personal note of Dwight D. Eisenhower, June 5, 1944. Dwight D. Eisenhower Library, Abilene, Kansas.

Excerpts from Operation Unthinkable Report, 1945. London *Daily Telegraph*, October 1, 1998.

U.S. Civil Service Commission Memorandum, November 13, 1962 and 1954 Article on Survival. Sue Schuurman, "A-Bomb Survival," http://weeklywire.com /ww/10-12/98/alibi.skeleton.html; Roger Bruns and George Vogt, *Your Government Inaction: Or in God We'd Better Trust*: New York: St. Martin's Press, 1981.

Memorandum of Gerard C. Smith to Undersecretary of State Christian C. Herter, August 13, 1958. National Archives and Records Administration, Record Group 59, Records of the Department of State; http://www.gwu.edu/nsarchive/nsa/ DOCUMENT/DOC-PIC/950509_1.gif

Instructions for Expenditure of Nuclear Weapons in Emergency Conditions, December 1959. Dwight D. Eisenhower Library, Abilene, Kansas; Office of Special Assistant for National Security Affairs, NSC Series, Atomic Weapons, Correspondence and Background for Presidential Approval.

Message Carried by John Glenn, on *Friendship 7*, February 1962. *New York Times*, September 16, 1999.

Draft of William Safire's speech for President Richard Nixon, 1974. National Archives and Records Administration, Nixon Presidential Materials Project, College Park, Maryland.

FORKS IN THE ROAD

Recollections of Frederick Douglass. Frederick Douglass, *Life and Times of Frederick Douglass* (Hartford, Connecticut: Park Publishing Company, 1881).

Diary Entries of John Wesley Powell, August 1869. J. W. Powell, *The Exploration of the Colorado River and its Canyons* (New York: Dover Publications, 1961); an unabridged work first published by Flood & Vincent in 1895 under the title *Canyons of the Colorado*.

Telegram of John Reid, *New York Times*, to Republican Leaders in Florida, Louisiana, and South Carolina, 1876. http://www.historybuff.com/ library/retilden.html.

Notes of Robert McNamara on Meeting with President Kennedy and Advisors, October 21, 1962. National Archives and Records Administration, Washington National Records Center, Suitland, Maryland, RG 330, OASD (C) A Files: FRC 71 A 2896, Misc. Papers Regarding Cuba.

Taped Conversation of President Kennedy with Solicitor General Archibald Cox, October 1, 1962. John F. Kennedy Library, President's Office Files, Presidential Recordings Transcripts, Integration of the University of Mississippi.

Memorandum of Watergate Prosecution Team, August 9, 1974. National Archives and Records Administration, Record Group 460, Records Relating to Richard M. Nixon, Records of the Watergate Special Prosecution Force.

FORTUITOUS OCCURRENCES

Excerpt of Letter of Thomas Jefferson to American Minister to Paris, April 18, 1802. Paul Leicester Ford, *The Writings of Thomas Jefferson, Volume VIII* (New York: G. P. Putnam's Sons, 1897).

Letter of Grace Bedell to Abraham Lincoln, October 15, 1860; Letter of Abraham Lincoln to Grace Bedell, October 19, 1860. Roy P. Basler, *The Collected Works of Abraham Lincoln*, Volume IV (New Brunswick, New Jersey: Rutgers University Press, 1953).

Excerpts from Robert E. Lee's Special Orders 191, 1862. http://www.lebmofo.com/antietam/so191.html

Speech of Theodore Roosevelt, October 14, 1912. *New York Times*, October 15, 1912.

Letter of Febb Ensminger Burn to Harry Burn, August 17, 1920. Paula Casey, "A Legacy of Leadership: Tennessee's Pivotal Role in Granting All American Women the Vote," http://gos.sbc.edu/c/casey.html

Letter of Albert Einstein to President Franklin Roosevelt, August 2, 1939. Franklin D. Roosevelt Library, Hyde Park, New York.

Letter of Philip Johnston to Commander of U.S. Marine Corps, September 12, 1942. National Archives and Records Administration; http://mprofaca.cro.net/navajolett.html

Deposition of FBI Informer on Kickback Payments to Vice President Spiro Agnew, 1973. National Archives and Records Administration, Mid-Atlantic Region, Philadelphia, Pennsylvania—NRBPA-118-1AGNEW(B).

CLOSE CALLS

Letter of George Washington to His Troops, March 15, 1783. John C. Fitzpatrick, ed., T*he Writings of George Washington from the Original Manuscript Sources, Volume 26* (Washington, D.C.: Government Printing Office, 1938).

Excerpt from Congressional Deliberations over the Tallmadge Amendment, February 1819. Annals of Congress, House of Representatives, 15th Congress, 2nd Session, February 1819.

Excerpts from the Memoirs of U. S. Grant, 1865. U. S. Grant, *Personal Memoirs* (New York: Charles L. Webster & Company, 1894).

***London Daily Mail*, December 24, 1931.** *London Daily Mail*, December 24, 1931.

Excerpts from Action Report on the Loss of the USS *PT-109*, August 1–2, 1943. National Archives and Records Administration, Action Report of the Loss of the USS *PT 109* on August 1, 1943, NWCTM-38-ACNRPTS-SERIAL006.

Excerpt from Interview with Dr. Richard W. Porter, 1945. Ernst Stuhlinger and Frederick I. Oredway III, *Wernher von Braun: Crusader for Space, A Biographical Memoir* (Malabar, Florida: Krieger Publishing Company, 1994).

An Aide's Memorandum on President Eisenhower's Heart Attack, September 1955. Dwight D. Eisenhower Library, Abilene, Kansas—NLE-EPRES-DDEJIARY-JAN-NOV55-DIARY92955.

Transcript of Communication from John Glenn's *Friendship 7*, 1962. National Archives and Records Administration, Southwest Region, Fort Worth, Texas, Records of the National Aeronautics and Space Administration.

Notarized Statement of Jane Rickover, Adm. Hyman Rickover's Daughter-in-law, 1979. http://www.antenna.nl/~wise/488/4840.html.

TWISTS OF IRONY

Letter of George Washington to Capt. Robert Mackenzie, October 9, 1774. Library of Congress Manuscript Division, George Washington Papers, Account Book 2.

Etching by James Whistler, 1855.

Cartoon by Thomas Nast, 1875.

Patent Drawing of Invention of Alexander Graham Bell, 1881.

Letter of Wilbur Wright to Smithsonian Institution, May 30, 1899. Smithsonian Institution, National Air and Space Museum.

Job application of Richard M. Nixon for Employment at the FBI, April 23, 1937.

Letter of Eleanor Roosevelt to Mrs. Henry N. Robert, DAR President, February 26, 1939. National Archives and Records Administration, NARA's American Originals Exhibit; http://nara.gov.

Boston *Globe*, November 28, 1942. Boston *Globe*, November 28, 1942.

The *Reporter*, September 14, 1954. Chalmers Roberts, "The Day We Didn't Go to War," The *Reporter* (September 14, 1954).

Answer to Plaintiff from *City of Memphis v. Martin Luther King, Jr.*, 1968. National Archives and Records Administration, Southwest Region, Atlanta, Georgia, Record Group 21, United States District Court, Western District of Tennessee—NRCA-21TWMCVCA2-C68(80)-ANSWPL.

FBI Memorandum on Efforts to Deport John Lennon, April 23, 1972. FBI Files on John Lennon, FBI Reading Room, Washington, D.C.; FBI's Freedom of Information Act Electronic Reading Room, www.fbi.gov.

Letter of Richard Nixon to Ronald Reagan, August 13, 1987. National Archives and Records Administration, Nixon Papers Project.

PLANS THWARTED

Telegram of William Henry Seward to Mayor of New York, November 2, 1864. *New York Times*, November 4, 1864.

Jefferson Davis to Brigade Commanders, May 2, 1865. Hudson Strode, *Jefferson Davis: Tragic Hero, the Last Twenty-Five Years* (New York: Harcourt, Brace & World, Inc., 1964).

The Last Public Speech of Abraham Lincoln. Roy Basler, ed., *The Collected Works of Abraham Lincoln, Volume VIII* (New Brunswick, New Jersey: Rutgers University Press, 1953).

Introduction to Proposed Agreement Between United States and Japan, November 26, 1941. Department of State Bulletin, Vol. V, No. 129 (December 13, 1941).

National Security Action Memorandum No. 263, October 11, 1963. John F. Kennedy Library, Columbia Point, Boston, Massachusetts—NLK-NSF-MM-NSAM-10JJJ.

CIA Memorandum, June 5, 1963. Lyndon B. Johnson Library, Austin, Texas.

Prepared Remarks of President John F. Kennedy for Delivery in Dallas, Texas, November 22, 1963. John F. Kennedy Library, Columbia Point, Boston, Massachusetts—NLK-SLNGR-PRESSRELEASES JFKFI-19631122-5GGG.

Excerpts from Report of the Inspector General on CIA plots to Assassinate Fidel Castro, 1967. CIA Report on Plots to Assassinate Fidel Castro, May 23, 1967 (released under Freedom of Information Act; redacted portions marked as "deleted").

OPPORTUNITIES MISSED; WARNINGS UNHEEDED

Speech of Abraham Lincoln Before the U.S. House of Representatives, December 22, 1847. Roy P. Basler, ed., *Abraham Lincoln: His Speeches and Writings* (Cleveland: World Publishing Company, 1946); and National Archives and Records Administration, RG 233, Records of the U.S. House of Representatives, HR 30 A-B 3.

Remembrances of Alexander Stephens of Aborted Confederate Plan, 1863. Alexander Stephens, *A Constitutional View of the Late War Between the States: Its Causes, Character, Conduct and Results Presented in a Series of Colloquies at Liberty Hall* (New York: Kraus Reprint Company, 1970).

Telephone Patent Filed by Elisha Gray, 1876.

Dispatch of Cuban Weather Forecasters to U.S. Weather Bureau, September 10, 1900. National Archives and Records Administration, Records of the Department of Agriculture, Weather Bureau, General Correspondence; Erik Larson, *Isaac's Storm: A Man, a Time, and the Deadliest Hurricane in History* (New York: Crown Publishers, 1999).

Wireless Message of the *Mesaba* to the *Titanic*, April 14, 1912, 7:50 P.M. http://www2.dynamite.com/au/rmstitanic.

Warnings Published in New York Newspapers from the German, May 1, 1915. *New York Times*, May 1, 1915.

Ho Chi Minh's Declaration of Independence for the Democratic Republic of Vietnam, September 2, 1945. Ho Chi Minh, *Selected Works*, Vol. 3 (Hanoi: Foreign Languages Publishing House, 1960–1962).

Ambassador to Japan Joseph Clark Grew to U.S. State Department, January 7, 1941. *Papers Relating to the Foreign Relations of the United States: Japan 1931–1941, Vol. 11* (Washington, D.C.: Government Printing Office, 1943).

Telegram of Senator Joseph McCarthy to President Harry S. Truman, February 11, 1950; Draft of Truman's Response to McCarthy. Harry S. Truman Library, Independence, Missouri.

Memorandum of Conference with President Eisenhower Following Soviet Launch of *Sputnik*, October 9, 1957. Dwight D. Eisenhower Library, Abilene, Kansas—NLE-EPRES-DDEDIARY-STAFOCS57920-MEMOCWP10857.

Excerpts from Report of Inspector General on FBI's Performance in Uncovering Espionage Activities of Aldrich Ames, April 21, 1997. Michael Bromwich, Inspector General, *A Review of the FBI's Performance in Uncovering the Espionage Activities of Aldrich Hazen Ames* (April, 1997); Department of Justice, http://www.usdoj.gov/oig/amesxsm1.htm

Coded Cable to United Nations from Maj. Gen. Roméo Dallaire, U.N. Force Commander in Rwanda, January 11, 1994; U.N. Response to Dallaire's Cable. http://www.pbs.org/wgbh/pages/frontline/shows/evil/warning.

VAGARIES OF WAR

Letter of Sir William Clinton to Gen. John Burgoyne, August 10, 1777. University of Michigan, Clements Library.

Memoir of Comte de Vergennes, February 1781. Mary A. Giunta, ed. *The Emerging Nation: A Documentary History of the Foreign Relations of the United States Under the Articles of Confederation, 1780–1789, Volume One* (Washington, D.C.: National Historical Publications and Records Commission, 1996).

Letter of Col. William Travis, February 24, 1836. http://www.lsjunction.com/docs/appeal.htm.

Exchange of Battlefield Notes Between James Longstreet and E. P. Alexander at Gettysburg Prior to Pickett's Charge, July 3, 1863. Library of Congress, Edward P. Alexander Papers; Lieutenant-General James Longstreet Gettysburg Documents, http://www.chickasaw.com/~rainbow/getty9.htm.

Orders of Brig. Gen. Albert Terry to Gen. George Custer, June 22, 1876. *Annual Report of the Secretary of War for 1876*, House Executive Document 1, Second Session of the Forty-fourth Congress (Serial volume 1742).

Excerpts from the Munson Report, November 11, 1941. Michi Weglyn, *Years of Infamy* (New York: Morrow Quill Paperbacks, 1976).

CODE-BREAKING CONSEQUENCES

Note from German Foreign Minister Arthur Zimmerman to the Mexican Government, January 19, 1917. National Archives and Records Administration, RG

59, General Records of the Department of State; http://www.nara.gov/exhall/originals/modern.html.

Decryptions by the American Black Chamber, November 28, 1921. Herbert O. Yardley, *The American Black Chamber* (Ameron House, 1931).

Report of Navy Code Breakers on Japanese Plans to Attack Midway Islands, from Diary of Lt. Burdick Brittin, May 30, 1942. Walter Lord, *Incredible Victory* (New York: Harper & Row Publishers, 1967).

SLIPPERY TRUTH

Excerpts from the Dahlgren Papers, 1864. *The War of the Rebellion: A Compilation of the Official Records of the Union and Confederate Armies, Series I: Volume XXXIII* (Washington, D.C.: Government Printing Office, 1891).

Excerpts from *The Backlash of War* by Ellen La Motte, 1916. Ellen N. La Motte, *The Backlash of War* (New York: G. P. Putnam's Sons, 1934).

Diary Entry of Harry S. Truman, July 25, 1945. Harry S. Truman Library, Independence, Missouri.

Memorandum of CIA Director Richard Helms, December 17, 1963. http://www.levity.com/aciddreams/docs/cyesonly.html.

URBAN LEGENDS

Excerpt from the Official Report on the Great Chicago Fire, 1871. "The O'Leary Legend," http://www.chicaohs.org/fire/oleary/essay-3.html.

***New York Evening Mail*, December 28, 1917.** *New York Evening Mail*, December 28, 1917.

***Boston Globe*, January 6, 1920.** *Boston Globe*, January 6, 1920.

LOUSY PREDICTIONS

***Scientific American*, January 2, 1909.** *Scientific American*, January 2, 1909.

***New York Times*, January 13, 1920.** *New York Times*, January 13, 1920.

Poll Results in Possession of Truman's Campaign, 1948. Harry S. Truman Library, Independence, Missouri, President's Secretary's Files.

***Popular Mechanics*, 1949.** "Brains that Click," *Popular Mechanics* (March 1949).

Index